Book Collecting:

The Book of First Books

Book Collecting:
The Book of First Books

By
Allen Ahearn

Quill & Brush
Rockville, Maryland
1986

Contents

Introduction

This book has been prepared to provide information for book collectors as well as librarians and book dealers.

It attempts to show that book collecting is enjoyable and a reasonably good investment over the long run. It explains some of the terms used in the trade and how to identify, purchase, care for, and sell first editions. Also included is my understanding of the rationale that drives collecting interests, which admittedly may appear to explain the unexplainable.

For those actively involved in the trade, the book includes opinions on the current retail value of first editions of first books by about 3,500 authors. These price estimates are not intended to be projections but representative of what are, one hopes, realistic current retail values based on the catalogs received, my own experiences in selling first editions, and discussions with collectors and dealers more knowledgeable than myself on values for books which have not appeared in catalogs or at auction since the last edition in 1983.

This is the fourth edition of the *Book of First Books*. The first edition of this book was published in 1975. It included current prices for the first books by approximately 1,000 authors. The second edition, in 1978, covered 2,000 authors. The third edition included approximately 2,500 first books. This edition inlcudes about 3,500 authors' first books and my estimate of the current retail prices for very good to fine copies of the books with a dustwrapper if published in 1920 or later; and in original bindings between 1800 and 1920.

I operate on the premise that the first edition of the first book often sets an upper level on the value of an author's first editions and therefore, the estimated prices in this book can assist in determining general values for later books by the authors listed.

The general comments on book collecting have been considerably enlarged in this edition. These comments, of course, reflect my own current perceptions.

The prices in this book are intended only as guides. Most dealers in collectable books do not handle rare books, per se; they handle scarce books. However, very fine copies of scarce books are actually rare. These fine copies command high prices from knowledgeable collectors and librarians because these individuals realize the true relative scarcity of such material. I am certainly not particularly knowledgeable about other collecting fields such as coins or stamps, but my impression is that if an individual wanted five very fine examples of a certain "rare" coin or stamp, and was willing to pay the going (not an inflated) price, they could be found within a relatively short time. On the other hand if an individual wanted to buy five very fine copies of a certain edition of a particular title it might take a few years. And this is not just for books costing thousands of dollars, it's true of books that sell for only a few hundred dollars (or less). The point is that many collectors, librarians and dealers are very aware of how scarce certain items are, and feel a price in a guide such as this one is useful for "getting in the ballpark'' as to whether a title is in the $50 or $500 range, but not whether a copy is a $500 or a $700 copy.

I have attempted to make the contents as complete and accurate as possible; however, errors and omissions are normal in projects such as this and correspondence thereon will be appreciated.

Book Collecting

There have been a number of books written on book collecting over the years. A few are listed in the Selected Bibliography. Their inclusion in the bibliography is appropriate, even if no direct quotations have been made, because I have read them and know my statements on book collecting have been influenced by them.

Book collectors start as readers. This may seem rather obvious but it is important to keep in mind; for the majority of book collectors collect authors or subjects which they are currently reading or have read and enjoyed. In fact, perhaps "enjoyed" is really not descriptive enough a term. Collectors do not just enjoy these books; they feel an affinity with the author, and admire the author as one of the best in the field. The author expresses the collector's thoughts and expresses them in ways the collector would if he or she had the talent; or takes them to a time and place the collector is interested in for historic reasons or a setting which removes the collector from the current world and cares.

The book reader makes the move to book collector when he or she finds that the book or books have become important as objects which they wish to own, admire, and enjoy at their leisure. This is an important point, for most readers are content with reading a library copy or a paperback reprint and have no desire to go beyond this point. I believe that in order to understand the drive of a book collector one must understand that most are attracted to book collecting for three reasons: the true enjoyment or fun of the search, the love of the book as an object, and the economics or investment potential. From my experience with collectors, and most dealers for that matter, all three motivations exist in varying degrees and each will be discussed below.

For the Fun of It

Book collecting seems to me to be more enjoyable than other collecting hobbies because the scope is broad and the availability of material is quite large. One can find bookstores in just about every town and reasonably priced books and even bargains can be found in most of them. But that's just the beginning, for there are also book fairs, garage sales, school, church and charity book sales, friends' attics and basements, antique shops and remainder sales (new books marked down to sell).

I haven't done any research but I suspect that the quantity, variety and availability far exceeds any other collecting field such as stamps, coins, glassware, furniture, etc. And there is another plus for hardback books, in that there are fewer price guides to the field than in any other field, which means it is not as regimented as coins, stamps, comic books or even paperback books, all of which have price guides covering the majority of the material. We are publishing price guides, which will be discussed later, and this book is a price guide and there are others,, but cumulatively all of these guides cover only a very small portion of the out-of-print book market and most of the prices require a fair amount of interpretation in order to arrive at a reasonable conclusion on the particular copy in hand. This absence of consistency and regimentation is an attractive feature for book collectors.

In addition, there are a vast array of personalities in the book field, including dealers, bookscouts, other collectors, librarians and the authors themselves, and over time you will meet many of them and the experience will hopefully add to your enjoyment. Certainly, there will be few towns you visit in the future where you won't find a bookstore to spend a few hours in and learn something about the owner, prices, editions, etc.

A. Edward Newton puts it as well as anyone has in *The Book-Collecting Game:*
"Book-collecting. It's a great game. Anybody with ordinary intelligence can play it: there are, indeed, people who think that it takes no brains at all; their opinion may be ignored. No great amount of money is required, unless one becomes very ambitious. It can be played at home or abroad, alone or in company. It can even be played by correspondence. Everyone playing it can make his own rules—and change them during the progress of the game. It is not considered 'cricket' to do this in other games."

And from *Book-Collecting as a Hobby* by P.H. Muir:
"Book-collecting is not exclusively a hobby for rich and leisured people. It is less a matter of money than of method. I know many people of quite modest means who have gathered valuable and important collections with no greater expenditure than casual book buying might entail."

The point is that the greatest pleasure for the collector is in the chase and if you can afford to buy an occasional new book, you can also afford to buy an occasional old book.

Books as Objects

It would seem that the move from reader to collector must be recognized as the perception of the book itself as an object, akin to art perhaps. Certainly, if you are going to pay $25 or $50 for a first edition when you could borrow a copy from the library or purchase a paperback reprint for $3.95 (and up), you have bought an object which you want to own and actually look at occasionally just as when you want to own an original painting or a signed limited print when there are copies available at significantly lower prices.

Economics

When I started to buy first editions years ago, the decision was based (rationalized) on a simple fact. If I bought a reprint or book club edition of a book by an author whose work I believed would stand the test of time, I knew that the most I would ever get for it when I sold it was a dollar or perhaps even less, if it was wanted at all. Whereas if I bought a first edition, I believed I would always be able to get back about one half of the cost and there was a good chance, over time, that I might get all of my cost back and even more. Therefore, if I were going to buy a copy of Salinger's *Franny and Zooey* at $4, and there was a choice between a first and second printing, obviously I would buy a first. The economics of buying the second printing made absolutely no sense to me. But admittedly, I enjoyed owning a first edition of the book as an object on my shelves, which was of value to me because I had made the transition from reader to collector.

Now the second step was a bit harder. I'd enjoyed Salinger's *Catcher in the Rye* and wanted a hardbound copy, but a first edition in the early 1960's was selling for $15 or $20, four to ten times what a hardback reprint would cost. A lot of money at the time, at least in my circumstances, but there still seemed little choice, given my feelings on the importance of the book, so I sprang for it. It turned out to be a good investment, relative to the purchase of a reprint whether it was a good investment relative to other investments, such as stock or real estate is certainly questionable but I wouldn't have made those investments anyway, so it's a moot point in my case.

Three things seem clear to me:

1) Two people can buy the same titles over a ten year period and each accumulate a library of 500 volumes, 50 a year, a book a week on average, and the person who was selective as to edition and condition will have a collection that is worth considerably more than the other, probably at no greater overall cost. It is no secret that very good to fine copies of recent books turn up on antiquarian bookstore shelves, as remainders in new book stores, or at booksales for a fraction of their published price.

2) We are talking about a relatively long period of time, probably five years at a minimum and more likely ten to twenty years for real growth value.

3) Collectors can set their own financial limits. They can spend $100 or $100,000 a year or anything in between. They can collect books that few people are currently collecting and the prices are low; or go for the big authors and "high-spots" where the competition is the keenest and the prices reflective of this fact.

In summary, if you are looking for a good investment for the short term, don't buy books, but if you want to spend a certain amount of money for books, or already spend a certain amount for books every year, I believe that a collection of good books will not only give you pleasure over the years but will also not disappoint you or your heirs when the time comes to sell them.

Investment

Ever since I first started collecting first editions I have been asked how many collected authors lose popularity over the years, and told that first edition collecting is a fad that will fade; that the market is false, the prices inflated and the bubble will burst any day. I have always wondered about these questions and comments myself and so for this edition I have tried to answer them.

From 1938 to 1941 the R.R. Bowker Company (NY) published *Trade Prices Current of American First Editions*, which was sub-titled "An indexing service for the American rare book trade." The authors included were all those listed in Merle Johnson's *American First Editions*, fourth edition, edited by Jacob Blanck. There were 206 authors included and to see how many of these authors are still collected I checked to see how many were included in the 1983 (third) edition of this book. The fact is that all but nine of these authors are still collected. The authors not included were:

Ray Stannard Baker (David Grayson)

Charles Egbert Craddock (M.N. Murfree)

Mazo de la Roche

Edgar Fawcett

William James

Morgan Robertson

Susan Rowson

Harriet Prescott Spofford

Henry Van Dyke

Aside from William James, whose first book was selling for $20, at the time the average price for the other authors' first books was $4. I would consider James and perhaps some of the others as oversights on my part as there is still interest in their work but I had not included them as of 1983. Nine out of 206 is less than 5%, leaving over 95% of the authors still being collected after 50 years or more.

The next question is whether or not the market prices have held up over the years for these 197 authors? *Trade Prices Current* indexed the catalog prices of the authors' books from 1937 to 1941. Given that the prices in *The Book of First Books* relies a great deal on dealer catalog prices it seemed reasonable to compare the prices for the first books in the *Trade Prices Current* to the prices in this edition. A complete comparison could not be made because *Trade Prices Current* did not record any first books for sale during this period for 31 of the authors on the list, but that still left a comparison on 166 authors, which I believe is a representative sample. The comparison was actually made on 182 books by the 166 authors because there were 16 authors where either separate editions of the first book were covered or first and second books were covered by both reference works. The results were that the 182 books in 1940 were catalogued for a total of $9,270, and their estimated prices in 1986 would be $913,500, an increase of 9850%. Now before we all dash for the used book stores lets refine these numbers somewhat by looking at the big drivers of the increases:

		1940	1985
Audubon	*The Birds of America* NY 1840-44	500	750,000
(Bryant)	*The Embargo* B 1809	20	750
Faulkner	*The Marble Faun* B 1924 (dw)	40	15,000
Faulkner	*Soldiers' Pay* NY 1926 (dw)	8	6,000
Pound	*A Lume Spento* (Venice) 1908	125	20,000
Sandburg	*In Reckless Ecstasy* 1904	150	6,000

Steinbeck	*Cup of Gold* NY 1929 (dw)	30	3,500
Thoreau	*A Week on the Concord...* B/C 1849	40	1,250
	Total	913	802,500

and, to be fair, an equal number of those pulling down the averages:

Cather	*April Twilights* B 1903	90	850
Dickinson	*Poems* B 1890	100	1,000
Dreiser	*Sister Carrie* NY 1900	150	800
Hearn	*Stray Leaves...* NY 1882	60	250
Herbert	*The Brothers* NY 1835	70	150
Irving	*Salamagundi* NY 1807-8	850	750
Millay	*Renascence* NY 1917 (vellum)	1,000	4,000
Millay	*Renascence* NY 1917 (dw)	125	500
	Total	2,445	8,300
	Total for both groups	3,358	810,800
	Original totals	9,270	913,500
	Adjusted Balance	5,912	102,700

Percentage increased 102,700/5912 = 1737%

This total seems to me to be a fair representation of the average increase in value for the titles and, by extention for first editions over a 45 year period. I don't believe that the inclusion of the 30 authors not included, due to lack of data, would reduce this percentage as these authors included Henry Adams, Hart Crane, Anna Katharine Green, Helen Hunt Jackson (H.H.), Joaquin Miller, John Muir and Edgar Allan Poe, whose first book prices would, I'm sure, have shown large increases were a comparison available.

So, at least, I'm satisfied that few authors go completely out of favor and the prices of first editions have shown steady increase, about seven (7) percent compounded annually for 45 years.

If your only concern is to make sure the books you buy will go up in value you probably shouldn't collect books. But if you decide to anyway you should stick with proven winners that have withstood the test of time. There are still no guarantees, but it is doubtful that the major masterpieces and rare first books in fine condition will fall in value, but none of them will be cheap either. You can make your own list, but books such as Crane's *Red Badge of Courage,* London's *Call of The Wild,* Fitzgerald's *The Great Gatsby,* Faulkner's *The Sound and The Fury,* Steinbeck's *Grapes of Wrath,* Mitchell's *Gone with The Wind,* Huxley's *Brave New World,* Graves' *Goodbye to All That,* Orwell's *1984,* Salinger's *Catcher in The Rye,* Merton's *Seven Storey Mountain* or Bradbury's *Martian Chronicles,* will more than likely hold a continuing interest in the foreseeable future and if you have 100 or more of these classics in fine condition in dust wrappers I would doubt that the bottom would fall out completely.

If you don't have much money you could consider collecting some of the author's first published in the 1960's or early 1970's that you happen to like. If 10 years ago, you had bought books by the authors whose first books were listed in the first edition of this book and were published in the 1950's or early

1960's you would find that most have increased in value. It makes sense that it would take 10 to 25 years for the collectors and critics to agree on the important authors, and that some of the more recent authors tend to become over-valued because of their success with the first book, but then go down in value when they publish the next few bombs.

I don't know whether the trend will continue. The inflationary period in the late 1970's and early 1980's affected book prices as it did everything else and inflation is down. But let's look at a few examples of first books which have shown very large increases in price in the last ten years.

Author's first books estimated (in the 1975 edition):

at $15:

     Edward Abbey, John Clellon Holmes, James Jones, Terry Southern

at $20-$25:

     Thomas Berger, Ian Fleming (U.S. edition), Ted Hughes, John Knowles

at $30-$50:

     Issac Asimov, Richard Brautigan, Arthur Clarke, Ralph Ellison, William Gaddis, Joseph Heller, Jack Kerouac, Bernard Malamud, Flannery O'Connor, Philip Roth, John Updike, Kurt Vonnegut

Admittedly these authors showed significant increases, but there are few of of the 1950's authors (listed in the first edition of this book (1975)) that have decreased in value.

On the other hand, the biggest risk would seem to be paying a good deal of money ($100 and up) for relatively recent trade editions. There are some that will be worth it, and more, but many of the recent first books may fade in popularity as later works fail to live up to the author's initial performance.

What To Collect

Book collecting allows you a wide choice. Most subjects have been covered by a number of authors. If your interests are in the labor movement, farming, espionage, chess, Americana, law, medicine, a foreign country, a state, a county, a city, railroads, wars, the military, artists, westerns, philosophy, sociology, grammar, writing, cooking, animals, cars, general or specific histories, the future, science fiction, utopias, detectives, slavery, etc. You will find that hundreds if not thousands of novels, poetry and non-fiction books have been written about the subject. And if you are interested in a non-fiction area don't overlook the fiction that has been written using the subject as a vehicle because you will find them interesting additions to your knowledge and library. If there was only one book in your life that you really enjoyed, don't overlook the possibility of collecting all the different editions of that book. There are really interesting collections of *The Rubaiyat, The Compleat Angler*, etc.

If you've found a subject or author that interests you the next decision is which edition to collect. You could decide to collect paperback editions because you have little money and the cover art interests you, or

- hardback editions with dust wrappers but not necessarily first editions
- first editions without dust wrappers
- first editions with dust wrappers
- hardback editions signed by the author
- first editions signed by the author
- all editions of an author's work including reprints, foreign editions and specially illustrated editions
- all first editions in English, including American, British, Canadian, Australian, etc.

As you can see there are many avenues and you should give some consideration to choices before starting. Although it is likely you will modify your initial decision as your collection grows.

First Editions

A first edition is the first printing of a book. It's true that a first edition may have one or more printings and that a second edition will normally only be noted if there are actual changes, usually major, in the text. But as far as a collector is concerned, a first printing is the only true first edition.

Within the first printing there can be differences that make the earlier books in the printing more valuable than the later books in the same printing. These differences are identified by "points," which are discussed elsewhere.

If it's difficult to explain book collecting in general, the reason for collecting first editions is even more difficult to explain to those who are not afflicted with the mania. Bob Wilson in his book *Modern Book Collecting* (Alfred A. Knopf, New York, 1980) deals with the question when he comments on book collecting in general:

"A great many people over a great number of decades, have written pamphlets, whole books even, to justify the collecting of books. This seems to me to be an unnecessary exercise. If you are predisposed to collect books, you don't need any ex-post-facto justification for having done so. And on the other hand, if you are not convinced before you start, the chances are that no argument is going to win you over."

Now, I believe there is a little more logic and reason than this, but his argument is not without merit. At any rate, for a collector, the first edition, was viewed by the author and public when it was first published, is the most desirable edition. It's the edition the author actually saw through production, the closest in time to the writing, and the edition most likely to represent the author's intent. This may seem a minor point, but one only has to read Ray Bradbury's Afterword to a later edition of his book *Farenheit 451* to become aware of what can happen to later printings/editions.

"Some five years back, the editors of yet another anthology for school readers put together a volume with 400 (count 'em) short stories in it. How do you cram 400 short stories by Twain, Irving, Poe...into one book?

Simplicity itself. Skin, debone, demarrow, scarify, melt, render down and destroy...

Every story, slenderized, starved, blue-penciled, leeched and bled white, resembled every other story...

Only six weeks ago, I discovered that, over the years, some cubbyhole editors at Ballantine Books, fearful of contaminating the young, had, bit by bit, censored some 75 separate sections from the novel (*Farhenheit 451*)...

All you umpires, back to the bleachers. Referees, hit the showers. It's my game, I pitch, I hit, I catch, I run the bases...

And no one can help me. Not even you."

I can only assume that many first edition collectors do not want to take a chance with their favorite authors.

First editions are identified by publisher. Each publisher has its own method of identification. Many publishers have changed their method of identification over the years; a few have been so inconsistent that one has to resort to individual author bibliographies to be sure one has the true first.

At present I am aware of only two books on the market (other than this one) which include a list of publishers and how each identifies first editions. They are *First Editions: A Guide to Identification* edited by Edward N. Zempel and Linda A. Verkley (The Spoon River Press, Box 3635, Peoria, IL 61614—$20); and *A Pocket Guide To The Identification of First Editions*, Third Revised Edition by Bill McBride, 157 Sisson Avenue, Hartford, CT 06105—$6.

Appendix A includes a summary of publisher methods of identifying first editions.

Proofs and Advance Review Copies

The publication date of a book is normally set sufficiently far in advance of the printing to allow the publisher to distribute copies of the book to reviewers, bookstore owners, store managers and others; and actually ship an initial order to bookstores so that the book will be available to customers when the reviews appear.

Prior to the trade edition (and limited edition, if one is involved), a book will take different forms. The most common forms which become available on the first edition market are galley proofs, uncorrected proofs, advance reading copies, and the normal trade edition with evidence that the particular book has been sent out in advance. The latter would usually contain a slip of paper or letter from the publisher stating that the copy is sent for advance reviews, or perhaps a publication date stamped on one of the preliminary pages.

As discussed previously, a first edition collector is always anxious to obtain the first issue within the first printing; therefore, it should come as no surprise that proofs or advance review copies of the first printing are also collected and bring a premium.

It is difficult to place a value on these "pre-publication" copies because there does not seem to be any consistent formula, but generally I find that trade editions containing advance review slips or other advance publication evidence will sell for perhaps 50% more than the regular trade edition; the advance review/reader copies in paperwraps will sell for twice the trade value; the uncorrected proofs (also in paperwraps but with "uncorrected" indicated) for somewhat more than the advance review copies; and the galley proofs (normally on long sheets either bound or unbound) will bring the most.

The recent "galleys," run off on copiers, are so easily duplicated that I don't feel they have much of a monetary value above duplication cost, but this is a personal view; and I must admit that they will prove very valuable to researchers as they do contain numerous corrections. This is an important consideration in forming a collection. If you are interested in the evolution of a writer's thoughts the page proofs and uncorrected proofs could prove very useful. If the collection is being formed with the thought in mind of eventual donation to a library, I believe the proofs should be included if at all possible. Also my thoughts on the proofs and advance copies are that the number of proofs is relatively low, 50 to 500 copies and if eventual scarcity is a determinent in future value a proof that was printed in an edition of 200 copies (and very fragile by nature) will certainly have more value than the first trade printing, which for popular authors can run from 100,000 to 800,000 copies (recent examples: Pat Conroy's *The Price of Tides*—first printing 250,000; James Michener's *Texas*—750,000 copies; and Stephen King's *It*—800,000 copies).

It should be noted that many publishers do not bother with paperbound proofs and only send out a number of trade editions with a review slip.

One recent example of a limited proof is James Clavell's *Noble House*. I understand the publisher xeroxed 4 copies on one side of the page only (8½" × 11"), and then 16 copies on both sides of the page. These copies were put in large three-ring binders, but after the first 20 copies they stopped. I assume they changed to sending out copies of the regular trade edition with review slips. I believe I know why they changed, as I handled one of the 16 copies, and it was about three inches thick and very unwieldy.

Shown below are three prepublication copies. On the left is a proof of James Baldwin's first book which is of special interest as the cover differs from the one finally selected for the book (the first trade edition is shown elsewhere). In the middle is an uncorrected proof of the first American edition of Adams' *Watership Down* (the true first edition is the English edition, which was and perhaps still is one of the most expensive trade first editions published in the 1970's). The book on the right is an advance reading copy of *Carrie* by Stephen King, who continues to be one of our best selling and most collected authors.

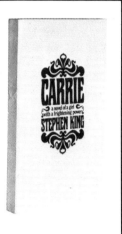

Limited Editions

The limited edition comes in varying forms as discussed below. A limited edition of a new book is usually signed, numbered and in a slipcase and costs three to five times the cost of the regular first edition, which is referred to as the trade, or first trade, edition. The first printing of the trade edition is still considered the first edition, so the collector must decide if both the limited signed and the first trade, are required or if only one is necessary for the collection.

"Limited editions" of 200 copies are usually still available when one has a hard time finding fine copies of first trade editions from the same period which were published in an edition of 5000 copies. This is because there is an aversion to throwing away a book signed and numbered by an author even if one has never heard of the author, but no aversion at all to throwing away novels, poetry, drama, detective stories, medical and scientific books by an author one has never heard of.

Limited Editions Club (LEC)—George Macy of department store fame, started the LEC in 1929. The books were printed on good paper and bound in various interesting and attractive covers, illustrated and signed by famous artists of the period, numbered and limited to 1500 copies (later 2,000). The books were issued in boxes or slipcases. They're very attractive and actually easy to read. The LEC issued one book a month until its problems of recent years when it changed hands a number of times (currently issuing books at a cost of $400 a volume). If we look at the total output, we find that one or two titles a year have gone up significantly in price and the balance can be purchased at reasonable prices, particularly at auction.

If you're interested in bindings and illustrated books, you should not overlook the LEC.

Heritage Press—editions are not limited, but are mentioned because the Heritage Press was an offshoot of the LEC. It produced the trade edition, so to speak. The Heritage editions were printed on good paper, nicely bound and issued in slipcases. The editions contained the same illustrations as the comparable LEC editions, but they were not signed or limited. You can still subscribe to the Heritage Press for $17.50 a volume; and buy most of the earlier editions in the series in used bookstores in the $5 to $25 range. If you like the classics in a very readable form, attractively bound and at a reasonable price, it would be hard to go wrong collecting these editions.

Franklin Press—a truly interesting recent phenomena is the Franklin Mint. Franklin publishes leather bound "limited editions." What I find interesting is that they publish literary titles and seem to have a bigger clientele than all the literary specialist bookdealers in the country combined. Of course, this is just a guess as the publishers do not disclose the quantities printed. But, one must assume the "limitation" is very large.

When the Franklin Press started advertising its Pulitzer Prize editions of fiction, a friend asked my advice on whether or not to purchase them. I told him that for less money he could probably buy first editions in very good condition of not only the fiction but also the poetry and drama winners. To date I have found about 150 titles and it has probably cost him $3,000.

Signed Limited Editions

Trade Book Publishers—When an author becomes popular the publisher may decide to issue a signed, numbered limited edition. This edition is usually 300 copies, plus or minus 50, but can be as little as 100 copies or as many as 1,000 copies. These books are composed of the first trade edition sheets bound up in a binding different than the trade edition binding and in a slipcase. There are people who are very happy with the trade edition, but if I thought James Michener was an important writer, as many people do, and I could buy one of 1,000 signed numbered copies of *Texas* for $75, versus one of the 750,000 copies of the trade edition at $15 to $25, depending on discount, I'd probably buy the signed limited, because at 750,000 copies it's hard to believe the trade edition will ever have much value. Of course, if the choice is between a first edition and a second printing for the same price, I'd still buy the first.

Private Press Publishers—When an author becomes popular with book collectors there are a number of small presses that publish signed limited editions of their work. Sometimes it is new material that has not been published before; or it may be a short story, novella, or poetry which have appeared previously in magazine or short story anthologies, and its publication by the press is considered the first separate edition/publication. These present real problems for the collector because these books come out in so many sub-editions, for example:

10 signed numbered copies for presentation
26 signed lettered copies
300 signed numbered copies
700 hardbound (not signed)

1,000 paperbound copies

All of the above are legitimate first editions, usually printed on the same paper at the same time, only bound differently; and in the case of the first three with an extra leaf with the limitation and signature. If you must have one of each you can see the problem and expense involved. If the author continued to remain popular the prices will probably rise proportionately, thus if one of the 26 copies sold at $100 and one of the 300 copies at $50, their respective values in the future might be $200 and $100. Published prices range from $50 to $150.

Fine Press Books —These are also private presses, similar to the last category, but the concentration is more on the classics, the quality of paper, binding and illustrations, and contain work and are signed by an artist of note. I have made them a separate group even though they are also private presses because there is a significant difference in the published price, usually ranging from $200 to $2,000.

THIS
SPECIAL
EDITION
IS LIMITED TO 310 COPIES
OF WHICH 300 ARE FOR SALE
EACH COPY
NUMBERED
& SIGNED
BY THE
AUTHOR
THIS IS
COPY
NUMBER
163

William Faulkner

Paperbacks or Paperwraps

The binding of most books published in this century varies from a paper cover weighing only slightly more than the pages of the book (paperwraps); to a completely stiff paper cover (boards) and finally to cloth and/or leather bound covers. The recent books in paperwraps are normally published after the original edition and are not particularly valuable. Presently, the first printings of these paper reprint editions are valued at 5% to 25% of the first edition. If, however, the paper edition contains a new introduction, or some major changes in the text, the value could approach the same value as the regular first edition. *The Paperback Price Guide* by Kevin Hancer (Overstreet Publications, Cleveland, TN 37311) is a helpful book for pricing individual titles.

In some cases the paper edition is the true first edition because no hardback edition was published; and this may become more common in the next few years as publishing costs continue to increase. Recently there has been a move to print the same sheets and bind some in hard cover and some in paperwraps. Over the next 10 to 20 years there may be a reversal of the ratio of original hardback to original paperback editions, with the paperback books becoming the normal medium and the hardback first editions becoming the exception.

Sources For Books

I believe that book collecting requires on-the-job training, particularly in the pricing area. As mentioned previously, the price guides in the field are not extensive and the best way to get a feel for prices is to visit a number of shops and obtain as many catalogs as possible. The first alternative may not be practical if you don't travel much, although you will find that book-collecting and travel go very well together, giving you a good excuse to take short trips to towns within a few hundred miles or so. For now, in addition to the tourist attractions, hotels and restaurants, you have the pleasure of looking over the stock of the bookstores in town.

Once you have decided what to collect and get a feel for prices, you need to spend some money. There's nothing like spending money to sharpen your wits and force you to take the whole business a little more seriously.

Catalogs

Catalogs can be obtained for the asking, at least initially. If you are going to collect books I would recommend you subscribe to the American Book Collector (ABC), a monthly publication with a subscription price of $30 a year (Box 867, Ossining, NY 10562-0867). It's a good magazine but more importantly for you as a novice, it includes in every issue a list of the catalogs received by ABC the previous month. The list includes the dealer's name, address, the catalog subject matter and price (if any). After looking over the list, you can write to the dealer issuing catalogs covering your field of interest. The vast majority of the dealers do not charge for their catalogs and will usually send you the current catalog and perhaps one or two more. There are many standard abbreviations and terms used in these catalogs and I have tried to cover many of them in Appendix B—Glossary. If you haven't purchased anything from these catalogs the dealers will drop you from their mailing list on the assumption that you just wanted the catalogs for pricing information or you are not really interested in the type of books they stock. If you are interested in their type of books but just don't find anything in the first two catalogs, you should ask if there is a subscription fee or if you can send them a list of exactly what you are looking for so the dealer(s) may quote you specific titles as they arrive. Keeping your name on mailing lists is very simple—just buy books. We have people who have asked for our catalogs every two years since we started in business and they have never bought a book. We assume they collect catalogs. We just received another request from a man who has received copies of our catalogs at various times over the last 20 years. If you read the letter you would never know he had ever heard of us before. He has not counted on my wife's long memory for people who cost us money, anywhere from $1 for a short list to $5 and up for a major catalog. I don't think she sent him another catalog.

General Used Book Stores and Sales

There are a great number of sources for books. There are garage sales; school, charity, library and church booksales; antique stores, and general used bookstores. Most of these are not particularly interested in either keeping up with current prices or trying to sell for the going market price. But you should keep in mind that occasionally these are also the places where you can get stung the worst as a beginner because there are always a few books that the owners or operators have heard are worth $100 and so they have priced their copy at $100 even though the condition is such that a specialist in the field might be embarrassed to ask more than $25 for the same book.

There are many dealers in Canada, England and the U.S., and with pricing being somewhat subjective, and collecting interests varying from one geographical location to another, there are always certain authors or subjects that bring premium prices in one region while commanding little interest elsewhere. If you are in a store which doesn't catalog there is a good chance that the books which don't sell well in that area will be priced much lower than the theoretical market.

Specialist Dealers

The next group includes the specialist dealer. These dealers may specialize in just one field or a number of collecting interests; but they don't consider themselves general book dealers and except for the occasional volume they will not try to stock books in other fields. Many have favorite authors or books that they insist on pricing more than the market and the authors and books they dislike and price lower than the market. Then there are the books a dealer has never seen before and assumes are extremely scarce and thus worth more than the market would indicate and the books everyone else seems to believe are scarce but which they know are not scarce because they have had 5 copies in the last two years and thus they mark the book lower than the market would indicate. But on 95 to 99% of the stock they're all pricing in the same range, plus or minus 20%.

There are a few dealers who claim (and fewer still who are right) that the condition of any book they carry is so superior to any other bookseller's copy, that the collector should not mind paying two or three times the going market price for their copy. So the collector should be very satisfied that the book received is in fact in very fine condition and worth the price; otherwise if the collector finds another copy in similar or better condition at a significantly lower price in the future, he will be disappointed not only in his copy but also in the dealer from whom it was purchased.

Auctions

For the book-collector there are a number of auction houses which handle books. Swann Galleries in New York City is probably the most active auction house as far as number of books are concerned because Swann has weekly sales. There are other houses such as Christie's and Sotheby's which have important (read expensive) book sales during the year; and many other houses which have monthly or quarterly sales. A few of these auction houses are listed in Appendix E.

Auction prices tend to vary widely. Many of the books at auction will sell for half the "market" price, particularly the cheaper books. And some sales, such as the recent sales at Christie's and Swann's of James Gilvarry's library, will garner prices for many lots that exceed the "market" prices.

There are auction houses around most cities and occasionally these auctions, which handle estate sales, contain books. These auctions are advertised in the local paper and it's possible to find some real bargains.

Knowledgeable Buying

In order to become a knowledgeable buyer you should be aware of issue points, bibliographies in your field and what pricing information may be available.

I believe strongly that one of the major drawbacks for a beginning book collector is the difficulty in finding out what is available by an author, how to identify the editions and what a reasonable price range is for individual books. The following will hopefully provide some information on these subjects.

First Issue or State and "Points"

There are a number of books, particularly those published before the turn of the century, where one can only differentiate between the first and later printings of a book by being aware of the changes made between printings. These changes can be in the text, the type used, the number of pages, the dates in the ads, the type of binding (cloth, leather, boards, wrappers) or elsewhere. In some cases the authors may have wished to make changes in the text themselves or the publisher may have run out of a certain color cloth for the covers and switched to another color. These differences are known as "points." The most common "points" are typographical errors that are discovered and corrected between printings or even midway through the first printing. For whatever reason, the changes are made and a "point" is created.

When these changes occur, the "points" indicate the first issue or first state of the printing. The glossary (Appendix B) includes a discussion of these terms, but it is worthwhile to quote P.H. Muir's *Book-Collecting as a Hobby* where the difference between issues and states is summarized as follows:

> "An 'issue' is caused by some change...after some copies have already been circulated, (while) a 'state' is caused by a...change before any copies of the book have been circulated."

In the list of First Books any "points" associated with a book will be mentioned. The difference in value between issues/states can be great. For instance, Hart Crane's *White Building* contains an introduction by Allen Tate. In the first issue Tate's name is spelled incorrectly on the title page. The correction was made by tipping in a new title page. The difference in value between the first and the second issue of that book is significant.

The First Edition collector and dealer must know the "points" connected with the books which they collect or deal in. These "points" are contained in reference books known as bibliographies. General bibliographies cover many authors or a wide field such as Americana or Black Literature. One of the most famous is Jacob Blanck's *Bibliography of American Literature* which has covered authors alphabetically through Stockton (seven [7] volumes). In addition to these general bibliographies there are specific bibliographies on individual authors. These include books written by or about the author, and, in many cases, also list the author's appearances in magazines, anthologies or as the contributor of an introduction or preface to a book written by another author.

Bibliographies

I would caution the buyer of bibliographies to make an attempt to examine a copy of the book before purchasing it. As a dealer, I maintain a large reference library of individual author bibliographies, and I must say that I am surprised at the number of "bibliographies" which, although extensive and expensive, do not assist one in identifying first editions.

The standard setter in modern bibliography, in my opinion, is Donald Gallup. In his book ON CONTEMPORARY BIBLIOGRAPHY (Humanities Research Center, University of Texas at Austin (1970)) Mr. Gallup states

"It is the bibliographer's first duty to make his bibliography useful...

And what exactly should be his job? His function as I see it may be summarized under three principal headings:

First, to establish the canon of the author's printed work;

Second, to identify and describe first and important later editions of the books, in their variants, states, and issues, with their various binding and dust jackets, explaining their significance where it is not readily apparent, and accounting, if possible, for any unusual aspects; and

Third, to establish for at least each major book the exact date of publication, date of composition (where this differs substantially), number of copies printed, and price at which the book sold when it was first published. He may, and doubtless will, do other things, but these seem to me to be the essentials."

There are books that are entitled "Checklists" which do not include precise information on how to identify the first printing, but these are not misleading, for they are billed as "Checklists" and not as "Bibliographies." But what do you do when you've bought a "Bibliography" and find that the bibliographer has not bothered to mention the existence of limited editions or how to identify the first editions?

The foregoing complaint was included in the last edition of this book (1983). Thereafter I decided that rather than complain (or in addition to) I would do something positive, so my wife and I started to publish a series of AUTHOR PRICE GUIDES (APG's).

Reasons for the APGs:

• In general there are no price guides available covering all of an individual author's books

• Bibliographies are expensive when published, remaindered within a few years, hard to find and sometimes expensive after five years or so and not economically worth up-dating and reprinting until another 10 or 15 years go by. Take Higginson's bibliography of Robert Graves for example: published in 1966, it is now a "rare" book bringing $100 to $150 when you can find one

- Many author bibliographies are available within large compilations such as the *Bibliography of American Literature* or *First Printings of American Authors*. These are excellent references but for someone, particularly the newer collector, who is only interested in a few or even one author, these compilations are just too expensive, and not available in local libraries in many parts of the country

The APGs include:
- A facsimile of the author's signature
- A very brief biographical sketch
- A separate listing for each issue of each book or pamphlet by the author. In other words, for each title there are separate listings for a limited lettered edition, a numbered edition, first American and first British edition, if applicable.
- Each individual listing includes the title, publisher, place of publication, date of publication, number of copies (if known), exact information for identifying the first printing, retail price estimates for the book with and without a dustwrapper; and a reference for the source of the bibliographical information.
- An author's "A" items, that is the books, pamphlets, and broadsides attributed to the author (147 titles and almost 300 items in the case of Robert Graves) and will be expanded over the years to include important "B" items. Proof copies will be included as seen or reported but only if the color or some means of differentiating them is known for I assume just about all books are preceeded by proofs.

The APGs are:
- Printed on 8½ × 11 inch paper that is mylar re-inforced and pre-punched for standard 3-ring binders
- Priced reasonably ($.50 to $9.00)

Given the nature of bibliographic research and the volatility of prices, each APG will be updated as necessary and it does not seem reasonable for the purchaser to have to pay full price for updates. Therefore, original purchasers of an individual APG will only be charged full price the first time they purchase; extra copies and subsequent updates will be available at half price if desired.

It is hoped that the APGs will prove useful as accurate, current and reasonably priced bibliographical checklists which include relatively accurate retail price estimates. The APGs will, of course, be improved over the years as collectors, librarians and dealers contribute new or revised information which will be incorporated in updates.

One of the major problems in arriving at a reasonable price for a first edition is, in our opinion, the lack of information on the number of copies actually printed. There are a number of reasons why it is difficult to obtain this information from publishers but whatever the reasons, it's obvious that cost should have some relation to quantity, as well as the number of collectors; therefore, we will try to obtain actual quanities printed from whatever sources we can.

A list of the APGs available is at the back of this book.

The following is the record on the first 67 APGs we compiled:

No bibliography exists 30
Current bibliography (within 5 years) 3
Bibliography 5 to 10 years old 27
Bibliography over 10 years old 7
Bibliographies (that are available) include—
    U.S. title page information* 35
    English title page information 23
    U.S. copyright page information** 34
    English copyright page information 22
    first printing quantities 5
    some first printing quantitites 4

*Indicates whether publisher, place and date actually appear on the title page.

**Indicates whether or not the copyright page states "First Printing," "First Edition," etc.

Here is a representative sample of 67 authors, all having some degree of collector interest. Three have current bibliographies available. Thirty, or 45% have never been covered by a bibliography. Only five of the existing bibliographies supply quantities printed, which I believe should provide some indication of scarcity, while two of the four, with partial quantities, relied on previous bibliographies dating from the 1930's and never obtained quantities thereafter, even though these authors published their work for another 30 years.

The most comprehensive bibliographies for our purposes in compiling the first Price Guides were:

Gallup, Donald, *T.S. Eliot A Bibliography*, Revised and Extended Edition, Harcourt, Brace & World, NY (1969)

Grimshaw, James A. Jr., *Robert Penn Warren A Descriptive Bibliography 1922-79*, University of Virginia, Charlottesville (1981)

Hanneman, Audre, *Ernest Hemingway A Comprehensive Bibliography*, Princeton University Press, Princeton, 1967 and Supplement.

Higginson, Fred H., *A Bibliography of the Works of Robert Graves*, Archon Books, Hamden, CT (1966).

The general sources for bibliographic information are:

First Printings of American Authors (FPAA) edited by Matthew G. Bruccoli, C.E. Frazer Clark, Jr., et al, Gale Research, Detroit (1977-1979). Four volumes—covers about 360 authors, both U.S. and English editions, with title page and first edition identification for all U.S. editions and the English editions for 50 authors (title, publisher, and dates for English editions of the other 310 authors). Of the 27 bibliographies 5 to 10 years old (above) 20 were covered in FPAA (with some overlap with other sources). In print and should be in most libraries.

A Bibliographical Introduction to Seventy-five Modern American Authors by Gary M. Lepper, Serendipity Books, Berkeley 1976—includes first edition identification for the U.S. editions by the 75 novelists and poets (unless a title was first published elsewhere in which case the foreign edition is included). Of the 27 bibliographies 5 to 10 years old (above), seven were covered by Lepper (with some overlap with other sources). Out of print.

Science Fiction and Fantasy Authors, A Bibliography of First Printings of Their Fiction, edited by L.W. Currey, G.K. Hall & Co., Boston (1979)—covers 216 authors' works including first edition identification. The book is excellent for all science fiction and fantasy titles (further checking will be required to obtain titles outside these fields).

Bibliography of American Literature (BAL) compiled by Jacob Blanck (Volumes 1-6) and edited and completed by Virginia L. Smyers and Michael Winship (Volume 7), Yale University Press, New Haven and London, (1955-1983)—seven volumes to date. Henry Adams through Frank Stockton, 238 authors with full bibliographical details. The coverage is up to the early part of this century. In print and at most libraries.

General sources for title, publisher and date, by author, would include the series *Contemporary Authors* (over 100 volumes—in most public libraries) and the general author compilations listed in the Selected Bibliography.

Price Guides

American Book Prices Current (ABPC)—An annual publication of the auction prices realized. You can find copies in the reference room of most university, city, or county libraries. The prices will vary greatly for the same title but you will be able to ascertain a range. The problem is that only a few of the currently collected authors will be included in ABPC, for the major auction houses can't afford to handle minor items, less than $75 to $100. And there will only be a few titles by each author.

Bookmen's Price Index—Edited by Daniel McGrath, a compilation of dealer catalog entries issued about every four to six months. There are 32 volumes available and the current price is $165 a volume. You'll find most titles but you may have to go through a number of volumes to find it and there are many titles that aren't covered at all, particularly the scarce ones which are sold without ever being catalogued. But it's a very useful reference and there should be a set somewhere in your local library system. My pet peeve with the publisher of this series is that they use many dealer catalogues, including ours, at no cost to them, and don't even offer these dealers a substantial discount.

The Book Collector's Handbook of Values—was compiled by Van Allen Bradley, who died last year. The 1982-1983 edition contained over 20,000 entries, primarily first editions in literature and Americana. We all complained about Bradley's pricing, either too high or too low, and there were some errors, but everyone in the trade used it because on the whole he did a good job. I have been told by a Putnam sales representative that a new edition will be available in the future. If so, it's affordable and worthwhile. If you are going to spend time looking for books anyway you may as well be aware of scarce books in other collecting areas in case you stumble across them.

Mandeville's Used Book Price Guide—A compilation of dealer catalog entries, well edited and concentrating on $10 to $100 books including many non-fiction titles. Very helpful for pricing general stock. This should also be in the reference room of most libraries. The 1983 edition is available for $79 from Price Guide Publishers, Box 525, Kenmore, WA 98028.

Miscellaneous—There are a number of price guides covering specific areas such as Americana, Law, the Civil War, the Occult, etc. Again, the local libraries should have copies or be able to locate them somewhere in the system. These are usually advertised in the *American Book Collector* as they are published, and if they cover your collecting interest you'd be well advised to pick them up.

Author Price Guides (APG)—have been described before. The advantage is that all of the books are listed, with identification points and price estimates. You only have to buy the APGs that interest you and the information is current. This is an unbiased recommendation, I swear to God.

Reprint Publishers and Book Clubs

There are certain publishers that normally only reprint books originally published by others. The most common are Grosset & Dunlap, A.L. Burt, Blakiston, Hurst, Modern Library, Sun Dial, Triangle and World's Tower Books (although the latter did publish two of Raymond Chandler's first editions). These reprints are not particularly valuable unless a new introduction is included in the edition, although some of the very early scarce titles by very popular authors are sought by collectors if they are fine in dustwrappers, principally because the dustwrappers on these reprints duplicated the front cover and spine of the original trade first editions.

I understand there have been over 800 book clubs in the United States during this century. Many of these, I assume, sent their members regular trade editions of a book. In the case of book clubs which printed their own editions, there is normally no problem identifying them if the book has a dustwrapper as the front flap of the dw will state that it is a book club edition and will not have a price on the dw flap.

If the book is by a publisher which states "First Edition" or "First Printing" on the verso of title page, the lack of this statement will make it easily identifiable as other than a First Edition. Book-of-the-Month Club editions, since 1949 or 50, although they look exactly like the publisher's edition and frequently state "First Edition/Printing," are also easy to identify even without the dw since they usually contain a small mark on the lower right corner of the rear cover. (Prior to 1949 it is difficult to differentiate the club's edition from the true first edition.) The mark can be a small black circle in earlier books or in more recent years merely a circular or square depression (blind stamp) in the lower right hand corner of the back cover. The Literary Guild book club editions also state "First Edition," but are actually books printed on plates rented from the original publisher. They are easy to identify as the spine and title page indicate "Literary Guild."

If a book club edition does not have a dw and is not a Book-of-the-Month Club edition, it may still be identified by the binding and paper which will be of poorer quality than a normal publishers' edition. The most difficult book club editions to identify are, in my opinion, those originally published by New Directions and Viking.

Pricing Variances

Pricing of out-of-print books, whether they be collectable or not, is primarily based on supply and demand. A dealer may price a book at $100 and feel confident it is a reasonable price, but if the book doesn't sell, the price will eventually be changed. The nature of the business is such that it can take one or even two years before the buyer comes along and many dealers are more than willing to wait to sell a scarce book.

The following comments are offered to indicate other factors that affect price.

Condition Isn't Everything—
It's the Only Thing

Vince Lombardi may have been talking about winning, but the book collectors could rephrase the quote. The condition of a first edition or any collectable book is the major determinant of its value. The retail prices I have estimated herein for an author's first book are for very good to fine copies (in dustwrappers after 1920). There is no doubt that certain collectors might pay two or perhaps three times this amount for an absolutely mint copy of a book.

First edition collectors are by nature very hard to please. They would like each of their first editions to look new. And they will pay for such copies. The reverse is also true. A book in poor condition is very difficult to sell. Books valued at $100 in fine condition are practically valueless if in very poor condition. If the book is rare it will of course have some value whatever its condition, but only a fraction of what it would be worth if it were a fine to mint copy.

Unless one is a book collector, dealer, or book scout, it is difficult to understand how to describe the condition of a book. Even within this group there can be wide differences of opinion, which only confirm the fact that condition descriptions are somewhat subjective.

Many people really believe that if a book is 20 or 30 years old it is in very good condition if the covers are still attached, and if the book is 100 years old one should not downgrade it just because the covers are no longer attached ("What do you expect, it's 100 years old!") I am sympathetic with their confusion but I am not interested in buying their books.

The following general gradings are used:

MINT—as new, unread

FINE—is close to new while showing slight signs of age, but without any defects

VERY GOOD—indicates a used book that shows some sign of wear but still has no defects

GOOD—is used for a book which shows normal wear and aging, still complete and with no major defects

FAIR—is a worn and used copy probably cover tears and other defects

READING COPY—a poor copy with text complete but not much else going for it

As a guide to condition I have included pictures of the book and dustwrapper of Charles Fort's first book, *The Outcast Manufacturers*, which was published in 1909—just to show what a 77-year-old book can look like.

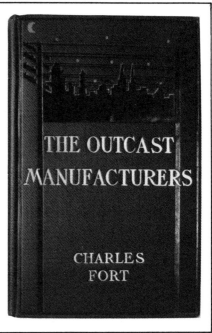

Dustwrappers or Dust Jackets

The dust jacket or dustwrapper (dw) that covers a book is a valuable part of a first edition. On recently published books, it is difficult to sell a first edition without a dustwrapper to a collector. On books 20 years old or older, the average increase in value added by the dustwrapper would be close to 400%, providing the dustwrapper is in fine condition. This rule would not apply to inexpensive books in the $5 to $20 range, where the dustwrapper value would be in the 50-100% range but is farily consistent on books valued above $25 without a dustwrapper. There are, of course, exceptions to this rule, the most obvious being the value added by the presence of a dustwrapper on the books of Hemingway, Faulkner or Fitzgerald. It's not unusual for these authors' books to sell for 5 to 10 times more with fine dustwrappers than without the dustwrapper. And at least one, Faulkner's *Soldiers Pay*, has been sold at 20 to 25 times the unjacketed price.

The condition of the dustwrapper is just as important, and perhaps as difficult to describe, as the condition of the book. It should be mentioned that *if a catalog entry does not specifically state a book is in a dustwrapper one must assume it is not.* A few examples of dustwrappers illustrate reasonably good condition.

Autographed Books

Authors' autographs in a book may be considered in various categories including limited signed editions, signed trade editions, and association copies.

Signed Trade Editions—are copies of the regular trade first edition signed by the author, with or without an inscription. If the original recipient of the book is not well known, or of general interest, some collectors prefer the author's signature without the inscription. These signed books will usually sell for at least twice as much as an unsigned copy, but the real determinant of price will be the value of the author's signature. Some authors are very generous in signing their books and as a result their signatures may only be worth $10 or $15 and this would be the price difference between a signed and unsigned copy of a first edition; or the price of a signed later printing. On the other hand, some authors very rarely sign a book and their signature alone may be worth $50 or more, and again this would establish a price. Further, some authors are very free with their signatures but very rarely inscribe copies of their books and therefore inscribed copies, even if the recipient is unknown, will command a premium.

Association Copies—are a category of signed books that include a signed inscription from the author to another famous personality or someone important within the framework of the particular author's life and work. These are known as "association copies" and will be valued more highly than the normal signed first edition, depending on the importance of the recipient involved.

- For Sylvia Beach, from Mr. Lowry. 1934.
With Love.

Association copy of a first book, Sylvia Beach, owner of Shakespeare and Company, Paris, from Malcolm Lowry (reduced).

Some Suggestions

The following comments may be of some help. They are basically my own feeling and may not be shared by others, but for what they are worth. . . .

Building a Collection

If you have decided to collect a number of currently popular authors whose books are not particularly scarce, and you want to do it fast, the best method would be to send a want list of the books to a number of specialist dealers including the minimum condition you will accept. You will receive a number of quotes and can choose among them. If you do buy a number of books on the first round, you should send a revised list, perhaps every month, to the dealers who responded so they will not be searching for books you have already bought and to remind them that you are still actively searching for certain titles.

If your budget only allows for a few books a month it would probably be wise to limit the want lists to a few dealers, explain your budget limitations and limit the number of books on the list. In other words if you have decided to spend $100 a month on your collection and most of the books you want are in the $20 to $40 range, you will only be buying 2 to 5 books a month and there is no sense obtaining quotes from dealers on hundreds of books. Also it will be hard to convince a dealer who quoted you once, to do it again if you didn't buy anything from the initial quotes. Alternatively, if you have found a dealer you believe has been fair with you and whom you trust, give him your complete want list, explain your budget limitation and ask him to buy for you. The dealer will see most of the catalogs that are issued every year and can work with you to build your collection. Make it clear that either the dealer will be the only one buying for you, or that you will also be buying at other local stores and from catalogs and you will keep your want list updated regularly so that the dealer can also keep current with your collection.

If you are interested in only a few authors who have produced a large body of work and have a number of scarce and expensive books in their canon, it seems to me advisable to limit the number of dealers searching for the books. If your job is such that you are tied up most of the day and evening the correspondence and telephone calls from 20 dealers can get on your nerves and spoil some of your enjoyment in building your collection. Also, there is always the possibility that if expensive items come up at auction the dealers might bid against each other to buy it for eventual sale to you at a higher price than you might otherwise have paid.

Caring for Books

Most dealers in scarce or rare books have taken up the practice of protecting the covers of books without dustwrappers by making a cover for the book out of a sheet of acetate, and protecting books with dust jackets by covering them with plain acetate or an acetate cover that is backed with acid-free paper. The latter are made by Bro-Dart and other companies and your dealer should be able to order some for you or tell you where you can buy them in your area.

From the viewpoint of the dealer the acetate cover improves the appearance of the books, but more important they protect the books and dustwrappers while they are on the dealers' shelves. The original dustwrappers are an expensive part of the book and it is easy to tear them on the edges just by taking them off the shelf, therefore it's only reasonable to go to the expense of putting on covers. There are dealers who don't like the idea or looks of the covers, a view I respect; but it is depressing to see a $200 copy of a book turn into a $50 copy after it has been handled by 50 or 100 people over a few months.

The collector who takes a book home may not feel the need to keep the covers on the books and if the books are not handled much and you don't like their appearance, I don't see any reason to leave them on. The covers do provide a measure of protection but they do age over time and probably should be changed after a number of years.

The best protection for a book is a specially made box, but these are labor intensive and expensive, in the $75 to $150 range, and are hardly worth the cost to protect a $50 book.

If boxes are not within your budget, or cost effective, I would recommend glass front bookcases as a good investment for your more valuable books.

The most important thing is to keep the books in a relatively clean environment at consistent temperature and humidity levels. This can be accomplished with air conditioning, a humidifier and perhaps an air cleaner.

It is also important to watch the little things like leaving a book out on a table where a visitor might set a glass on it or something could be spilled nearby and spread to the cover before the book can be picked up; shelving books too tightly so that the top edges are torn when a book is removed; leaving acid content paper such as newsprint stored in the books, which will darken the pages; or putting thick sheaves of paper in the book which can loosen the bindings.

Books are fragile but the worst made of them have resided in attics for decades without serious damage; so worry more about dampness than dryness, avoid direct sunlight which can fade the covers badly and don't put stickers or gummed labels directly on the covers as they will discolor. The latter is mentioned because I've seen a number of book collections marked with different colored labels.

Insurance and Appraisals

As far as insurance is concerned I understand that most homeowner policies have a limit on collectables and you may have to purchase a special rider on the policy to cover your books. If the books are covered under your basic insurance policy or a rider is required your company will normally require an appraisal for its files. The easiest and least expensive way to obtain an appraisal is to type an itemized list of your books or at least the ones which have a vlue over $25.00. Include the author, title, publisher, place, date, edition and very brief description and leave room on the right margin for the dealer to add the appraisal prices. After you've completed this list visit a bookdealer, hopefully one that you have actually bought some books from, and ask him what he will charge to appraise the books on the list. The dealer will have to visit your home to actually look at the books, unless he or she is familiar enough with your collection to make the appraisal without a visit. If you have 1,000 books and only 100 of them have a value over $25, just list the 100 books and then add a miscellaneous category for hardbacks and paperbacks, so that these can be included. Many people don't feel the lesser books are worth the trouble but if you have 800 hardback books with an average value of $10 each, it would be nice to get the $8,000 if there ever was a fire in your house.

Credit

Most specialist dealers carry VISA, MASTERCARD, CHOICE, DISCOVER and/or AMERICAN EXPRESS. If they don't have charges and the amount of the purchase is relatively large the dealer will usually allow you 30 days to pay and may arrange longer time payments if necessary.

Even if the dealer does take credit cards, he or she might be interested in allowing payment terms because the credit charge will be 3 to 5%. Many times an expensive book will not have a large margin and 5% could equate to 25 to 50% of the profit.

Examining the Book

When buying a book make sure it's complete, and if there are 'points', check them. This may seem obvious but dealers do make mistakes, particularly on modern books where there are no plates or maps to collate. It is possible to find blank pages, back endpapers missing, a page torn, or a page missing. Someone actually neatly cut out one story in a short story collection (we did notice this one). The point is that dealers handle a great number of books and they don't expect a 1975 mass produced book that looks almost new to have a page missing, and if you discover it much later it may be too late or not worth the bother to return.

Bargaining

Bargaining with a dealer is not unheard of and if a book has been on the shelf for a year or so, the dealer might be willing to accept an offer of something less than the marked price, but the collector should be careful because dealers have different attitudes about this and some will never discount. You should ask the dealer very straightforwardly and politely if an offer on a specific title would be acceptable. One must understand that most banks have little confidence in books as collateral and so all the books on the shelf have probably been paid for and the nature of the business is to wait for the right buyer to come along, even if this takes over a year in some cases.

There is also a danger in continual bargaining if you are a serious collector, because if a scarce book you have wanted for years comes into the store and the dealer has other customers for the book, you can rest assured that you will not be offered the book first if you have established a pattern of bargaining in the past.

Discounts

My observation after cataloging for twenty years, having an open shop for ten years, and visiting hundreds of other shops is that an antiquarian bookstore is a great negative cash flow business. Many, but by no means all, of the owners are getting along on a relatively low income, particularly if you compute it on an hourly basis. This is not a complaint as the vast majority of the owners are perfectly aware that they could be doing something else, but don't have any desire to work in another field.

There are reciprocal discounts within the trade because dealers purchase much of their inventory from other dealers. There are no warehouses stocking inscribed copies of Fitzgerald's books and if you have a customer for one, your best chance of finding it is on the shelves of another dealer. You, as a collector, don't offer the dealer the long range opportunities to buy saleable inventory and therefore there is no compelling reason to give you a discount, which seems to come as a shock to certain collectors, fortunately a minority.

Selling Your Books

The antiquarian book field represents a true marketplace. A book is worth what someone will pay for it. Prices can vary over a wide range for the same book during the same year. When selling a book to a dealer, the value of the book will depend on what the dealer believes to be a reasonable resale value in his particular market. If the book is scarce or rare and the dealer has a ready market for the particular book, the dealer may be willing to pay close to the retail value of the book. If the dealer has no immediate market for the book, but is confident that it will sell within a few months he will probably offer about 30% to 50% of the retail value. If he is uncertain of selling the book within the year he may only be willing to pay 10% to 20% of the value or not be interested at all.

The best market for a collector is another collector. If another collector is not available, one might investigate the possibility of advertising the book(s) for sale in the "Books for Sale" section of the *Antiquarian Bookman*, P.O. Box AB, Clifton, NJ 07105; or putting the books at auction.

Authors Most Often Requested

The following is a list of authors that appear to be the most in demand at this time. But keep in mind that even these authors have titles that are very common and those titles will not bring high offers from dealers. Also, it should be noted that my selection is influenced by my customers, and that other dealers, particularly in other geographic areas, may have substantially different lists.

Ambler, Eric
Beckett, Samuel
Bradbury, Ray
Brooks, Gwendolyn
Burroughs, Edgar Rice
Cather, Willa
Chandler, Raymond
Christie, Agatha
Churchill, Sir Winston
Crane, Stephen
Davies, Robertson
Dickens, Charles
Doyle, Arthur Conan
Dubois, W.E.B.
Faulkner, William
Fitzgerald, F. Scott
Fleming, Ian
Francis, Dick
Frost, Robert
Graves, Robert
Greene, Graham
Grey, Zane
Hammett, Dashiell
Heaney, Seamus
Hemingway, Ernest
Howard, Robert E.

Hughes, Langston
Joyce, James
Kennedy, John F.
Kennedy, William
Kerouac, Jack
King, Stephen
LeCarre, John
LeGuin, Ursula
Leonard, Elmore
Lewis, Wyndham
London, Jack
Lovecraft, H.P.
Lowry, Malcolm
Ludlum, Robert
MacDonald, Ross
McMurtry, Larry
Matthiessen, Peter
Melville, Herman
Mencken, H.L.
Michener, James
Mishima, Yukio
Moore, Marianne
Morrison, Toni
Nabokov, Vladimir
Niedecker, Lorine
Nin, Anais

O'Brien, Tim
O'Connor, Flannery
Orwell, George
Parker, Robert B.
Poe, Edgar Allan
Pound, Ezra
Powell, Anthony
Pynchon, Thomas
Rand, Ayn
Roethke, Theodore
Salinger, J.D.
Sayers, Dorothy
Shepard, Sam
Smith, Stevie
Stein, Gertrude
Steinbeck, John
Stone, Robert
Stevens, Wallace
Stoppard, Tom
Stout, Rex

Theroux, Paul
Thomas, Ross
Thoreau, Henry David
Tolkien, J.R.R.
Twain, Mark
Tyler, Anne
Updike, John
Verne, Jules
Vonnegut, Kurt
Walker, Alice
Warren, Robert Penn
Waugh, Evelyn
Welty, Eudora
Williams, Tennessee
Williams, William Carlos
Wilson, Edmund
Wodehouse, P.G.
Woolrich, Cornell
Woolf, Virginia
Yeats, W.B.

First Books

My definition of a first book is any single title publication containing more than one page, regardless of size or format, that is bound, stapled or laid in covers. I do not consider broadsides to be books and thus I have not included James Joyce's first publication, *Et Tu, Kelly*, published in 1891 or 1892, as his first book.

I do consider as first books those that represent a collaboration with one other author, although in the first book list I also include the author's first separate book, as I suspect many collectors may not consider collaborations as valid first books.

I have also included books edited and translated by an author if they preceded the first book written by the author. I do not consider these to be first books, but assume some collectors may consider them as the first, as these books are the first to include the author's name on the title page.

In many cases I have included the author's second book. Normally in these cases the first was written anonymously, written under a pseudonym; is so rare as to be unobtainable; or because I felt like it.

It should be understood that in many cases I have never seen these books and have merely listed first books and values as I have come upon them in dealer catalogs or auction catalogs. this means that there are many authors not covered because of the simple fact that I have not encountered listings of their first books and don't feel comfortable listing a price.

My definition of a first book is necessary to understand my selection in the first book list. there is no real agreement among collectors on what constitutes a first book and this is probably just as well as it means the collector must buy three or four titles by certain authors to cover all bets.

General

In my opinion, in most cases an author's first book puts an upper limit on the value of his or her books. This is why the value of the first book can often be used as a rough guide to estimating later books. If a current catalog price or auction record is available it would, of course, be more reliable. But, if such records are not available, and you find two books by the same author, one published in 1930 and one in 1940, the one published in 1930 would normally be valued higher and it will be important to know if the author's first book was published in 1900 or 1929. This rule applies to unsigned trade editions only (often a limited signed edition of a later book will be valued more highly than the first or earlier book). There are exceptions, e.g. when a first or early book had a large printing or when a later book is much scarcer and/or acclaimed as an important book with lasting literary value.

Estimated Values

The dollar values shown are my estimates of the retail value of the book in very good to fine condition with a dustwrapper for those published in 1920 and after. Estimated values of books published between 1800 and 1920 are for very good to fine copies without dustwrappers but in original bindings. Therefore if you have a book prior to 1920 with a complete dustwrapper the value would be higher than the value shown. Estimates for books before 1800 are for rebound copies. The estimated values are believed to be accurate, plus or minus 20%. this may seem to be a very wide range, but it's not unusual to see the same book in different dealer catalogs or at auction with that wide a range (or even wider) within the same year. If you prefer, you can consider the range to represent the difference in condition between a very good copy and a fine copy of the individual book. It's also not unusual for an absolutely mint copy of a book to bring twice the price of a very good to fine copy. On the other hand, copies with even minor defects might sell for as little as 50% of the values shown, worn and chipped copies (books and/or dustwrappers) might only be worth 25% to 30% of the values shown, and books without dustwrappers (after 1920) would normally sell for 15% to 25% of the values shown.

The price listed for any particular title should be considered only as a guide. In some cases the books are truly rare and the fact that I have estimated a price based on a catalog or auction entry that may have been a few years old does not mean this price is accurate. As many dealers will tell you, when you have found a book on their shelves for $100 that is listed in a pricing guide for $50, "go buy it from them."

THE
FIRST
BOOK
LIST

The format of the entries shows the author's name or the title the book was published under (if written anonymously); the title of the author's first book; the city of publication as shown on the title page; the date that appeared on the title page; and any "points" that are applicable. If the city or date do not appear on the title page, they are shown in brackets; i.e. "(NY) 1965" denotes that the date is shown on the title page but not the city and "NY (1965)" denotes that the city is shown, but not the date.

HOMEWARD ❧
SONGS BY ❧❧❧
THE WAY. A. E.

DUBLIN. WHALEY ❧❧
46 DAWSON CHAMBERS 46
MDCCCXCIV. PRICE 1/6 ❧❧

A.E. (George Russell) see E., A.

A., T.B. (Thomas Bailey Aldrich) THE BELLS... B/NY 1855   150

Abbey, Edward JONATHAN TROY NY (1954)   175

Abbott, Anthony (Charles Fulton Oursler) ABOUT THE
            MURDER OF GERALDINE FOSTER NY (1930)   75

Abel, Lionel SOME POEMS OF RIMBAUD NY (1939) wraps
                        (translated by L. Abel)   60

Abercrombie, Lascelles INTERLUDES AND POEMS 1908   75

Abish, Walter DUEL SITE NY 1970 wr (300 cc)   75

Ableman, Paul I HEAR VOICES P (1958)   40

Abrahams, Peter A BLACKMAN SPEAKS OF FREEDOM Durban 1938   150
                 DARK TESTAMENT L 1942   125

Abrahams, William INTERVAL IN CAROLINA NY 1945   30

Abse, Dannie AFTER EVERY GREEN THING L 1949   60

ACELDAMA... (Aleister Crowley) L 1898 wraps   500

Achebe, Chinua THINGS FALL APART L 1958   75
                                    NY 1958   35

Ackerly, J.R. THE PRISONERS OF WAR L 1925 wraps   125

Ackroyd, Peter LONDON LICKPENNY L 1973 wr (26 sgd ltr cc) 50

Acton, Harold AQUARIUM L 1923 (plain dw)   200

Adam, Helen (Douglas) THE ELFIN PEDLAR 7 TALES TOLD
                        BY PIXIE POOL L 1923   100

Adamic, Louis ROBINSON JEFFERS: A PORTRAIT Seattle 1929
                                             wraps   75

Adams, Alice CARELESS LOVE (NY 1966)   350

Adams, Andy THE LOG OF A COWBOY B 1903
             i -map at page 28 not in list of illus.   125

Adams, Ansel TAOS PUEBLO Grabhorn Press SF 1930
                            with Mary Austin   12,000

Adams, Charles Francis RAILROAD LEGISLATION B 1868 wr   75

Adams, Douglas THE HITCHHIKER'S GUIDE TO THE GALAXY
                                      L 1979   30
                                      NY 1980   25

Adams, Edward C.L. CONGAREE SKETCHES... Chapel Hill 1927
                                  (200 sgd no cc)   75

Adams, Frederick Upham PRESIDENT JOHN SMITH C 1897   50

Adams, Henry (Brooks) CIVIL SERVICE REFORM B 1869 wraps 1,000

Adams, Herbert THE SECRET OF BOGEY HOUSE L 1924   50

Adams, James Truslow MEMORIALS OF BRIDGEHAMPTON 1916   75

Adams, Leonie THOSE NOT ELECT NY 1925   200

Adams, Ramon F. COWBOY LINGO B 1936   150

Adams, Richard WATERSHIP DOWN L 1972   600
                               NY 1972   40

Adams, William Taylor see Warren T. Ashton

Addams, Charles DRAWN AND QUARTERED NY (1942)   75

Ade, George CIRCUS DAY CH (1896) (5 prev annonymous
                       offprints from Chicago Quarterly) 300
             ARTIE, A STORY OF... Ch 1896   60

Adeler, Max (Charles Heber Clark) OUT OF THE HURLEY-
             BURLY Ph 1874 (also first book illus by
                                      A.B. Frost)   75

Adler, Edward NOTES FROM A DARK STREET NY 1962   20

Adler, Reneta SPEEDBOAT NY (1970)   20

ADVENTURES OF HARRY FRANCO (THE) (Charles Frederick
                       Briggs) NY 1839 2 vol   150

ADVENTURES OF TIMOTHY PEACOCK...(THE) (Daniel Pierce
                       Thompson) Middlebury 1835   400

ADVENTURES OF A YOUNGER SON (Edward John Trelawny)
                       L 1831 bds 3 vol   350

Agee, James PERMIT ME VOYAGE NH 1934   600

Ai (Florence Ogawa) CRUELTY B 1973   35

Aiken, Conrad(Potter) EARTH TRIUMPHANT NY 1914   200

Ainsworth, William Harrison see SIR JOHN CHIVERTON

Akins, Zoe INTERPRETATIONS L 1912   50

ALARIC AT ROME (Matthew Arnold) A Prize Poem Recited at
                Rugby School, 12 pp wr Rugby, Eng 1840 5,000

Albee, Edward THE ZOO STORY AND THE SANDBOX (NY 1960) wr 150
               THE ZOO STORY, THE DEATH OF BESSIE SMITH,
                             THE SANDBOX NY 1960   125
                                       L (1962)   100

Alcott, Amos Bronson OBSERVATIONS ON THE PRINCIPLES AND
               METHODS OF INFANT INSTRUCTION B 1830 wraps 850

Alcott, Louisa May FLOWER FABLES B 1855   gift binding 250
                                      regular binding   125

ALCUIN: A DIALOGUE (Charles B. Brown) NY 1798 wraps   300

```
Aldington, Richard  IMAGES  (L 1915)  wraps                    250
                           B 1916 wraps                         75

Aldiss, Brian W(ilson)  THE BRIGHTFOUNT DIARIES  L (1955)       75

Aldrich, Thomas Bailey  see T.B.A.

Aldridge, James  SIGNED WITH THEIR HONOUR  L 1942              30
                                           B 1942              25

Aldridge, John W.  AFTER THE LOST GENERATION  NY (1951)        30

Alger, Horatio, Jr.  BERTHA'S CHRISTMAS VISION  B 1856        850

Algren, Nelson  SOMEBODY IN BOOTS  NY (1935)               1,000

Ali, Ahmed  TWILIGHT IN DELHI  L 1940 (prev. privately
                      printed books in Urdu)                   60

Allbeury, Ted   A CHOICE OF ENEMIES  L 1973                   40

Allen, Gracie  HOW TO BECOME PRESIDENT  NY (1940)             75

Allen, (Charles) Grant  BABYLON  L 1885                       50

Allen, William Hervey  BALLADS OF THE BORDER (El Paso)
         1916 wraps (name misspelled "Hervy" on
                             copyright page)                  600
         WAMPUM AND OLD GOLD  NH 1921 stiff wraps              75

Allen, James Lane  FLUTE AND VIOLIN AND OTHER KENTUCKY
                                      TALES   NY 1891
                i -sheets bulk 1 1/6"                          40
               ii -sheets bulk 15/16"

Allen, Woody  DON'T DRINK THE WATER  French  NY 1967  wraps    40
                                 Random House NY (1967)        60

Alling, Kenneth Slade  CORE OF FIRE  NY (1939) wraps          75
                                     NY 1940 cloth            40

Allingham, Margery (Louise)  BLACK'ER CHIEF DICK  L (1923)    250
                                             GC 1923          200

Allott, Kenneth  POEMS  Hogarth Press  L 1938                60

Alpert, Hollis  THE SUMMER LOVERS  NY 1958                   25

Alpha and Omega (Oliver St. John Gogarty) BLIGHT, THE
                      TRAGEDY OF DUBLIN  D 1917              200

Alther, Lisa  KINFLICKS  NY 1976                             20

Altsheler, Joseph Alexander  THE SON OF SARATOGA  NY 1897   150

Alvarez, A.  (POEMS)  O 1952 wr  FANTASY POETS #15           75

Amado, Jorge  THE VIOLENT LAND  NY 1945 (1st Eng trans)      40

Ambler, Eric  THE DARK FRONTIER  L 1936                   1,500

Amis, Kingsley (William)  BRIGHT NOVEMBER  L (1947)         300

Amis, Martin  THE RACHEL PAPERS  L 1973                      40

Ammons, A(rchie) R(andolph)  OMMATEUM, WITH DOXOLOGY
                    Ph (1955) 300 cc, 200 destroyed          800
```

Anderson, Alston LOVER MAN L (1959) (Graves intro)   30

Anderson, Forrest SEA PIECES+ NY 1935 (155 cc)   125

Anderson, Frederick Irving ADVENTURES OF THE
                    INFALLIBLE GODAHL NY (1914)   200

Anderson, J(ohn) Redwood THE MUSIC OF DEATH Clifton/L
                                        1904 wraps   75

Anderson, Maxwell YOU WHO HAVE DREAMS NY 1925 (1,000 cc)
                                25 sgd no. cc   300
                                975 no. cc   60
            (Four collaborations in 1924/25)

Anderson, Patrick A TENT FOR APRIL Montreal 1945 stiff
            wr & dw first reg publ book, preceded by
                    two publ items in his teens   100

Anderson, Poul VAULT OF THE AGES Ph (1952)   50

Anderson, Sherwood WINDY McPHERSON'S SON NY 1916   250

Andrews, Jane THE SEVEN LITTLE SISTERS... B 1861   100

Andrews, William Loring A CHOICE COLLECTION OF BOOKS FROM
                    THE ALDINE PRESSES NY 1885
                            wraps (50 copies)   400

Angell, Roger THE STONE ARBOR+ B (1960) (Edw. Gorey dw)   40

Angelo, Valenti NINO NY 1938   75

Angelou, Maya I KNOW WHY THE CAGED BIRD SINGS NY (1969)   35
            i -text bulks 15/16", top stained magenta

ANONYMOUS (Michael Fraenkel) P (1930) wr (first Carrefour
                    Editions book, with Walter Lowenfels) 150

Anstey, Christopher see THE NEW BATH GUIDE...

Anstey, F. (Thomas Anstey Guthrie) VICE VERSA L 1882   75

Anthony, Peter (Peter & Anthony Shaffer) THE WOMEN IN
                    THE WARDROBE L (1951)   100

Antin, David   MARTIN BUBER'S TALES OF ANGELS, SPIRITS AND
                    DEMONS NY 1958 tr by Antin & Jerome
                            Rothenberg wraps   60
                DEFINITIONS (NY 1967) stiff wraps (spiral
                            bound) (300 cc)   60

Antin, Mary FROM PLOTZK TO BOSTON B 1899 cloth   250
                                        wraps   150

Antoninus, Brother see William Everson

Apple, Max INTRODUCING THE ORANGING OF AMERICA (NY 1973) wr 75
            THE ORANGING OF AMERICA+ NY 1976   30

Appleton (Publisher) CRUMBS FROM THE MASTER'S TABLE
            NY 1831 by W. Mason (first book of press)   100

ARCHITEC-TONICS...NY 1914 (includes first book illus by
                            Rockwell Kent)   75

Arden, John Serjeant MUSGRAVE DANCE L 1960   35

Ardizzone, Edward IN A GLASS DARKLY by J. Sheridan Le Fanu
                   L 1929 (1st book illus by Ardizzone)   125

Arensberg, Ann SISTER WOLF NY 1980   20

Arensberg, Walter Conrad POEMS B/NY 1914   60

Arion Press PICTURE/POEMS... SF 1975 By Andrew Hoyem
                              (first book of press)   75

Arkham House THE OUTSIDER+ by H. P. Lovecraft SC 1939   900
     (there is a reprint dw not as clear as original)

Arlen, Michael THE LONDON VENTURE L (1920) ("1919"
                        reportedly printed later)   125
                                        NY (1920)   50

Armour, Richard YOURS FOR THE ASKING B (1942)   35

Armstrong, Martin EXODUS+ L 1912   50

Arno, Peter WHOOPS, DEARIE! (NY 1927)   75

Arnold, Matthew see ALARIC AT ROME
                  CROMWELL... O 1843 wraps   1,000
                  THE STRAYED REVELLER L 1849   400

Arnow, Harriette (Louisa Simpson) See Harriette Simpson,
     HUNTER'S HORN NY(1949) 2nd book - 1st under real name   50
                                (states first edition)

Arthur, T(imothy) S(hay) see INSUBORDINATION...

Asbury, Herbert UP FROM METHODISM NY 1926   90

Ashbery, John (Lawrence) TURANDOT+ NY 1953 wr (300 cc)   750
                          SOME TREES NH 1956   150
     preceded by THE HEROS (Living Theatre NY 1952)
     mimeographed legal sheets in folder

Ashdown, Clifford (R. Austin Freeman) THE ADVENTURES
          OF ROMNEY PRINGLE L 1902 with J.J. Pitcairn   1,000

Asher, Don THE PIANO SPORT NY 1966   25

Ashton, Warren T.(William Taylor Adams) HATCHIE, THE
                              GUARDIAN SLAVE B 1853   75

Asimov, Isaac PEBBLE IN THE SKY NY 1950   150
               I ROBOT NY 1950   350

Asquith, Cynthia THE GHOST BOOK... L 1926   350

Astrachan, Sam AN END TO DYING NY (1956)   35
                              L (1958)   35

Athas, Daphne THE WEATHER OF THE HEART NY (1947)   40

Atherton, Gertrude see Frank Lin HERMIA SUYDAM NY (1889)
                    wraps 2nd book, 1st under own name   100

Atkinson, Justin Brooks SKYLINE PROMENADES NY 1925
                    50 no. cc in bluish-gray
                                        cloth   100
                    1950 no. cc in blue cloth
                              & patterned bds   75

POEMS

BY

W. H. AUDEN

LONDON

FABER & FABER

24 RUSSELL SQUARE

Atlee, Philip THE INHERITORS NY 1940   125

Attaway, William LET ME BREATHE THUNDER NY 1939   150

Atterley, Joseph (George Tucket) A VOYAGE TO THE MOON
                                            NY 1827   500

Atwood, Margaret (Eleanor) DOUBLE PERSEPHONE Toronto 1961
                                          wraps 1,200
                        THE EDIBLE WOMAN T (1969)   200
                                          B (1969)   60

Aubrey-Fletcher, Henry Lancelot see Henry Wade

Auchincloss, Louis (Stanton) see Andrew Lee
        THE INJUSTICE COLLECTORS B 1950 2nd bk (1st under
                                        own name)   75

Auden, W(ystan) H(ugh) POEMS (Hampstead, Eng 1928) wr
                              12 cc recorded 10,000
                        POEMS L(1930) stiff wr in dw   350
                        POEMS NY (1934)   125

Audubon, John James   THE BIRDS OF AMERICA FROM ORIGINAL
      DRAWINGS L 1827-1838 87 parts or 4 double elephant
                folios containing 435 plates (no text) 750,000

Auel, Jean M. THE CLAN OF THE CAVE BEAR NY (1980)   50

Auslander, Joseph SUNRISE TRUMPETS NY 1924   35

Austen, Jane see SENSE AND SENSIBILITY

Austin, Jane Goodwin FAIRY DREAMS... B (1859)   60

Austin, Mary (Hunter) THE LAND OF THE LITTLE RAIN B 1903   200

AUTHORSHIP OF THE IMPRECATORY PSALMS   (Thomas Bulfinch)
                                    B (1852) wraps   300

AUTOBIOGRAPHY OF AN EX-COLORED MAN (James W. Johnson) B 1912 350

Awahsoose the Bear (Rowland Evans Robinson) FOREST AND
                    STREAM FABLES NY (1886) wraps   200

Axelrod, George BEGGAR'S CHOICE NY 1947   75

Ayrton, Michael GILES OF RAIS by Cecil Gray   L (1945)
         1st book illus by Ayrton stiff wr & dw
                              (200 sgd no. cc)   250

B., J.K. (John Kendrick Bangs) THE LORGNETTE NY (1886)   300

Bach, Richard STRANGER TO THE GROUND NY (1963)   35

Bacheller, Irving THE MASTER OF SILENCE NY 1892   75

Bacon, Josephine Dodge SMITH COLLEGE STORIES NY 1900   40

Bacon, Leonard THE BALLAD OF BLONAY... Vevy 1906 wr   250

Bacon, Peggy THE TRUE PHILOSPHER + B 1919   60

Bagnold, Enid A DIARY WITHOUT DATES L 1918   35

Bahr, Jerome ALL GOOD AMERICANS NY 1937 (Hemingway intro)
            blue cloth (yellow cloth publ in 1939)   150

Bailey, H(enry) C(hristopher) MY LADY OF ORANGE   L 1901   35

Bainbridge, Beryl A WEEKEND WITH CLAUD (L) 1967   40

Baird, Thomas TRIUMPHAL ENTRY NY (1962)   40

Baker, Asa (Davis Dresser) MUM'S THE WORD FOR MURDER
                              NY 1938   75

Baker, Carlos H. SHADOWS IN THE STONE Hanover 1930
                125 sgn no. cc, wraps   125

Baker, Dorothy YOUNG MAN WITH A HORN (B) 1938   50

Baker, Elliott A FINE MADNESS NY (1964)   50
                               L (1964)   30
Balchin, Nigel see Mark Spade

Baldwin, James (Arthur) GO TELL IT ON THE MOUNTAIN
                              NY 1953   400
                               L 1954   100

Baldwin, Joseph G. THE FLUSH TIMES OF ALABAMA AND
                MISSISSIPPI NY 1853   200

Baldwin, Michael THE SILENT MIRROR L (1951)   40

Ballantine, Sheila NORMA JEAN THE TERMITE QUEEN NY 1975   30

Ballantyne, Robert Michael HUDSON'S BAY... Edin 1848 1,000
                              Edin/L 1848   350

Ballau, Jenny SPANISH PRELUDE B 1937   30

Bambara, Toni Cade   GORILLA, MY LOVE NY 1972   40
            (edited two books previously)

```
Bancroft, George  PROSPECTUS OF A SCHOOL... (C 1823)
                  (with J.C. Coggswell)  wraps        350
              POEMS  C 1823                           100

Bancroft, Irving  THE MASTER OF SILENCE  NY 1892      125

Bangs, John Kendrick  see J.K.B.
              ROGER CAMERDEN  NY 1887  wraps          125

Banyan Press  see Gil Orlovitz

Barbellion, W.N.P.  (Bruce Frederick Cummings) THE JOURNAL
                  OF A DISAPPOINTED MAN   L 1919      100
                                         NY 1919       75

Barfield, Owen  HISTORY IN ENGLISH WORDS  L 1926 (8 pp ads)  75

Barker, Eric (Wilson)  THE PLANETARY HEART  Mill Valley 1942  90

Barker, George (Granville)  ALANNA AUTUMNAL  L 1933   125
                  THIRTY PRELIMINARY POEMS
                                    L 1933            100

Barker, Shirley  THE DARK HILLS UNDER  NH 1933         50

Barnes, Arthur K.  INTERPLANETARY HUNTER  NY (1956)    20

Barnes, Djuna  THE BOOK OF REPULSIVE WOMEN  (NY 1915) wr  400

Barnes, Julian  see Dan Kavanagh  METROLAND  L (1980)   50

Barney, Natalie C(lifford)  QUELQUES PORTRAITS  P 1900  300

Barnsley, Alan  THE FROG PRINCE +  Aldington 1952  wr   60

Barnum, Phineas Taylor  THE LIFE OF P. T. BARNUM  NY 1855  150

Barr, Robert  see Luke Sharp

Barrett, Clifton Waller  BLUEPRINT FOR A BASIC... (NY) 1944
                              mimeographed sheets      60

Barrie, James M.  BETTER DEAD  L 1888  wraps          400

Barstow, Stan(ley)  A KIND OF LOVING  L (1960)         40

Barth, John (Simmons)  THE FLOATING OPERA  NY (1956)  300
                       L (1968) revised edition        40

Barthelme, Donald  COME BACK DR. CALIGARI  B (1964)   150
                                    L (1966)           75

Barthelme, Fredrick  RANGOON  NY 1970  cloth           60
                                    wraps              25

Bartlett, John  A BOOK OF HYMNS FOR YOUNG PERSONS  C 1854  100
            also see A COLLECTION OF FAMILIAR QUOTATIONS

Barton, Bruce  MORE POWER TO YOU  NY 1917             25

Bartram, William  TRAVELS THROUGH NORTH & SOUTH CAROLINA
                              Ph 1791              8,000
                               L 1792              4,500

Barzun, Jacques Martin  SAMPLINGS AND CHRONICLES
              (edited by JMB)  NY 1927  (500 cc)      100

Basso, Hamilton  RELICS AND ANGELS  NY 1929           75
```

with sincere regards to Mr. and Mrs. Bull from

TWO BIRD-LOVERS IN MEXICO

BY

C. WILLIAM BEEBE

Curator of Ornithology of the New York Zoölogical Park and Life Member of the New York Zoölogical Society; Member of the American Ornithologists' Union

C. William Beebe.

ILLUSTRATED WITH PHOTOGRAPHS
FROM LIFE TAKEN BY THE AUTHOR

Mary Blair Beebe

BOSTON AND NEW YORK
HOUGHTON, MIFFLIN AND COMPANY
The Riverside Press, Cambridge
1905

46

```
Bates, H. E.    THE LAST BREAD   L (1926)   wraps              150

Bates, Ralph   SIERRA   L 1933                                  60

Baum, L(yman) Frank   THE BOOK OF HAMBURGS   Hartford 1886    1,500
                      MOTHER GOOSE IN PROSE   Ch (1897)
                      (first Maxfield Parrish illus)           1,200

Bax, Clifford   TWENTY CHINESE POEMS   Hampstead 1910           75

Baxter, Richard   POETICAL FRAGMENTS   L 1821                  150

Bayliss, John   THE WHITE KNIGHT +   L 1944                     40

Beach, Abel  see AN EARLY PIONEER

Beach, Joseph Warren   SONNETS OF THE HEAD AND HEART   B 1903   50

Beach, Rex (Ellingwood)   PARDNERS   NY 1905                    60

Beagle, Peter S.   A FINE AND PRIVATE PLACE   NY 1960           75

Beard, Charles Austin   THE OFFICE OF THE JUSTICE... NY 1904
                                                        wraps   75

Beasley, Gertrude   MY FIRST THIRTY YEARS... (P 1925) wraps    400

Beaton, Cecil   THE TWILIGHT OF THE NYMPHS   L 1928 1200 cc
                    Book by Pierre Louys, Illus by Beaton      100
               THE BOOK OF BEAUTY   L (1930)                   250

Beaton, George (Gerald Brenan)   JACK ROBINSON   L (1933)       75

Beattie, Ann   CHILLY SCENES OF WINTER   GC 1976               75
               DISTORTIONS   GC 1976 (publ simultaneously)     75

Beaumont, Charles (Charles Nutt)   THE HUNGER + NY (1957)       75

Beaumont Press   TIDES by John Drinkwater   L 1917             75

Becke, Louis   BY REEF AND PALM   L 1894   wraps               75

Becker, Stephen   THE SEASON OF THE STRANGER   NY (1951)        50

Beckett, Samuel (Barclay)   WHOROSCOPE   Hours Press   P 1930
                      stapled wraps   100 sgd cc             2,250
                                      200 unsgd cc           1,000
                      PROUST   L 1931                          300
                               P 1931 wraps                   300
                               NY (1957) 250 sgd no cc        200
                               (issued w/o dw)

Bedichek, Roy   ADVENTURES WITH A TEXAS NATURALIST   GC 1947   100

Beebe, (Charles) William   TWO BIRD-LOVERS IN MEXICO   B 1905
          i   -Charles M. Beebe on cover                    1,500
          ii  -C. William Beebe on cover                      250
          iii -gold sky background lacking                    125
          iv  -lacks pictorial design, just lettered           60

Beebe, Lucius   FALLEN STARS   B 1921                         100

Beecher, Harriet Elizabeth   PRIZE TALE: A NEW ENGLAND
                      SKETCH   Lowell, MA   1834   wraps       500

Beecher, John   AND I WILL BE HEARD   NY (1940)   wraps        75

Beeding, Francis (John Leslie Palmer & Hilary Saunders)
                      THE SEVEN SLEEPERS   L 1925              60
```

```
Beer, Patricia  LOSS OF THE MAGYAR  L 1959 (glassine dw)        50

Beer, Thomas  THE FAIR REWARDS  NY 1922                        150

Beerbohm, Max  THE WORKS OF MAX BEERBOHM  NY 1896
                         1000 cc--400 pulped                   225
                                      L 1896                   150

Beeton, Isabella  THE BOOK OF HOUSEHOLD MANAGEMENT  L 1861
                 i -"18 Bouverie St." on woodcut title pg      500

Behan, Brendan  THE QUARE FELLOW  L 1956                       150
                NY (1956)  Boards (100 no. cc) no dw           100
                                             wraps              25

Behn, Noel  THE KREMLIN LETTER  NY (1966)                       35

Behrman, Samuel Nathaniel  BEDSIDE MANNER  NY 1924
                           (with J.K. Nicholson) wraps          50
                           THE SECOND MAN  NY 1927
                                stiff wraps in dw              100
                                             L 1928             75
                 (Another collaboration 1926)

Belitt, Ben  THE FIVE FOLD MESH  NY 1938                        60

Bell, Acton (Ann Bronte)  AGNES GREY  L 1847 (third
                vol of Wuthering Heights) (1000 cc)          3,000

Bell, Clive  ART  L 1914                                        75

Bell, Currer, Ellis and Acton (Charlotte, Emily and Ann
      Bronte)  POEMS  L 1846 (publ by Aylott and Jones)      7,500
                     L 1846 (publ by Smith, Elder)             750

Bell, Currer (Charlotte Bronte)  JANE EYRE  L 1847  3 vols   6,000
                i-Bell as editor, 36 page catalog in vol one
                            dated June and October

Bell, DeWitt  RAVENSWOOD+  Hanover 1963 (250 cc)                50

Bell, Ellis (Emily Bronte)  WUTHERING HEIGHTS  L 1847
                           2 vols (1000 cc)                  5,000
           plus AGNES GREY by Acton Bell (making 3 vols)     8,000

Bell, Josephine (Doris Bell & Collier Ball)  MURDER
                            IN HOSPITAL  L 1937                 50

Bell, Julian  CHAFFINCHES  C 1929  wraps                        75

Bell, Quentin  ON HUMAN FINERY  Hogarth  L 1947                 40

Bell, Robert  THE BUTTERFLY TREE  Ph (1959)                     35

Bellah, James Warner  SKETCH BOOK OF A CADET FROM GASCONY
                                              NY 1923           75
Bellamy, Edward  see SIX TO ONE

Belli, Melvan M.  BELLI LOOKS AT LIFE AND LAW IN JAPAN
                                     Ind (1960)                 30

Belloc, Hillaire  VERSES AND SONNETS  L 1896                  400

Bellow, Saul  DANGLING MAN  NY (1944)                         600
                            L 1946                            250

Bemelmans, Ludwig  HANSI  NY 1934                             250
```

```
Benchley, Nathaniel  SIDE STREET   NY 1950                          35

Benchley, Robert C.   OF ALL THINGS  NY 1921                       300
                                     L 1922                        150

Benefield, Barry  THE CHICKEN WAGON FAMILY  NY (1925)               25

Benet, Laura  FAIRY BREAD  NY 1921                                  50

Benet, Stephen Vincent  FIVE MEN AND POMPEY  B 1915
                        i--purple wraps (trial)                    350
                        ii--brown wraps                             75

Benet, William Rose  MERCHANTS FROM CATHAY  NY 1913                 35

Bennett, E. A(rnold)  A MAN FROM THE NORTH  L 1898                 250

Bennett, Emerson  THE BRIGAND... NY 1842 wraps                     400

Bennett, Hal  A WILDERNESS OF VINES  GC 1966                        40

Benson, Arthur Christopher  see Christopher Carr
     WILLIAM LAUD, ARCHBISHOP OF CANTERBURY  L 1887
            (second book first under own name)                    100

Benson, E(dward) F(redric)  DODO  L 1893  2 vols                   100

Benson, R.H.  THE LIGHT INVISIBLE  L 1903                           60

Bentley, E(dmund) C(lerihew)  see E. Clerihew
                    TRENT'S LAST CASE  L (1913)                    125
                    THE WOMAN IN BLACK  NY 1913
                                    (new title)                    75

Bentley, Eric Russell  A CENTURY OF HERO WORSHIP
                        Ph/NY (1944)                                40

Benton, Thomas Hart  EUROPE AFTER 8:15  NY 1914 (First
                    illus--with Mencken, Nathan and
                                    W.H. Wright)
                    i - cloth stamped in blue                      100
                    ii - cloth stamped in gold                      75

Berge, Carol  THE VULNERABLE ISLAND  Cleveland 1964
                                    wraps                           50

Berger, John  A PAINTER OF OUR TIME  L 1958                         75

Berger, Thomas (Louis)  CRAZY IN BERLIN  NY (1958)                 175

Bergman, Andrew  THE BIG KISS-OFF OF 1944  NY (1974)                35

Berkeley, Anthony  see THE LAYTON COURT MYSTERY

Berkson, Bill  SATURDAY NIGHT  NY 1961 wraps (300 cc)               60

Bernstein, Aline  THREE BLUE SUITS  NY  1933
                        (600 sgd cc--boxed)                        100

Berriault, Gina  THE DESCENT  NY 1960                               30

Berrigan, Daniel  TIME WITHOUT NUMBERS  NY 1957                     50

Berrigan, Ted (Edmund J.)  THE SONNETS (NY) 1964  (300 cc)
                        Stapled mimeographed sheets                 60
                        Grove Press  NY (1964) wr                   25
         (preceded by at least two priv printed pamphlets)

Berry, Don  TRASK  NY 1960                                          30
```

MOUNT ZION

OR

IN TOUCH WITH THE INFINITE

BY

JOHN BETJEMAN

LONDON
THE JAMES PRESS

Berry, Francis   GOSPEL OF FIRE   L 1933   60

Berry, Wendell (Erdman) see FIVE YOUNG AMERICAN POETS
                         NATHAN COLTER   B 1960   200

Berryman, John   POEMS   N (1942)   bds (500 cc)   250
                                    wr (1500 cc)   75

Bessie, Alvah Cecil   DWELL IN THE WILDERNESS   NY (1935)   100
                      (previous translations)

Bester, Alfred   THE DEMOLISHED MAN   Ch (1953) signed cc   250
                                               unsigned   150
                                            L (1953)   60

Betjeman, John   MOUNT ZION OR IN TOUCH WITH... L (1931)
                                       issued w/o dw
               i -blue and gold pattern cover   450
              ii -striped paper cover   350

Betts, Doris   THE GENTLE INSURRECTION+   NY 1954   100

Beveridge, Albert Jeremiah   THE RUSSIAN ADVANCE   NY 1903   50

Beynon, John (John Beynon Harris)   THE SECRET PEOPLE
                                          L (1935)   400

Bezzerides, A.I.   LONG HAUL   NY (1938)   40

Bierce, Ambrose (Gwinnett)   see Dod Grile

Biggers, Earl Derr   IF YOU'RE ONLY HUMAN   1912   100
                     SEVEN KEYS TO BALDPATE   I (1913)   75

Binns, Archie   LIGHTSHIP   NY (1934)   60

Binyon, Laurence   PERSEPHONE   L 1890 wr (Newdigate Prize) 300
                   LYRIC POEMS   L 1894   150
                   POEMS   O 1895 (200 cc) wraps   125

Bird, Bessie Calhoun   AIRS FROM THE WOOD WINDS   Ph (1935)
                       (only book) 25 sgd ltr cc   150
                                   300 sgd no. cc   50

Bird, Robert Montgomery   see CALAVAR

Birmingham, Stephen   YOUNG MR. KEEFE   B 1958   35

Birney, (Alfred) Earle   see E. Robertson
                       DAVID+   T 1942   (500 cc)   200

Birrell, Augustine   see OBITER DICTA

Bishop, Elizabeth   NORTH AND SOUTH   B 1946 (1000 cc)   350

Bishop, John Peale   GREEN FRUIT   B 1917   150

Bishop, Zealia   THE CURSE OF YIG   SC 1953   75

Bissell, Richard   A STRETCH OF THE RIVER   B 1950   40

Black, (Harvey) MacKnight   MACHINERY   NY 1929   75

Black, E.L. (Sir John Ellerman)   WHY DO THEY LIKE IT...
                                 (Dijon 1927) wr   200

Black Manikin Press   see Ralph Cheever Dunning

Black, Mansell (Elleston Trevor)   SINISTER CARGO   L 1951 100

Black Sparrow Press   NOT MEANING NOT TO SEE by Bernard A.
                      Forrest   (LA 1967)   (75 sgd cc)   150

Blackburn, Paul   PROENSA (M) 1953 wraps (translation)   225
                  THE DISSOLVING FABRIC (M) 1955 wraps   175

Blackmore, Richard Doddridge   see Melanter

Blackmur, R(ichard) P(almer)   T.S. ELIOT (C) 1928 wr   100
                  (off-print from "Hound and Horn")
                  DIRTYHANDS OR THE TRUE BORN CENSOR C 1932 wr 150

Blackwood, Algernon   THE EMPTY HOUSE+   L 1906   200
                                         NY 1917   75

Blackwood, Caroline   FOR ALL THAT I FOUND THERE   L 1973   35

Blaikie, John Arthur   see Edmund Gosse

Blanding, Don   LEAVES FROM A GRASS-HOUSE (Honolulu 1923) wr   50

Blatty, William   WHICH WAY TO MECCA, JACK   NY 1960   35

Blake, Nicholas (C. Day-Lewis pseudonym)   A QUESTION
                  OF PROOF   L 1935 (first under this name)   300

Blechman, Burt   HOW MUCH?   NY (1961)   40

Blish, James (Benjamin)   JACK OF EAGLES   NY (1952)   100

Bloch, Robert   SEA KISSED   (L 1945) wr
                  i - 39 pp "Printed in Great Britain" on p.39   250
                  ii - 36 pp "Printed in Eire" on p.36   200
                  THE OPENER OF THE WAY   SC 1945 (2000 cc)   150

Block, Herbert   THE HERBLOCK BOOK   B 1952   35

Blum, Etta   POEMS   NY 1937   40

Blunden, E(dmund) C(harles)   POEMS 1913 AND 1914 (Horsham
                                       1914) wr (100 cc)   300

Blunt, Wilfred Scawen   see PROTEUS SONNETS AND SONGS

Bly, Robert (Elwood)   THE LION'S TAIL AND EYES   Madison 1962
                               (with J. Wright & W. Duffy)   100
                       (previous broadside in 1961)
                       SILENCE IN THE SNOWY FIELDS   Middleton
                                          (1962) cloth   125
                                             wrappers   50

Bodenheim, Maxwell   MINNA AND MYSELF   NY 1918
                  i -"Posner" for "Poisoner" p 67   75
                  (also Ben Hecht's first book)

Bodkin, M(atthais) McDonald   WHITE MAGIC   L 1897   150
                  PAUL BECK: THE RULE OF THUMB
                                   DETECTIVE   L 1898   500

Bodley Booklets #1   THE HAPPY HYPOCRITE: A FAIRY TALE
                       by Max Beerbohm   NY/L 1897
                  i -period on cover, colophon dated Dec 1896   200

Bogan, Louise   BODY OF THIS DEATH   NY 1923   250

Bogner, Norman   IN SPELLS NO LONGER BOUND   L (1961)   40

Boles, Robert   THE PEOPLE ONE KNOWS   B 1964   30

Bolitho, William LEVIATHAN L 1923   30

Bolt, Robert (Oxton) FLOWERING CHERRY L 1958   50
        (first play, A Man For All Seasons not
        publ until 1961)

Bolton, George G. A SPECIALIST IN CRIME L 1904 (only book) 150

Bond, Nelson (Slade) MR. MERGENTHWIRKER'S LOBBLIES+ NY 1946 60

Bontemps, Arna (Wendall) GOD SENDS SUNDAY NY 1931   175

Booth, Evangeline Cory LOVE IS ALL NY (1908)   50

Booth, Philip LETTER FROM A DISTANT LAND: POEMS NY 1957   35

Borrow, George (Henry) see CELEBRATED TRIALS

Bottrall, Ronald THE LOOSENING+ C 1931 (tissue dw)   50

Boucher, Anthony (William Anthony Parker White)   THE
            CASE OF THE SEVEN OF CALVARY NY 1937   150

Boulle, Pierre THE BRIDGE OVER THE RIVER KWAI (first trans
                            in English) L 1954   100
                                         NY 1954   50

Bourdillon, Francis W. AMONG THE FLOWERS+ L 1878   75

Bourjaily, Vance (Nye) THE END OF MY LIFE NY 1947   75

Bourne, Randolph S(illiman) YOUTH AND LIFE B 1913   125

Bova, Ben STAR CONQUERORS Ph (1959)   150

Bowen, Elizabeth ENCOUNTERS L1923   750

Bowen, Marjorie (Gabrielle M.V. Long) THE VIPER OF MILAN
                                        L 1906   100

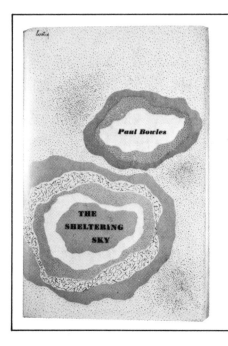 

```
Bowles, Jane   TWO SERIOUS LADIES   NY (1943)              400
                                    L 1965                  75

Bowles, Paul (Frederick)   TWO POEMS  (NY 1934)   wraps    600
                           NO EXIT  NY 1946  wr Bowles'
                                     trans of Sartre        75
                           THE SHELTERING SKY  L (1949)    250
                                             (NY 1949)     150

Boyd, James   DRUMS   NY 1925                             200
                      NY (1928) illus - N.C. Wyeth        125

Boyd, Thomas   THROUGH THE WHEAT   NY 1923               125

Boyd, William   A GOOD MAN IN AFRICA   L 1981            75
                                       NY 1982            30

Boyle, Jack   BOSTON BLACKIE   NY (1919)                 100

Boyle, Kay   SHORT STORIES   P 1929 wraps in tied folder
                         15 signed numbered copies     1,000
                        150 numbered copies              350
             WEDDING DAY +  NY (1930) (new title)         75
             (two spine variants noted:  "KAY/BOYLE/
             WEDDING/DAY/&/OTHER/STORIES" & "SHORT/
             STORIES/KAY/BOYLE" o/w the same -priority
                                          unknown)

Boyle, Patrick   LIKE ANY OTHER MAN   L 1966            40

Boyle, T. Coraghessan   DESCENT OF MAN   B (1979)       40
```

54

SHORT STORIES

BY

KAY BOYLE

THE BLACK SUN PRESS
EDITIONS NARCISSE
RUE CARDINALE
PARIS
MCMXXIX

BOZ (Charles Dickens) see SKETCHES BY "BOZ"

Brackenridge, H(ugh) H(enry) see A POEM ON THE RISING
                                         GLORY...

Bradbury, Malcolm (Stanley) EATING PEOPLE IS WRONG L 1959   50

Bradbury, Ray (Douglas) DARK CARNIVAL   SC 1947   500
                                         L (1948)   250

Braddon, Mary Elizabeth LADY AUDLEY'S SECRET L 1862
                                         (3 vols.)   400

Bradford, Gamaliel TYPES OF AMERICAN CHARACTER NY 1895   50

Bradford, Richard RED SKY AT MORNING Ph (1968)   35

Bradford, Roark OL'MAN ADAM AND HIS CHILLUN NY 1928   75

Bradley, David SOUTH STREET NY 1975   75

Bradley, Edward COLLEGE LIFE Oxford 1849/50
                                         (6 parts in 5)   600

Bradstreet, Anne see THE TENTH MUSE...

Braine, John (Gerard) ROOM AT THE TOP L 1957   100
                                         B 1957   25

Braithwaite, E. R. TO SIR, WITH LOVE Englewood Cliffs
                                         (1959)   35

Braithwaite, William Stanley LYRICS OF LIFE AND LOVE
                                         B 1904 (500 cc)   150

Bramah, Ernest (Ernest Bramah Smith) ENGLISH FARMING...
                                         L 1894 stiff wraps   150

Brammer, William THE GAY PLACE B 1961
                  i -rear dw flap has name of designer   100
                 ii -rear dw flap has name of designer
                                         covered by design   60
                iii -rear dw flap has name of designer
                                         removed   40

Branch, Anna Hempstead THE HEART OF THE ROAD+ B 1901   40

Brand, Christianna (Mary Christianna Lewis) DEATH IN
                                 HIGH HEELS L 1941   60

Brand, Max (Frederick Schiller Faust) THE UNTAMED NY 1919   75

Brand, Millen THE OUTWARD ROOM NY 1937
              i -pictorial dw, S. Lewis blurb   30
             ii -pr dw, Lewis, Dreiser and Hurst blurbs   15

Brashler, William THE BINGO LONG TRAVELING... NY (1973)   30

Brautigan, Richard THE RETURN OF THE RIVERS (SF 1958) wr 1,000

Bremser, Ray POEMS OF MADNESS (NY) 1965 wr   30
              (Ginsberg intro)

Brenan, Gerald see George Beaton

Brennan, Joseph Payne HEART OF EARTH Prairie City (1949)   125
                       NINE HORRORS AND A DREAM SC 1958   90

```
Breslin, Jimmy  see Jimmy Demaret
          SUNNY JIM...FITZSIMMONS  GC 1962          40

Brett, Simon  CAST, IN ORDER OF DISAPPEARANCE  L 1975     40
                               NY (1976)        25

Brewster, Ralph H.  THE GOOD BEARDS OF ATHOS   Hogarth
                                          L 1935        100

Bridges, Robert  POEMS  L 1873 (suppressed by author
                                    in 1878)        400

Briggs, Charles Frederick  see THE ADVENTURES OF HARRY FRANCO

Brinnin, John Malcolm  THE GARDEN IS POLITICAL  NY 1942     50

Brisbane, Albert  SOCIAL DESTINY OF MAN... Ph 1840        300

Brissman, Barry  SWING LOW  NY (1972)                25

Bristow, Gwen  THE INVISIBLE HOST   NY 1930  with
                               Bruce Manning        50

Brittain, Vera M.  VERSES OF A V.A.D... L 1918        75

Brodeur, Paul (Adrian)  THE SICK FOX  B (1963)        35

Brodkey, Harold  FIRST LOVE & OTHER SORROWS  NY 1957     100

Bromell, Henry  THE SLIGHTEST DISTANCE  B 1974        25

Bromfield, Louis  THE GREEN BAY TREE  NY 1924        250

Bromige, David (Mansfield)  THE GATHERING BUFFALO  (NY)
                          1965  wraps (350 cc)        50

Bronk, William  LIGHT AND DARK  (Ashland)  1956  wraps    150

Bronte Anne, Charlotte & Emily  see Acton, Currer &
                               Ellis Bell

Brookner, Anita  THE DEBUT  NY 1981                25

Brooke, Jocelyn  SIX POEMS  O 1928  wraps            300
                DECEMBER SPRING  L 1946            75

Brooke, Rupert  THE PYRAMIDS  Rugby 1904 wraps      6,000
                THE BASTILLE  A.J. Lawrence  Rugby 1905 wr  4,000
                     George E. Over  Rugby 1905 (1920) wr   200
                POEMS  L 1911 (first commercial publ)
                               issued w/o dw        200

Brooks, Gwendolyn  SONG AFTER SUNSET 1936 (one known cc)  3,000
               A STREET IN BRONZEVILLE   NY 1945     250

Brooks, Jeremy  THE WATER CARNIVAL  L 1957        50

Brooks, Richard  THE BRICK FOXHOLE  NY (1945)        50

Brooks, Van Wyck  see VERSES BY TWO UNDERGRADUATES
               THE WINE OF PURITANS  B 1908        75

Brophy, Brigid  THE CROWN PRINCESS +  L 1953        50

Brossard, Chandler  WHO WALK IN DARKNESS  (NY 1952)    75
                               L (1952)        60

BROTHERS (THE): A TALE OF THE FRONDE (Henry William
          Herbert)  NY 1835  2 v  i -brown cl        150
```

```
Broughton, James (Richard)   SONGS FOR CERTAIN CHILDREN
                                     SF 1947        350
                        THE PLAYGROUND... (SF) 1949      60

Broun, Heywood  SEEING THINGS AT NIGHT  NY 1921         100

Brown, Alice  see STRATFORD-BY-THE-SEA

Brown, Bob (Robert Carlton)   THE REMARKABLE ADVENTURES OF
                        CHRISTOPHER POE   CH 1913       350
                        WHAT HAPPENED TO MARY   NY 1913  150

Brown, Cecil  THE LIFE & LOVES OF MR. JIVEASS NIGGER
                                     NY 1969         30

Brown, Charles Brockton  see ALCUIN...

Brown, Claude  MANCHILD IN THE PROMISED LAND  NY (1965)   30
                                     L (1966)        50

Brown, Frank Landon  TRUMBULL PARK  CH (1959)           40

Brown, Fredric  THE FABULOUS CLIPJOINT  NY 1947        200

Brown, George Douglas  THE HOUSE WITH THE GREEN SHUTTERS
                                     L 1901         50
```

```
Brown, H. Rap   DIE NIGGER DIE!   NY 1969                        40

Brown, Harry   THE END OF A DECADE   N (1940)   bds in dw        35
                                                   wraps         15

Brown, Lloyd (Lewis)   IRON CITY   NY 1951   cloth              75
                                              wraps             40

Brown, Rita Mae   THE HAND THAT CRADLES THE ROCK   NY 1971      40

Brown, Rosellen   SOME DEATHS IN THE DELTA   U. Mass. Press
                                        (1970)   cloth         30
                                                 wraps         15

Brown, Sterling A.   SOUTHERN ROAD   NY (1932)                 750

Brown, Wesley   TRAGIC MAGIC   NY (1978)                        20

Brown, William Wells   CLOTEL: OR, THE PRESIDENT'S
                                    DAUGHTER   L 1853        1,500
                       CLOTELLE: A TALE OF THE SOUTHERN
                       STATES (new title) B/NY (1864) wr     1,200

Brown, Zenith Jones   see David Frome

Browne, Howard   WARRIOR OF THE DAWN   CH (1943)               75

Browning, E(lizabeth) B(arrett)   THE BATTLE OF MARATHON
                                              L 1820       12,000

Browning, Robert   see PAULINE: A FRAGMENT OF A CONFESSION
                       PARACELSUS   L 1835                   1,000

Brownjohn, Alan (Charles)   TRAVELERS ALONE   Liverpool
                                              1954  wr         75

Brownson, Orestus Augustus   AN ADDRESS, ON THE FIFTY-
                             FIFTH..Ithaca 1831  wraps         300

Brownstein, Michael   BEHIND THE WHEEL   C Press (1967)
                       (200 cc)  wraps  6 sgd ltr cc          150
                               10 sgd no. cc                 125
                               184 unsigned                  50

Bruce, Leo (Rupert Croft-Cooke)   CASE FOR THREE DETECTIVES
                             (first mystery)   L 1936          75

Brunner, John   see Gill Hunt

Bryant, Edward   AMONG THE DEAD   NY (1973)                    15

Bryant, William Cullen   see EMBARGO
                       THE EMBARGO   B 1809 (2nd ed)
                       i - wraps                              750
                       ii - wraps stitched                   500

Bryher see Annie Winfred Ellerman

Buchan, John   ESSAYS AND APOTHEGMS OF FRANCIS BACON
                       L (1894)   edited by                   175
               SIR QUIXOTE OF THE MOORS   L 1895              250
                                    NY 1895                   125

Buck, Howard   THE TEMPERING   NH 1919   wr (first title in
                       Yale series of Younger Poets)          40

Buck, Pearl   EAST WIND, WEST WIND   NY (1930)                300

Buckler, Ernest   THE MOUNTAIN & THE VALLEY   NY 1952         75
```

```
Buckley, William F.  GOD AND MAN AT YALE   CH 1951          75

Buechner, (Carl) Frederick  THIS IS A CHAPTER FROM A LONG
                            DAY'S DYING..  NY (1949) wr      175
                            A LONG DAY'S DYING  NY 1950       50

Bukowski, Charles  FLOWER, FIST AND BESTIAL WAIL  (Eureka,
                   CA 1959) wraps (two prev broadsides 1956
                                            and 1950)        350

Bulfinch, Thomas   see AUTHORSHIP

Bullen, Frank T.  THE CRUISE OF THE "CACHALOT"  L 1898       200
                                                NY 1899       75

Bullett, Gerald (William)  THE PROGRESS OF KAY  L 1916        60

Bullins, Ed  HOW DO YOU DO...Mill Valley (1967) wraps         30

Bull-us, Hector (James K. Paulding)  THE DIVERTING HISTORY
                            OF JOHN BULL... NY 1812          600

Bulwer-Lytton, Edward George  ISMAEL: AN ORIENTAL TALE
                                           L 1820           300

Bulwer-Lytton, Edward Robert  see CLYTEMNESTRA

Bumpus, Jerry  ANACONDA  Western Springs (1967)              30
                        (issued w/o dw)

Bunner, H(enry) C(uyler)  A WOMAN OF HONOR  B 1883           60
                 (previous pamphlets and collaborations)

Bunin, Ivan  THE GENTLEMAN FROM SAN FRANCISCO  B 1918 (publ
                            with Andreyev's LAZARUS)         75
                      Hogarth Press  Richmond 1922          175

Bunting, Basil  REDIMICULUM MATELLARUM   Milan 1930       2,000

Burdette, Robert J(ones)  THE RISE AND FALL OF THE
                          MUSTACHE +  Bur IA 1877            50

Burford, William  MAN NOW  Dallas 1954                      75

Burgess, Anthony  (John Anthony Burgess Wilson)  TIME FOR
                                      A TIGER   L 1956       350

Burgess, (Frank) Gelett  THE PURPLE COW  (SF 1895)
                    i -printed on both sides of paper        200
                    ii -printed on one side only              75

Burke, James  FLEE SEVEN WAYS  L 1963                        30

Burke, Kenneth (Duva)  THE WHITE OXEN +  NY 1924            200

Burke, Leda (David Garnett)  DOPE-DARLING  L 1919
                              (2nd book)                    125

Burke, Thomas  VERSES (Guilford 1906)  wraps (25 cc)      1,000
               NIGHTS IN TOWN  L 1915                        100

Burnett, Frances Hodgson  THAT LASS O'LOWRIE'S  NY 1877     100

Burnett, W(illiam) R(iley)  LITTLE CAESAR  NY 1929          500

Burnett, Whit  THE MAKER OF SIGNS  NY 1934                   60

Burnham, David  THIS OUR EXILE   NY 1931                     40
```

Burns, John Horne THE GALLERY NY (1947)   75

Burns, Robert POEMS, CHIEFLY IN THE SCOTTISH DIALECT
                    Kilmarnock Edition 1786   6,000
          Edinburgh 1787 i -"Skinking" p 263   500
                    ii -"stinking" p 263   250

Burnshaw, Stanley POEMS Pittsburgh 1927   200

Burroughs, Edgar Rice TARZAN OF THE APES McClurg CH 1914
                    i -printer's name on c in Old
                              English letters 1,000
                    L (1917) ads dated Autumn   300

Burroughs, John NOTES ON WALT WHITMAN AS POET AND PERSON...
                                              NY 1867
               i -leaves trimmed to 6-9/16", cl & wraps 200
              ii -leaves trimmed to 7-1/4"   75

Burroughs, William (Seward) see William Lee
               NAKED LUNCH P 1959 wraps & dw (green
               border on title pg. "Francs : 1500"
                         on back cover of book)   250
                    NY (1962) (3500 copies)   50

Burroway, Janet DESCENT AGAIN L 1960   30

Burt, (Maxwell) Struthers IN THE HIGH HILLS B 1914   50

Burton, Sir Richard F(rancis) GOA, AND THE BLUE MOUNTAINS..
                                              L 1851
               i -light fawn cloth, 5 x 8-1/8"   750
              ii -light blue cloth, 4-3/4 x 8"   400

Busch, Frederick   I WANTED A YEAR WITHOUT FALL L (1971)   60

Buss, Kate JEVONS BLOCK B 1917   50

Butler, Arthur G(ardiner) LEPIDOPTERA EXOTICA L 1874   400

Butler, Ellis Parker see PIGS IS PIGS
               PIGS IS PIGS NY 1906 (second edition)   30

Butler, Frances Anne (Kemble) POEMS Ph 1844   150

Butler, Samuel A FIRST YEAR IN CANTERBURY SETTLEMENT
                                              L 1863
               i - 32 pgs of ads, light brown end papers   400

Butler, William THE EXPERIMENT L (1961)   75

Butts, Mary (Francis) SPEED THE PLOW + L (1923)   500

Byles, Mather A POEM ON THE DEATH OF HIS LATE
               MAJESTY KING GEORGE (B 1727)   1,000

Bynner, (Harold) Witter AN ODE TO HARVARD + B 1907   50
                    (three different bindings)

Byrd, Richard SKYWARD NY 1928 (500 sgd copies,boxed)   150
                    NY 1928 - first trade edition   35

Byrd, William see A DISCOURSE...

Byrne, (Brian Oswald) Donn STORIES WITHOUT WOMEN NY 1915   75

Byron, Robert EUROPE IN THE LOOKING GLASS... L 1926   300

```
Cabell, James Branch  THE EAGLE'S SHADOW  NY 1904
                i -dedication to "M.L.P.B."                      100
                ii -dedication to "Martha Louise
                                         Branch"                 50
                         NY 1923 revised edition                 30

Cable, George Washington  OLD CREOLE DAYS  NY 1879
                i -no ads in back                               150
                ii -ads in back                                  75

Cahan, Abraham  YEKL...  NY 1896                                150

Cain, George  BLUESCHILD BABY  NY (1970)                         50

Cain, James M(allahan)  OUR GOVERNMENT  NY 1930                 250
                THE POSTMAN ALWAYS RINGS TWICE
                                         NY 1934                750
Cain, Paul (George Sims)  FAST ONE  GC 1933                     400

CALAVAR... (Robert Montgomery Bird)  Ph 1834  2 v wraps         400

Calder, Alexander  ANIMAL SKETCHING  NY (1926)                  350

Caldwell, Erskine  THE BASTARD  NY (1929)  (1100 cc)
                         200 signed cc                          400
                         900 unsigned cc                        175

Caldwell, James  PRINGLE +  Denver (1948)  wr (400 cc)           40

Caldwell, Taylor  DYNASTY OF DEATH  NY 1938                      50

Calisher, Hortense  IN THE ABSENCE OF ANGELS  B 1951            75
                                         L 1953                  60

Calkins, Clinch  POEMS  NY 1928                                  40

Callaghan, Morley (Edward)  STRANGE FUGITIVE  NY 1928           200

Calvert, George Henry  ILLUSTRATIONS OF PHRENOLOGY  BA 1832     100
                (edited by Calvert)

Calvin, Ross  SKY DETERMINES...  NY 1934                        100

Calvino, Italo  THE PATH TO THE NEST OF SPIDERS  B (1957)        75

Cameron, Norman  THE WINTER HOUSE +  L 1935                      60

Campbell, J. Ramsey  THE INHABITANT OF THE LAKE...  SC 1964
                                         (2000 cc)               75

Campbell, John W., Jr.  THE ATOMIC STORY  NY (1947)             75
                THE MIGHTIEST MACHINE  Providence
                                         (1947)                  75

Campbell, Roy  THE FLAMING TERRAPIN  L (1924)                   150
                                         NY 1924                 75

Campbell, Walter S.  see Stanley Vestal

Campbell, Will  BROTHER TO A DRAGONFLY  NY 1977                  25

Camus, Albert  THE OUTSIDER  L (1946) (C. Connolly intro)      125
                THE STRANGER (new title) NY 1946 (does not
                                 include Connolly intro)         75

Cane, Melville  JANUARY GARDEN  NY (1926)                        35

Canning, Victor  THE CHASM  L 1947                              35
```

Cantwell, Robert LAUGH AND LIE DOWN NY 1931   75

Capa, Robert DEATH IN THE MAKING NY (1938)   150

Capek, Karl THE MAKROPOLOUS AFFAIR L 1922 (1st
                          English translation)   200
                                       B 1925   125

Capote, Truman OTHER VOICES, OTHER ROOMS NY (1948)   150
                                          L 1948   100

Carleton, William M. FAX: A CAMPAIGN POEM CH 1868 wraps   750

Carlile, Clancy AS I WAS YOUNG AND EASY NY 1958   25

Carlyle, Thomas THE LIFE OF FRIEDRICH SCHILLER L 1825   850

Carmen, Bliss (Bliss Carman) LOW TIDE ON GRAND PRE
                          Toronto (1889-90?) 13 pp
                          (name misspelled) wraps   2,500
                                       NY 1893 cloth   400
                                       L 1893   200

Carmer, Carl FRENCH TOWN New Orleans (1928) (500 cc)
     stiff wraps (prev textbook collaboration + edited bks)   100

Carnevali, Emanuel A HURRIED MAN (P 1925) wraps (300 cc)   150

Carpenter, Don HARD RAIN FALLING NY (1966)   35
                                    L (1966)   30

Carpenter, Edmund NARCISSUS + L 1873   200
               (Preceded by his Burney Prize Essay)

Carr, Christopher (A.C. Benson) MEMOIRS OF ARTHUR HAMILTON
                                                L 1886   100

Carr, John Dickson IT WALKS BY NIGHT NY 1930   750

Carrefour Press see ANONYMOUS

Carrier, Constance THE MIDDLE VOICE Denver (1955)   40

Carroll, James MADONNA RED B (1976)   20

Carroll, Jim ORGANIC TRAINS (NY 1968) wraps   125

Carroll, Paul THE POEM IN ITS SKIN CH (1968)   30
               (edited DAHLBERG READER in 1966)

Carruth, Hayden THE ADVENTURES OF JONES NY 1895   50

Carruth, Hayden THE CROW AND THE HEART NY 1959 wraps   40

Carryl, Charles E. THE RIVER SYNDICATE NY 1899   40

Carryl, Guy Wetmore FABLES FOR THE FRIVOLOUS NY 1898   50
                          (prev pamphlets)

Carson, Rachael UNDER THE SEA WIND NY 1941   150

Carter, Angela UNICORN Leeds 1966   150
                SHADOW DANCE L 1966   60
                HONEYBUZZARD NY (1966) (new title)   40

Carter, Hodding CIVILIAN DEFENSE... NY (1942) (with
                                       Col Dupuy)   50
                LOWER MISSISSIPPI NY (1942)   50

Carter Ross S. THOSE DEVILS IN BAGGY PANTS NY (1951)   40

Cartier-Bresson, Henri THE DECISIVE MOMENT NY (1952)   450

Cartland, Barbara JIG-SAW   L (1925)   300

Caruthers, William Alexander THE KENTUCKIAN IN NEW YORK...
                               NY 1834 2 vols   300

Carver, Raymond   NEAR KLAMATH Sacramento 1968 wraps   500
                  WINTER INSOMNIA (Santa Cruz 1970)
                                   (1000 cc) wraps   125
                  noted in green & yellow and green
                          & white (less often)

Cary, Arthur (Joyce) VERSE Edinburgh 1908 (also see next
                                            entry)   2,500

Cary, (Arthur) Joyce AISSA SAVED L 1932   400

Casey, John AN AMERICAN ROMANCE NY 1977   20

Casey, Michael OBSCENITIES NH 1972   75

Cassady, Carolyn HEART BEAT Berkeley 1976 (150 sgd no cc)   75

Cassidy, John A STATION IN THE DELTA NY (1979)   25

Cassill, R(onald) V(erlin) THE EAGLE ON THE COIN
                               NY (1950)   30

Castlemon, H(arry) C. (Charles Austin Fosdick) FRANK, THE
                               YOUNG NATURALIST CI 1865   150

Castaneda, Carlos THE TEACHINGS OF DON JUAN BE 1968   90

Cather, Willa APRIL TWILIGHTS B 1903   850

Caute, David AT FEVER PITCH L 1959   40

Cawein, Madison Julius BLOOMS OF THE BERRY Louisville
                               1887 (500 cc)   75

CELEBRATED TRIALS AND REMARKABLE CASES (Geo. Barrow)
                               L 1825 6 vol   500

Celine, Louis Ferdinand JOURNEY TO THE END OF THE
                               NIGHT B 1934   50

Centaur Press SONG OF THE BROAD AX by Walt Whitman
                               Ph 1924   100

Chambers, Robert W(illiam) IN THE QUARTER CH 1893   150

Chandler, Raymond THE BIG SLEEP NY 1939   1,750

Channing, William Ellery THE DUTIES OF CHILDREN
                               B 1807 wraps   250

Chaplin, Sid THE LEAPING LAD + L 1946   60

Chapman, Arthur OUT WHERE THE WEST BEGINS B 1917   25

Chapman, John Jay see THE TWO PHILOSOPHERS
                    EMERSON AND OTHER ESSAYS NY 1898   50

Chappell, Fred IT IS TIME, LORD NY 1963   100

APRIL
TWILIGHTS

POEMS BY

Willa Sibert Cather

ARTI ET VERITATI

Boston: Richard G. Badger

The Gorham Press: 1903

```
Chappell, George S.   COLONIAL ARCHITECTURE IN VERMONT
                                      NY 1918   wr          50

CHARLES AUCHESTER (Elizabeth Sara Sheppard)  L 1853  3 vol  300

Charteris, Hugo  A SHARE OF THE WORLD  L 1953              50

Charteris, Leslie (Charles Bowyer Lin)  X ESQUIRE  L 1927  300

Charyn, Jerome  ONCE UPON A DROSHKY  NY (1964)            40

Chatwin, Bruce  IN PATAGONIA  L 1977                     125

Chayefsky, Paddy  TELEVISION PLAYS  NY 1955               35

Cheever, John  THE WAY SOME PEOPLE LIVE  NY (1943)       500

Cheever, Susan  LOOKING FOR WORK   NY (1979)             15
                                   L 1979                 15

Chesnutt, Charles W(addell)  THE CONJURE WOMAN  B 1899
                    150 Large paper copies      1,000
                             Trade Edition        250

Chester, Alfred  HERE BE DRAGONS  P 1955 wraps
                        125 deluxe cc            125
                        1000 regular cc           75

Chester, George Randolph  GET-RICH-QUICK-WALLINGFORD
                                      NY 1908              75

Chesterton, Cecil  GLADSTONIAN GHOSTS  L (1905)           60

Chesterton, G(ilbert) K(eith)  GREY-BEARDS AT PLAY  L 1900  250

Child, Lydia Marie  HOBOMOK... B 1824                    400

Childress, Alice  LIKE ONE OF THE FAMILY  Brooklyn (1956)  100

CHINESE POEMS (Arthur Waley)  L 1916 wraps (about 50cc)  1,500

Chivers, Thomas Holley  THE PATH OF SORROW  Franklin
                                      (Tenn) 1832         850

Christie, Agatha (Mary Clarissa)  MYSTERIOUS AFFAIR
                        AT STYLES  NY 1920       2,000
                             L (1920)            2,000

Chubb, Ralph  MANHOOD  Curridge 1924 (200 cc) wraps      125

Chubb, Thomas Caldecott  THE WHITE GOD+  NH 1920 stiff wr  35

Churchill, Sir Winston S.   THE STORY OF MALAKAND FIELD
                        FORCE  L 1898 errata slip
                             preceding first map   1,000

Churchill, Winston (American author)  THE CELEBRITY
                                      NY 1898              35

Churton, Henry (Albion W. Tourgee)  TOINETTE  NY 1874
                                   (first novel)         100

Chute, Carolyn  THE BEANS OF EGYPT, MAINE   NY 1985       60

Ciardi, John (Anthony)  HOMEWARD TO AMERICA  NY 1940      75

Cicellis, Kay  THE EASY WAY  (Sackville-West intro) L 1950  35
                                   NY (1950)              35
```

CITY LIGHTS   see L. Ferlinghetti

Clampitt, Amy MULTITUDES, MULTITUDES NY (1973) wr   90

Clark, Austin C. THE SURVIVORS OF THE CROSSING T 1964   60

Clark, Charles E.   PRINCE AND BOATSWAIN Greenfield, MA
                (1915) (edited and three chapters by
                              Marquand & J. M. Morgan)   175

Clark, Eleanor THE BITTER BOX GC 1946   75

Clark, Tom TO GIVE A PAINLESS LIGHT   1963 typescript
                                carbon (3 copies)   500
               THE SAND BURG L(1966) wr (60 sgd no cc)   75
                                          (440 cc)   35
               AIRPLANES (Essex England) 1966 wraps
                                    4 sgd no. cc   150
                (priority in 1966 uncertain)   trade   40

Clark, Walter Van Tilburg CHRISTMAS COMES TO HJALSEN
                                (Reno 1930) wraps   350

Clarke, Arthur C(harles) INTERPLANETARY FLIGHT L 1950   100
                                          NY (1951)   60

Clarke, Austin THE VENGEANCE OF FIONN D 1917   100

CLASS POEM (James Russell Lowell) (C) 1838 wraps   600

Claude (Claude Durrell) MRS. O' L(1957) (Lawrence's
                                      third wife)   40

Clavell, James KING RAT   B (1962)   150
                           L (1963)   100

Cleaver, Eldridge SOUL ON ICE NY (1968)   25
                                 L 1969   25

Clemens, Samuel Langhorne see Mark Twain

Clement, Hal (Harry C. Stubbs) NEEDLE GC 1950   75

Clemons, Walter THE POISON TREE B 1959   60

Clerihew, E. (E.C. Bentley) BIOGRAPHY FOR BEGINNERS
        L (1905) illus by G.K. Chesterton wraps   250
                        (also issued in cloth?)

Clifton, Mark THEY'D RATHER BE RIGHT NY (1957)
                        (with Frank Riley)   60

CLOCKMAKER (THE) (Thomas Chandler Haliburton)
                        Halifax 1836   750

Clough, A(rthur) H(hugh) A CONSIDERATION OF OBJECTS...
                                     O 1847   500
                (2 previous pamphlets at Rugby)

Clouston, J(oseph) Storer THE LUNATIC AT LARGE L 1899   50

CLYTEMNESTRA... (Edw. Robert Bulwer Lytton) L 1855   350

Coates, Robert M(yron) THE EATER OF DARKNESS (P 1926)
                                         wraps   450
                                         NY 1929   350

Cobb, Humphrey PATHS OF GLORY NY 1935 (only book)   50
                                L (1935)   50

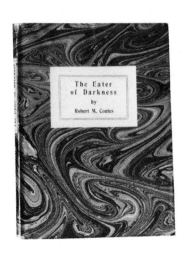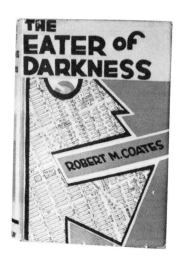

Cobb, Irvin Shrewsbury BACK HOME NY (1912)
    i -"Plimpton Press" on c p & publ name in 3 lines   60

Coblentz, Stanton A(rthur) THE WONDER STICK NY 1929   75

Codrescu, Andrei LICENSE TO CARRY A GUN CH (1970)   25

Coester, A. (Arthur Koestler) see Dr. A. Costler

Coetzee, J(ohn) M. DUSKLANDS Johannesburg 1974   125

Coffey, Brian THREE POEMS P 1933 (250 cc) wraps   175

Coffin, Robert Peter Tristram CHRISTCHURCH NY 1924   75

Cohen, Arthur A. THE CARPENTER YEARS (NY 1967)   35

Cohen, Leonard (Norman) LET US COMPARE MYTHOLOGIES
                              Montreal (1956)   450

Cohen, Marvin THE SELF-DEVOTED FRIEND NY 1967   25

Cohen, Octavus Roy THE OTHER WOMAN   NY 1917 (with
                                 J. U. Giesy)   60

                  THE CRIMSON ALIBI NY 1919   60

Coker, Elizabeth Boatwright DAUGHTER OF STRANGERS NY 1950 75

Cole, G(eorge) D(ouglas) H(oward) THE BROOKLYN MURDERS
                                    L 1923   350

```
Cole, Tom  AN END TO CHIVALRY  B (1965)                              25

Coleman, Wanda  ART IN THE COURT OF THE BLUE FAG      SB 1977
                                                       wraps       15
        MAD DOG BLACK LADY  SB 1979
                   26 sgd ltr cc                                  60
                   200 sgd no. cc                                 25

Coleridge, Hartley  POEMS (vol 1, all publ) Leeds 1833           250

Coleridge, Samuel Taylor  THE FALL OF ROBESPIERRE  L 1794        500

Coles, Manning (Cyril Henry Coles and Adelaide Manning)
                   DRINK TO YESTERDAY  L (1940)                   600

COLLECTION OF FAMILIAR QUOTATIONS (A) (John Bartlett)
                                      C 1855                      250

Colette, (Gabrielle Claudine)  THE VAGRANT  L 1912                60

Collier, John  HIS MONKEY WIFE  L 1930                           350
                                NY 1931                          200

Collins, Michael (Dennis Lynds)  ACT OF FEAR  NY 1967             30

Collins, Wilkie  MEMOIRS OF THE LIFE OF WILLIAM COLLINS
                                      L 1848   2 vol.            450

Colony, Horatio  A BROOK OF LEAVES  B 1955                        35

Colter, Cyrus  THE BEACH UMBRELLA  Iowa City (1970)               25

Colton, James (Joseph Hansen)  LOST ON TWILIGHT ROAD
                                Fresno (1964)  wr                 50

Colum, Mary  FROM THESE ROOTS  L 1935                             50

Colum, Padriac  THE LAND  D 1905                                  75

Colwin, Laurie  PASSION AND AFFECT  NY 1974 (14 stories)          40
                DANGEROUS FRENCH MISTRESS   L (1975)
                            new title (10 stories)                30

Combs, Tram  PILGRIM TERRACE... San German PR 1957 wr             40

Comfort, Alex (Ander)  THE SILVER RIVER  L 1937                   75

Compton-Burnett, Ivy  DOLORES  L 1911 (written with her
                                       brother)                  400
                      PASTORS AND MASTERS  L 1925               250

Condon, Richard (Thomas)  THE OLDEST CONFESSIONS  NY (1958)       30

CONFESSIONS OF AN ENGLISH OPIUM-EATER (Thomas DeQuincey)
                   L 1822 (ad leaf at end)                       750
                          (w/o ad leaf)                         500

CONFESSIONS OF HARRY LORREQUER (THE)   (Charles Lever)
                   D (1839) boards                              250
                            cloth                               150

Congdon, A. Kirby  IRON ARK  (NY 1962) wraps (500 cc)            30

Connell, Evan S. (Helby)  THE ANATOMY LESSON +  NY 1957          60
                                      L (1958)                   40

Connelly, Marc(us)  DULCY  NY 1921 (with G.S. Kaufman)          125

Connett, Eugene V.  see DERRYDALE PRESS
```

```
Connolly, Cyril   THE ROCK POOL   P 1936   wraps                    350
                                          NY 1936                   150
                     (new postscript) L 1947                         50

Connolly, James B(rendan)   JEB HUTTON   NY 1902                    100

Conquest, (George) Robert (Acworth)   POEMS   L 1955                 50

CONQUEST (THE)... By A Negro Pioneer (Oscar Micheaux)
                                  Lincoln, NE 1913                  125

Conrad, Barnaby   THE INNOCENT VILLA   NY (1948)                     40

Conrad, Joseph (Theodor Jozef Konrad Korzeniowski)
            ALMAYER'S FOLLY   L 1895   i - "e" missing in
            "generosity" and "of" omitted in penultimate
                                      line p.110   1,000
                                  NY 1895   (650 cc)                600

Conroy, Frank   STOP-TIME   NY (1967)                               40
                            L (1968)                                30

Conroy, Jack (John Wesley)   THE DISINHERITED   (NY 1933)          150
                     (prev co-edited three books)

Conroy, Pat   THE BOO   Verona (1970) (2000 cc)                    150
              THE WATER IS WIDE   B 1972                            75

CONSIDERATIONS ON SOME RECENT SOCIAL THEORIES (Charles
                               Eliot Norton)   B 1853              125

Cooke, John Esten   see LEATHER STOCKING AND SILK

Coolbrith, Ina Donna   A PERFECT DAY +   SF 1881
                                  Folio issue                      150
                                  regular issue                     60

Coolidge, Dane   HIDDEN WATER...   CH 1910                          75

Cooper, Clarence   THE SCENE   NY (1960)                            25

Cooper, James Fenimore   see PRECAUTION

Cooper, Madison   SIRONIA, TEXAS   B 1952   2 vols - (350 cc
              with sgd page - only seen with second pr
                                  of first vol)                    200
                                  regular edition                   60

Cooper, William   see H(arry) S(ummerfield) Hoff

Coover, Robert   THE ORIGIN OF THE BRUNISTS   NY (1966)            125
                                  L (1967)                          75

Coppard, A(lfred) E(dgar)   ADAM & EVE & PINCH ME   Waltham
                     1921   (also first Golden
                                  Cockerel Press)
                     i -white buckram (160 cc)                     300
                    ii -salmon boards (340 cc)                     150
                                  NY (1922) (350 cc)               100

Corby, Herbert   HAMPDENS GOING OVER   L 1945                       30

Corle, Edwin   MOJAVE   NY 1934                                    100

Corley, Edwin   FIVE PLAYS FOR TWO MEN   n-pl 1951 wraps
                     (with Claude Hubbard)                          75

Corman, Cid (Sidney)   SUBLUNA (Dorchester, MA 1944)
                                  wraps   (400 cc)                  75
```

```
Cornford, Frances  see F.C.D.
                 POEMS  Hampstead  (1910)                        150

Cornford, John  A MEMOIR  L 1938  posthumously published
                              edited by Pat Sloan                 75

Corso, (Nunzio) Gregory  THE VESTAL LADY ON BRATTLE +
                    C 1955  wraps  (500 cc)                      200

Cortazar, Julio  THE WINNERS  NY (1965)                          35

Corvo, Baron (Frederick William Rolfe)  see TARCISSUS...
                 STORIES TOTO TOLD ME  L 1898                    400

Cossery, Albert  MEN GOD FORGOT  Cairo (1944) wraps             125

                              (BE) 1946                          50

Costler, Dr. A. (Arthur Koestler)  ENCYCLOPEDIA OF SEXUAL
                         KNOWLEDGE  L (1934)                     250
                 THE PRACTICE OF SEX   L (1936)
                 ("Coester" on title page)                      200

Cotton, John  GOD'S PROMISE... L 1630                           750

Coulette, Henri  THE WAR OF THE SECRET AGENTS+  NY (1966)        20

Cournos, John  A DILEMMA... Ph 1910  trans of Leonid
                 Andrei Yeff's book by Cournos                   75
             THE MASK   L 1919                                  100

Coward, (Sir) Noel (Pierce)  I'LL LEAVE IT TO YOU   L 1920
                                              wraps             300

Cowen, William Joyce  MAN WITH FOUR LIVES  NY (1934)            50

Cowley, Malcolm  RACINE  P 1923  (150 to 200 cc but most
                        burned per author)  wraps             3,500
             ON BOARD THE MORNING STAR by R. MacOrlan
                 NY 1924 (translated by Cowley)                200
             BLUE JUNIATA  NY (1929)                           300

Cox, A(nthony) B(erkeley)  see THE LAYTON COURT MYSTERY

Cox, Palmer  SQUIBS OF CALILFORNIA  Hartford 1874              75

Coxe, George Harman  MURDER WITH PICTURES  NY 1935
                              (first hardbound)                250

Coxe, Louis O(sbourne)  UNIFORM OF FLESH  Princeton 1947
                        mimeographed sheets in stiff
                        wraps (with R.H. Chapman)              100
                 THE SEA FARING +  NY (1947)                    50

Coyle, Kathleen  PICADILLY  L 1923                             200

Cozzens, Frederick Swarthout  see Richard Haywarde

Cozzens, James Gould  CONFUSION  B 1924  (2000 cc)            500
                 i -grey-green cloth, top edge red

Crackanthorpe, Hubert  WRECKAGE  L 1893 (16 pp ads
                              dated Oct 1892                    75

Craik, Dinah Marie Mulock  see THE OGILVIES

Cranch, Christopher Pearse  A POEM DELIVERED IN THE
                 FIRST CONGREGATION CHURCH...
                              B 1840  wraps                    200

                                                                71
```

White Buildings:
Poems by Hart Crane

With a Foreword by
ALLEN TATE

BONI & LIVERIGHT, 1926

```
Crane, Hart  WHITE BUILDINGS  (NY) 1926 (500 cc in total)
             i -Allen Tate's name incorrectly spelled on
                       title page as "Allan"        2,500
             ii -tipped in title page corrected spelling    1,250
                       P 1930  wraps + dw  (200 cc)        600

Crane, Nathalia  THE JANITOR'S BOY + NY 1924 (500 sgd cc)    75

Crane, Stephen  see Johnston Smith  BLACK RIDERS+  B 1895
                       50 cc on Japan paper    1,000
                              trade (500 cc)      300
                    MAGGIE NY 1896  i - title in Gothic     200
                                   ii - title in Roman      125
                                        L 1896              200

Cranston, Alan  THE KILLING OF PEACE  NY 1945               30
                (preceded by a translation of MEIN KAMPF)

Crapsey, Adelaide  VERSE  Rochester, NY 1915               75

Crawford, F(rancis) Marion  OUR SILVER... NY 1881 wraps    300
                           MR. ISAACS  NY 1882              40

Crawford, Lucy  THE HISTORY OF THE WHITE MOUNTAINS...
                       White Hills  1846                   125

Crawford, Max  WALTZ ACROSS TEXAS  NY (1975)               25

Crawford, Stanley  GASCOYNE  NY (1966)                     40

Creasey, John  SEVEN TIMES SEVEN    L 1932                 250

Creekmore, Hubert  PERSONAL SUN  Prairie City 1940 wraps   50

Creeley, Robert (White)  LeFOU,POEMS  Columbus 1952  wraps
                                              (500 cc)     500

Crevecoeur, Michael Guillaume Jean de  see LETTERS

Crews, Harry  THE GOSPEL SINGER   NY 1968                  200

Creyton, Paul (John Townsend Trowbridge)    PAUL CREYTON'S
            GREAT ROMANCE! KATE THE ACCOMPLICE... B (1849)
                                              wraps      1,500

Crichton, (John) Michael  see John Lange

Cripps, Arthur Shearly  LYRE EVANGELISTICA   O/L 1909      60
                                     (S. African)

Crisp, Quentin  COLOUR IN DISPLAY  L 1938                 100

Crispin, Edmund (Robert Bruce Montgomery)   THE CASE OF
                       THE GILDED FLY  L 1944             150
                    OBSEQUIES AT OXFORD  Ph (1945)
                                    (new title)           75

Croaker, Croaker & Co. & Croaker, Jr. (Joseph Rodman Drake
          & Fitz-Green Halleck)  POEMS   NY 1819         750

Crockett, S(amuel) R(utherford)  THE STICKIT MINISTER...
                                          L 1893          50

Croft-Cooke, Rupert  SONGS OF A SUSSEX TRAMP  Steyning 1922
            (600 no. cc) (also see Leo Bruce)            100

Crofts, Freeman Wills  THE CASK  L 1920  2 pages ads at
                  back and "Spring List, 1920"         1,500
```

```
Cronin, A(richibald) J(ospeh)    DUST INHALATION BY HEMATITE
                                 MINERS (L) 1926 wraps -
                                            offprint       300
                                 INVESTIGATIONS IN FIRST-AID
                                 ORGANIZATION... L 1927 wr     250
                                 HATTER'S CASTLE  L 1931       125

Crosby, Caresse  CROSSES OF GOLD  P 1925  (100 cc)            750
                       Exeter (Eng) 1925  wraps               150

Crosby, Henry Grew (Harry)  ANTHOLOGY  (P 1924) wraps         750

Cross, Amanda  (Carolyn G. Heilbrun)  IN THE LAST ANALYSIS
                                            NY (1964)          75

Crothers, Samuel McChord  MISS MUFFET'S CHRISTMAS PARTY...
                                 St. Paul 1891  wraps         250

Crowder, Henry  HENRY MUSIC  P 1930 (100 sgd no. cc)
                                 issued in tissue dw        2,500

Crowley, (Edward Alexander) Aliester  see ALCEDAMA

Crowley, Mart  THE BOYS IN THE BAND  NY (1968)                40

Crumley, James  ONE TO COUNT CADENCE  NY 1969               150

Crump, Paul  BURN, KILLER, BURN  CH (1962)                   25
```

```
Cullen, Countee  COLOR  NY 1925                              250

Cummings, Bruce Frederick  see W.N.P. Barbellion

cummings, e(dward) e(stlin)  THE ENORMOUS ROOM   NY (1922)
              i - word not blacked out page 219 last line    600
             ii - word blacked out p 219                     400
                                            L (1928)          200

Cummings, Ray(mond King)  THE GIRL IN THE GOLDEN ATOM
                                            L (1922)          350

Cummington Press  FIVE CUMMINGTON POETS  Cummington, MA
                             1939 300 cc wraps               250

Cunard, Nancy  OUTLAWS  L 1921                              600

Cuney, Waring  PUZZLES  Utrecht 1960 (175 cc in slipcase)   250

Cunningham, A(lbert) B(enjamin)  MURDER AT DEER LICK
                                            NY 1939          200

Cunningham, J(ames) V(incent) THE HELMSMAN  SF 1942
                  (300 cc in total)    cloth               600
                                       wraps               250

Cunningham-Graham, R.B.  NOTES ON THE DISTRICT OF MENTEITH
                                    L 1895   wraps          150

Cuppy, William J(acob)  MAROON TALES  CH 1910               35

Curley, Daniel  THAT MARRIAGE BED... B (1957)               25

Curley, Thomas  IT'S A WISE CHILD  NY (1960)                40

Curran, Dale  A HOUSE ON A STREET  NY (1934)                40

Curtis, George William  see NILES NOTE OF A HOWADJI

Curtis, Jack  GREEN AGAIN (Mexico City 1951) wraps (500
                                    no. copies)             40

Curwood, James Oliver  THE COURAGE OF CAPTAIN PLUM
                                    I (1908)                50

Cushman, Dan  STAY AWAY, JOE  NY 1953                       40

Custance, Olive  OPALS  L 1897                              150

D.,F.C. (Frances Crofts Darwin Cornford)  THE HOLTBURY
                        IDYLL n-pl, n-d (c1908)           1,500

D.,H. (Hilda Doolittle)  CHORUSES FROM IPHIGENEIA IN AULIS
                    Cleveland 1916 wraps (40 no. cc)      1,250
                                            L 1916          250
                    SEA GARDEN  L 1916  wraps               350
                        B 1916 (Eng sheets)                200
                                    B 1917                  125

Dabbs, James McBride  THERE IS A LAD HERE   (Louisville
                                      1943?)                50
                    WHEN JUSTICE AND EXPEDIENCY MEET
                            (Columbia 1947) wraps           25

Dahl, Roald  THE GREMLINS   NY (1943)                      300
                            L (1944)                        250
            OVER TO YOU... NY (1946)                        100
                            L 1946                          100
```

OUTLAWS

BY
NANCY CUNARD

LONDON
ELKIN MATHEWS, CORK STREET
MCMXXI

EDWARD DAHLBERG

BOTTOM
DOGS

WITH AN INTRODUCTION BY
D. H. LAWRENCE

LONDON
G. P. PUTNAM'S SONS

```
Dahlberg, Edward  BOTTOM DOGS  L (1929) (520 cc)          250
                              NY (1930)                   150

Daly, Thomas Augustine  CANZONI  Ph 1906  i-"feety" p 17   50

Dana, Richard Henry  see TWO YEARS BEFORE THE MAST

Dane, Clemence (Winifred Ashton)  A REGIMENT OF WOMEN
                                   L 1917                   35

Daniels, Jonathan  CLASH OF ANGELS  NY 1930                60

Dannay, Frederic  see Ellery Queen

Darrow, Clarence (Seward)  A PERSIAN PEARL  CH 1899
                                    (edited by)           125
                         RESIST NOT EVIL  CH 1903    --   150

Darwin, Charles  JOURNAL OF RESEARCHES...  L 1839       1,250

Davenport, Guy (Mattison) THE INTELLIGENCE OF LOUIS AGASSIZ
                B (1963) edited & intro by Davenport      125

Davey, Frank  D-DAY AND AFTER  Oliver (B.C.) (1962)
                              (400 no. cc)                 75

Davidman, Joy  LETTER TO A COMRADE  NH 1938                75

Davidson, Donald  AN OUTLAND PIPER  B 1924                200

Davie, Donald (Alfred)  PURITY OF DICTION IN ENGLISH VERSE
                                   L 1952                  75
                        (POEMS) FANTASY POETS  O 1954
                                        cloth             150
                                        wraps              50

Davies, Rhys  THE SONG OF SONGS + L(1927)  wraps (1000 cc)
                                100 sgd cc                150
                                900 unsgd cc               40

Davies, Robertson  SHAKESPEARE'S BOY ACTOR  L (1939)      500

Davies, W(illiam) H.  THE SOUL'S DESTROYER + (L 1905) wr  600

Davies, William  SONGS OF A WAYFARER  L 1869               50

Daviot, Gordon (Elizabeth MacKintosh)  THE MAN IN THE QUEUE
                              L 1929 1st mystery          200
                              NY 1929                     125

Davis, Angela  IF THEY COME IN THE MORNING  NY 1971        40

Davis, Burke  WHISPER MY NAME  NY 1949                     60

Davis, Dorothy Salisbury  THE JUDAS CAT  NY 1949           25

Davis, H(arold) L(enoir)  HONEY IN THE HORN  NY 1935       50

Davis, Rebecca Harding  MARGRET HOWTH  B 1862              50

Davis, Richard Harding  ADVENTURES OF MY FRESHMAN  Beth
                        (Penna)(1883)  wraps             600
                        GALLEGHER +  NY 1891 i- no ads for
                        "Famous Women..." in back  wraps  200
                                            cloth          75
                                            L 1891         75
```

```
Dawson, Fielding  A SIMPLE WISH FOR A SINCERE... Black Mtn
                                           (1949)  wr      250
                   6 STORIES OF THE LOVE OF LIFE   Black Mtn
                                           (1949)  wr      225

Day, Clarence (Shepard)  DECENNIAL RECORD OF THE CLASS OF
                                      1896  NY 1907         75
                         THE '96 HALF-WAY BOOK  NY 1915     35
                         THIS SIMIAN WORLD NY 1920         150
                                      L (1921)            125

Day, John (Publisher)  THE MUSIC FROM BEHIND THE MOON  NY
                       1926 by James Branch Cabell (boxed)  30

Day-Lewis, C(ecil)  BEECHEN VIGIL +  L(1925)  wraps       350
                    (at least one cc in cloth)
                    Also see Nicholas Blake

Dean, Capt. Harry  see Sterling North

DeBeauvoir, Simon E.  THE BLOOD OF OTHERS  L 1948 (first
                                        Eng trans)         75
                                        NY 1948            35

DeCasseres, Benjamin  THE SHADOW EATER  NY 1915 (Boni)
                                     150 sgd cc            75
                                     650 unsgd cc          50
                             NY 1917 (Wilmarth)            25

DeCasseres, Walter  THE SUBLIME BOY  NY 1926 deluxe (100 cc)  75
                                            regular        40

DeForest, John W(illiam)  HISTORY OF THE INDIANS OF
                          CONNECTICUT... Hartford 1851
                          i - p vii misnumbered iiv       150

Deck, John  ONE MORNING FOR PLEASURE  NY (1968)           30

Deeping, Warwick  UTHER AND IGRAINE  L 1903               75
                                     NY1903               50

Dehn, Paul  THE DAY'S ALARM  L (1949)                     35

Deighton, Len  THE IPCRESS FILE  L (1962)  i -no reviews
                                 on front dw flap         150
                                 NY 1963                  75

DeJong, David Cornel  BELLY FULLA STRAW  NY 1936          35

De La Mare, Walter  see Walter Ramal
                    HENRY BROCKEN  L 1904
                    i - without top edges gilt            75

DeLand, Margaret  THE OLD GARDEN +  B 1886               100

Delaney, Shelagh  A TASTE OF HONEY  NY(1959)  50 no. cc
                                 issued w/o dw  wraps     100

Delany, Samuel R(ay)  THE JEWELS OF APTOR  NY (1962) wr
                      bound dos-a-dos with a James White
                                             novel        40

Delbanco, Nicholas  THE MARLET'S TALE  PH (1966)          50

De Lillo, Don  AMERICANA  B 1971                          60

Del Rey, Lester  "...AND SOME WERE HUMAN"  Ph 1948
                      (hand-ltr title page)               75
                                 Ph 1949                  50
```

Dell, Floyd WOMEN AS WORLD BUILDERS CH 1913 (a few
                    hundred according to author)   150

Del Vecchio, John M. THE 13TH VALLEY (CHAPTER 26)
                            NY (1981) wr   60
                    THE 13TH VALLEY NY 1982   25

Demaret, Jimmy MY PARTNER BEN HOGAN NY (1954) (ghost
                    written by Jimmy Breslin)   50

Demby, William BEETLECREEK NY 1950 (preceded by pub-
            lication of this book in Italian in Milan)   60

DeMorgan, William Frend JOSEPH VANCE... L 1906   75

Denby, Edwin IN PUBLIC, IN PRIVATE Prairie City (1948)
                            i -Blue cloth   300
                           ii -Grey cloth   175

Derleth, August TO REMEMBER Vermont 1931 wr (129 page
                            pamphlet)   300
            MURDER STALKS THE WAKELY FAMILY NY 1934   200
            DEATH STALKS THE WAKELY FAMILY L 1937   125

Derrydale Press MAGIC HOURS by Eugene V. Connett
            NY 1927 (100 cc)(First book of press)   7,500

DeQuincey, Thomas see CONFESSIONS OF AN ENGLISH OPIUM-EATER

DERRY, DERRY DOWN (Edward Lear) L (1846) wraps (175 cc) 2,000
            (first book for children)

Desani, G(ovindas) V(ishnoodes) ALL ABOUT H. HATTERR
                            L (1948)   40

DESCENDANT THE (Ellen Glasgow) NY 1897 i - author's
            name not on spine NY imprint only
                    last ad is Tom Sawyer Abroad   100

DESPERATE REMEDIES (Thomas Hardy) L 1871 3 vol (500 cc) 3,000
            NY 1874 ("author's edition") (yellow cloth)   250

Deutsch, Babette BANNERS NY (1919)   50

Devlin, Denis INTERCESSIONS : POEMS L (1937) pc   40

De Voto, Bernard THE CROOKED MILE NY 1924   75

De Vries,Peter BUT WHO WAKES THE BUGLER? B 1940   200

Dew, Robb Forman DALE LOVES SOPHIE TO DEATH NY 1981   25

Dewey, John PSYCHOLOGY NY 1887   350

DIARY OF SECTION VIII AMERICAN AMBULANCE FIELD SERVICE
                    (William Seabrook) (B) 1917   75

Dibdin, T(homas) F(rognall) POEMS L 1797 (500 cc)   500

Dick, Philip K(endred) A HANDFULL OF DARKNESS L 1955
            i -blue bds ltr in silver   600
           ii -orange bds ltr in black   400

Dick, R.A. (Josephine A. Leslie) THE GHOST AND MRS. MUIR
                            CH/NY (1945)   50

Dickens, Charles see SKETCHES BY "BOZ"

80

```
Dickens, Monica  ONE PAIR OF HANDS  NY 1939                    60

Dickey, James (Lafayette)  DROWNING WITH OTHERS  Middleton,
                                   Conn 1962  cloth           150
                                              Wraps          100

Dickey, William  OF THE FESTIVITY  NY 1959                    40

Dickinson, Emily  POEMS  B 1890 (500 copies)              1,000
                         L 1891 (480 cc)                    500

Dickinson, Patrick  THE SEVEN DAYS OF JERICHO  L (1944) wr    30

Didion, Joan  RUN RIVER  NY (1963)                           75

Di Donato, Pietra  CHRIST IN CONCRETE  Esquire Publ
                   CH (1937) pictorial bds in glassine dw    60
                   Ind (1939) (expanded) sgd tipped-in leaf  40
                                            regular ed       20

Dillard, Annie  TICKETS FOR A PRAYER WHEEL  Columbia (Mo)
                                               (1974)        60

Dillon, George  BOY IN THE WIND  NY 1927                     50

Diment, Adam  THE DOLLY DOLLY SPY  L 1967                    50

Dinesen, Isak (Karen Blixen)  SEVEN GOTHIC TALES  NY 1934
                   1010 no. cc in slipcase
                                       leather              250
                                   black cloth              150
                          regular trade edition             100
                          L 1934 - Rex Whistler dw          150

Di Prima, Diane  THIS KIND OF BIRD FLIES BACKWARD  (NY
                                       1958)  wraps          40

DISSERTATION ON THE HISTORY...OF THE BIBLE...
                (A) (Timothy Dwight)  NH 1772 wr            250

Disney, Doris Miles  A COMPOUND FOR DEATH  GC 1943           30

Dixon, Stephen  NO RELIEF  Ann Arbor (1976) stiff wr         25

Dixon, Thomas, Jr.  THE LEOPARD'S SPOT... NY 1902
                    presentation issue sgd                   90
                    regular                                  30

Dobie, James Frank  A VAQUERO OF THE BRUSH COUNTRY  Dallas
                    1929 i -"Rio Grande River" on map       300

Dobson, Austin  VIGNETTES IN RHYME...  L 1873               125

Doctorow, E(dgar) L(awrence)  WELCOME TO HARD TIMES NY 1960 150
                    BAD MAN FROM BODIE  L 1961
                                   (new title)              125

Dodge, M.E. (Mary Mapes Dodge)  THE IRVINGTON STORIES
                                          NY 1865           125

Dodge, David  DEATH AND TAXES  NY 1941                       75

Dodge, Mary Abigail  see Gail Hamilton

Dodson, Owen  POWERFUL LONG LADDER  NY 1946                  75

Donaldson, Stephen R.  LORD FOUL'S BANE  NY 1977             40
```

```
Donleavy, J. P.  THE GINGER MAN  P (1955)  wraps          350
                                  L 1956                  100
                          P 1958 cloth
         i - original dw flaps                           100
        ii - dw flaps glued on                            50
                          NY (1958)                       50

Donne, John  PSEUDO-MARTYR...  L 1610                   5,000

Donnelly, Ignatius   ATLANTIS...  NY 1882                150
              (pamphlets preceded)

Donovan, Dick (Joyce E. Muddock)  THE MAN HUNTER  L 1888  250

Doolittle, Hilda  see H.D.

Dorn, Ed(ward) Merton)  WHAT I SEE IN THE MAXIMUS POEMS
                     (Ventura CA) 1960 wraps            150

Dos Passos, John (Roderigo)  ONE MAN'S INITIATION-1917
                          L (1920) (750 copies
                          bound for English ed)         600
                          NY 1922 (500 cc from
                               English sheets)          500
       i -both have the word "flat" obliterated p.35:32

Douglas, Ellen  (Josephine Haxton) A FAMILY AFFAIR  B 1962  100
                                  L (1963)                50

Douglas, Keith  ALAMEIN TO ZEM ZEM  L 1946             100
```

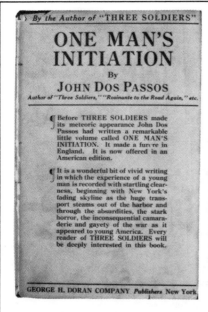
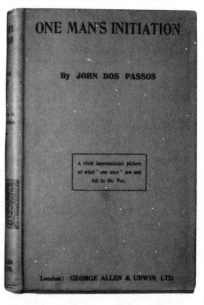

Sister Carrie

By
Theodore Dreiser

NEW YORK
Doubleday, Page & Co.
1900

Douglas, Lord Alfred POEMS P 1896 wraps (prev trans)
                          20 Hollande paper   450
                               Trade ed   150

Douglas, Norman see Normyx

Douskey, Franz INDECENT EXPOSURE NH 1976 wr   30

Doves Press DE VITA ET MORIBUS...by C. Tacitus L 1900
                          5 cc vellum   3,000
                          regular (225 cc)   850

Dowden, Edward A WOMAN'S RELIQUARY Churchtown Dumdrum
                          (Ireland) 1913 (300 cc)   150

Dowdy, Andrew NEVER TAKE A SHORT PRICE NY (1972)   25

Dowell, Coleman THE GRASS DIES L (1968)   75
               ONE OF THE CHILDREN IS CRYING NY 1968   40
                          (new title)

Downes, Quentin (Michael Harrison) NO SMOKE NO FLAME
                               L 1952   40

Dowson, Ernest VERSES L 1896 (30 lpc in imitation vellum) 1,500
                          trade edition   200

Doyle, Arthur Conan A STUDY IN SCARLET L 1888 wr
               i -"younger" spelled correctly
                          in Preface   15,000
               ii -"youuger"   10,000
                          PH 1890 wraps   2,500
                               cloth   1,500

Drabble, Margaret A SUMMER BIRD-CAGE L 1963   150
                          NY 1964   75

Drake, Joseph Rodman see Croaker THE CULPRIT FAY +
                          NY 1835 leather   125
                          various cloths   60

Drake, Leah Bodine A HORNBOOK FOR WITCHES SC 1950   750

DREAM DROPS...BY A DREAMER (Amy Lowell) B (1887)
               cloth - white linen spine (99 cc)   2,500
                          wrappers (151 cc)   1,500

Dreiser, Theodore SISTER CARRIE NY 1900 (about 1000 cc)   800
                               L 1901   350

Drexler, Rosalyn I AM THE BEAUTIFUL STRANGER NY (1965)   35

Drinkwater, John POEMS Birmingham, England 1903   150

DuBois, W(illiam) E(dward) B(urghardt) SUPPRESSION OF THE
                     AMERICAN SLAVE TRADE NY 1896   750
Dubus, Andre THE LIEUTENANT NY 1967   50

Duer, Alice (Later Miller) POEMS NY 1896 (with Caroline
                               Duer)   30

Dugan, Alan GENERAL PROTHALAMION IN POPULOUS TIMES (NH
                     1961) Broadside (100 cc)   90
               POEMS NY 1961 cloth   50
                          wraps   20

Duggan, Alfred KNIGHT WITHOUT ARMOUR L 1950   60

84

```
Dujardin, Edouard  WE'LL TO THE WOODS NO MORE  NY 1938        75

Duke, Osbourne   SIDEMAN  NY (1956)                           40

Dulles, Allen (Welsh)  GERMANY'S UNDERGROUND  NY 1947         40

DuMaurier, Daphne  THE LOVING SPIRIT  L 1931                 100

DuMaurier, George  PETER IBBETSON  NY 1892                   100
                             L 1892  2 vol                   150

Dunbar, Paul (Laurence)  OAK AND IVY  Dayton, Ohio 1893
                                          (500 cc)           350

Duncan, Robert (Edward)  HEAVENLY CITY, EARTHLY CITY
        (BE) 1947  green cloth (100 signed copies)           750
                    white pictorial boards in dw             500

Duncan, Ronald (Frederick)  THE COMPLETE PACIFIST  L (1937)
                                                    wraps     75

Duncan, Sara Jeanette  A SOCIAL DEPARTURE  NY 1890            50

Dunn , Nell  UP THE JUNCTION  L 1963                          40
                        Ph 1966                               30

Dunn, Waldo H.  THE VANISHED EMPIRE  Ci 1904                  50

Dunne, Finley Peter  see MR. DOOLEY IN PEACE AND WAR

Dunne, John Gregory  DELANO...  NY (1967)                     25

Dunning, Ralph Cheever  ROCOCO  Black Manikin Press  P 1926  200
                        (first book of this press)

Dunphy, Jack  JOHN FURY  NY (1946)                           40

Dunsany, Lord (Edward J.M.D.P.)  THE GODS OF PEGANA  L 1905
                i -drummer blind-stamped on front cover      150
               ii -without above                             100

Durant, Will  PHILOSOPHY AND THE SOCIAL PROBLEM   NY 1917     50

Durham, Marilyn  THE MAN WHO LOVED CAT DANCING  NY (1972)     25

Durrell, Claude  see CLAUDE

Durrell, Gerald  THE OVERLOADED ARK  L (1953)                 75
                            NY 1953                           30

Durrell, Lawrence (George)  QUAINT FRAGMENT  (L) 1931
            blue wr or red bds (fewer than 10 cc)         12,000
            TEN POEMS  L 1932 (12 sgd cc)                   4,000
                            wraps                           2,000
            THE PIED PIPER OF LOVERS  L 1935 (1st
                                     novel)                 2,000
            (four other items from 1932-35)

Dwight, Theodore  AN ORATION, SPOKEN BEFORE THE SOCIETY
                        OF THE CENCINNATI  H 1792            125

Dwight,Timothy  see A DISSERTATION...

Dykeman, Wilma  THE FRENCH BROAD  NY(1955)                   50

Dyment, Clifford  FIRST DAY  L 1935                          40

E. A. (George W. Russell)  HOMEWARD: SONGS BY THE WAY
                        O 1894  wraps                        250
```

```
EARLY PIONEER (AN) (Abel Beach)  WESTERN AIRS... Buffalo
                                 1895 (600 no. cc)          40

Eastlake, William (Derry)  GO IN BEAUTY  NY (1956)         125
                                         L 1957             75

Eberhart, Mignon G(ood)  THE PATIENT IN ROOM 18  GC 1929   150

Eberhart, Richard  A BRAVERY OF EARTH  L (1930)            250
                             NY (1930)(Eng sheets)         150

Eckert, Allan W.  THE GREAT AUK  B/T (1963)                 50

Economou, George  THE GEORGIC   LA 1968  wraps
                                 50 sgd no. cc              75
                                250 sgd no. cc              35

Eddington, Arthur Stanley  STELLAR MOVEMENTS... L 1914     125

Eddison, E(ric) R(ucker)  POEMS, LETTERS AND MEMORIES OF
                            PHILIP SIDNEY NAIRN   L 1916
                            (109 pg intro by Eddison)      150
                          THE WORM OUROBOROS   L (1922)
                          i -no blindstamped windmill on
                                          rear cover       250
                          ii - with windmill               200
                                             NY 1926       150

Eddy, Mary (Morse) Baker  see Mary Baker Glover

Edgar, Patrick Nisbett  THE AMERICAN RACE-TURF REGISTER...
                        NY 1833 (vol 1 - all publ)         750

Edman, Irwin  HUMAN TRAITS...   NY 1919  wraps             100
                                NY 1920  cloth              50

Edmonds, Walter D(umaux)  ROME HAUL  B 1929                200

Edson, Russell  APPEARANCES  Stamford  1961  wr            50

Edward, Junius  IF WE MUST DIE  GC 1963                     50

Edwards, Dorothy  RHAPSODY  Wishart  L 1927                 60

Edwards, Page  THE MULES THAT ANGELS RIDE  CH 1972          35

Edwards, S. W.  GO NOW IN DARKNESS  CH 1964 wraps (dw)      35

Eggleston, Edward  THE MANUAL: A PRACTICAL GUIDE TO SUNDAY-
                                   SCHOOLWORK  CH 1869
                   i -with "A. Zeese" imprint on copr. page 150
                   MR. BLAKE'S WALKINGSTICK  CH 1870  wraps  200
                   (one previous anonymous pamphlet)

Ehrlich, Max  THE BIG EYE  GC 1949                          60

Eigner, Larry (Lawrence Joel)  POEMS  Canton, MA 1941
                                wraps (25 cc)            2,000
                               FROM THE SUSTAINING AIR
                               n-pl 1953  (250 cc)  wr     300

Eiseley, Loren  THE IMMENSE JOURNEY  NY (1957)              75

Eliot, George (Mary Ann Evans) see David Friedrich Strauss
               SCENES OF CLERICAL LIFE  L 1858  2 vols     750

Eliot, T(homas) S(tearns)  PRUFROCK +  L 1917 (500 cc) wr 2,000
```

Elkin Mathews, Publisher see Richard LeGallienne

Elkin, Stanley (Lawrence) BOSWELL NY (1964)   100

Ellenbogen, George WINDS OF UNREASON Montreal (1957)   50

Ellerman, Annie Winifred REGION OF LUTANY + L 1914 wraps   750

Ellerman, Sir John see E.L. Black

Ellet, Mrs. E(lizabeth) POEMS Ph 1835 (prev. trans.)   125

Ellin, Stanley DREADFUL SUMMIT NY 1948   75

Elliott, George P(aul) PARKTILDEN VILLAGE B (1958)   50

Elliott, Janice CAVE WITH ECHOES L 1967   35

Elliott, Sumner Locke CAREFUL, HE MIGHT HEAR YOU NY 1963
                       author's name on spine of dw in red
                                    or black (variant)   30

Elliott, William ADDRESS TO THE PEOPLE OF ST HELENA
                   PARISH Charleston 1832 wraps   150

Ellis, A. E. THE RACK L 1958   50

Ellis, Havelock THE NEW SPIRIT L 1890   100

Ellison, Harlan (Jay) THE DEADLY STREETS NY (1958) wr   60

Ellison, James Whitfield I'M OWEN HARRISON HARDING
                                              NY 1955   20

Ellison, Ralph THE INVISIBLE MAN NY (1952)   200
                                   L 1953   100

Ellson, Hal DUKE NY 1949   40

Ely, David (David Ely Lilienthal) TROT NY (1963)   25

EMBARGO...(William Cullen Bryant) B 1808 12 pp wraps   4,000

Emerson, Ralph Waldo LETTER FROM THE REV R. W. EMERSON
                                TO... B (1832) wraps   250
                      A HISTORICAL DISCOURSE... Concord
                                               1835   250
                      also see NATURE

Emmons, Richard THE FREDONIAD B 1827 4 vol   200

Empson, William POEMS L 1935   125

Endore, S. Guy CASANOVA: HIS KNOWN AND UNKNOWN LIFE
                                     NY (1929)   40
                                     L (1930)   40

England, George Allan DARKNESS AND DAWN B (1914)   75

Engle, Paul (Hamilton) WORN EARTH NH 1932   125
                        (co-edited anthology in 1931)

Enslin, Theodore (Vernon) THE WORK PROPOSED (Ashland, MA)
                           1958 (ltd to 250 cc) stiff wr   175

Epstein, Seymour PILLAR OF SALT NY(1960)   60

Ertz, Susan MADAME CLAIRE L 1923   75

```
Eshleman, Clayton  MEXICO & NORTH  (NY/SF 1961)
                        wraps (26 ltr cc)         75
                        regular edition           40

EUPHRANOR, A DIALOGUE ON YOUTH (Edward Fitzgerald)  L 1851    300

Evans, Donald  DISCORDS  Ph 1912                    100

Evans, E. Everett  MAN OF MANY MINDS  Reading (1953)
                        (300 sgd no. cc)           60
                        i  -blue cloth             25
                        ii -boards                 15

Evans, John  ANDREWS' HARVEST  NY 1933              75

Evans, Margiad  COUNTRY DANCE  L 1932               75

Evans, Walker  THE CRIME OF CUBA  Ph (1933)  Book by
               Carlton Beals.  First book appearance
                        of Evans' photos          150

Everett, Edward  A DEFENCE OF CHRISTIANITY  B 1814  100

Everson, William (Oliver) (Brother Antoninus) THESE ARE
               THE RAVENS  San Leandro, CA 1935 wraps   400

Ewart, Gavin  POEMS AND SONGS  L (1939)            150

Ewing, Max  TWENTY-SIX SONNETS FROM THE PARONOMASIAN...
                        (NY 1924) wraps            50

Exley, Frederick  A FAN'S NOTES  NY (1968)         50
                                 L (1970)          50

F.,M.T. (Katherine Anne Porter)  MY CHINESE MARRIAGE
                        NY 1921                   400

Fabes, Gilbert  THE AUTOBIOGRAPHY OF A BOOK  L (1926)  75

FAIR DEATH (A)  (Sir Henry Newbolt)  L (1881)  wraps  100

Fainlight, Harry  SUSSICRAN  (L 1965) wraps  50 sgd cc  75
                                 100 unsigned      35

Fair, Ronald L.  MANY THOUSANDS GONE  NY (1965)    60

Fairless, Michael  THE GATHERING OF BROTHER HILARIUS  L 1901  50

Fairman, Henry Clay THE THIRD WORLD...  Atlanta 1895  200
                                         NY 1896   100

Falkner, J. Meade  THE LOST STRADIVARIUS  L 1895    75

FANNY  (Fitz-Greene Halleck)  NY 1819 grey wraps   300

FANSHAWE: A TALE (Nathaniel Hawthorne)  B 1828   12,000

Fante, John  WAIT UNTIL SPRING, BANDINI  NY (1938)  125

Farina, Richard  BEEN DOWN SO LONG IT LOOKS LIKE UP TO ME
                        NY (1966)                  50

Farjeon, Eleanor  PAN-WORSHIP +  L 1908            60

Farmer, Philip Jose  THE GREEN ODYSSEY  NY (1957)  cloth  850
                                                   wraps   30

Farnol, (John) Jeffery  MY LADY CAPRICE  L 1907     35
```

Farrell, Henry   WHAT EVER HAPPENED TO BABY JANE?   NY (1960)   35

Farrell, J. G.   A MAN FROM ELSEWHERE   L 1963   125

Farrell, James T(homas)   YOUNG LONIGAN   NY 1932   250
        reissued in 1935 with new intro by F. Thrasher
           inserted, title page still dated 1932   100

Farren, Julian   THE TRAIN FROM PITTSBURGH   NY 1948   25

Fauset, Jessie Redmond   THERE IS CONFUSION   NY 1924   100

Fast, Howard (Melvin)   TWO VALLEYS   NY 1933   250

Faulkner, John   MEN WORKING   NY (1941)   60

Faulkner, William   THE MARBLE FAUN   B (1924)   15,000
            SOLDIER'S PAY   NY 1926   6,000
                     L 1930   750

Faust, Frederick see Max Brand

Faust, Irvin   ENTERING ANGEL'S WORLD...   NY 1963   50
           ROAR LION ROAR +   NY (1964)   40

Faust, Seymour   THE LOVELY QUARRY   NY 1958   wraps   20

Favil Press   GLEANINGS by Clifford Bax   Kensington 1921
                        (40 cc)   100

Fay, Theodore Sedgwick   see DREAMS AND REVERIES...

Fearing, Kenneth   ANGEL ARMS   NY 1929   200

Feibleman, James   DEATH OF THE GOD IN MEXICO   NY (1931)   150

Feibleman, Peter S.   A PLACE WITHOUT TWILIGHT   Cleveland
                        (1958)   50

Feifer, Jules   SICK, SICK, SICK   NY 1958   40

Feikema, Feike (Frederick Manfred)   THE GOLDEN BOWL
                St. Paul   1944   100

Feinstein, Elaine   IN A GREEN EYE   L 1966 (30 sgd no. cc)   60

Feinstein, Isidor   see I. F. Stone

Feldman, Irving (Mordecai)   WORKS AND DAYS +   L (1961)   75
                              B (1961)   60

Fenton, James   OUR WESTERN FURNITURE   O (1968)   wr   125

Ferber, Edna   DAWN O'HARA   NY (1911)   50

Ferguson, Helen (Helen Woods)   A CHARMED CIRCLE   L (1929)   350

Ferlinghetti, Lawrence   PICTURES OF THE GONE WORLD   SF
                (1955) 25 sgd hardbound cc   500
                wraps (500 cc) (price $.65)   200
                (first City Lights book)

Ferril, Thomas Hornsby   HIGH PASSAGE   NY 1926   75

Ferrini, Vincent   NO SMOKE   Portland 1941   50

Fessier, Michael   FULLY DRESSED AND IN HIS RIGHT MIND
                        NY 1935   50

YOUNG LONIGAN

A Boyhood in Chicago Streets

by

JAMES T. FARRELL

Introduction by
FREDERIC M. THRASHER
Associate Professor of Education, New York University
Author of "The Gang"

NEW YORK
THE VANGUARD PRESS
1932

```
Ficke, Arthur Davidson  (and Thomas Newell Metcalf)
                THEIR BOOK  (CH 1901)  (50 no. cc)         150
                FROM THE ISLES (Surrey) 1907 wraps         100

Fiedler, Leslie (Aaron)  AN END TO INNOCENCE  B (1955)      25

Field, Ben  THE COCK'S FUNERAL  NY (1937)                  40

Field, Edward  STAND UP, FRIEND  NY (1963)                 20

Field, Eugene  TRIBUNE PRIMER  (Denver 1881) wraps      5,000
                                Brooklyn 1882            300

Field, Rachel Lyman  RISE UP,JENNIE SMITH  NY (1918) wr   125

Fielding, Gabriel  see Alan Barnsley


Fields, James T(homas)  ANNIVERSARY POEM... B 1838  wr      50
                        POEMS  B 1849                       50

Finch, Amanda  BACK TRAIL... NY 1951 wr                     50

Finlay, Ian H(amilton)  THE SEA-BED +  Edinburgh (1958)
                                          wr (dw)          200

Finney, Charles G.  THE CIRCUS OF DR. LAO  NY 1935        175

Finney, Jack (Walter Braden Finney)  5 AGAINST THE HOUSE
                                          GC 1954          75

Finney, Sterling (E.B. White)  LESS THAN NOTHING...  NY
                                (1927) issued w/o dw       250

Firbank, (Arthur Annesly) Ronald  ODETTE D'ANTREVERNES
                and A STUDY IN TEMPERMENT  L 1905
                          10 LPC vellum sgd             1,000
                          wraps  (500 cc)                  250

FIRST LESSONS IN GRAMMAR... (Elizabeth Peabody) B 1830    150

Fish, Donald   AIRLINE DETECTIVE   L 1962 (Ian Fleming
                                          intro)           75

Fish, Robert L(loyd)  THE FUGITIVE  NY 1962                50

Fisher, Alfred Young  THE GHOST IN THE UNDERBLOWS  LA 1940
                                          (300 cc)        125

Fisher, Bud (Harry Conway)  THE MUTT AND JEFF CARTOONS
                                          B 1910          100

Fisher, M(ary) F(rances) K(ennedy)  SERVE IT FORTH  NY 1937  150

Fisher, Roy  CITY  Worcester 1961  wraps                   75

Fisher, William  THE WAITERS  NY/CL 1953                   35

Fisher, Vardis  SONNETS TO AN IMAGINARY MADONNA  NY 1927   150

Fiske, John  TOBACCO AND ALCOHOL  NY 1869                  50

Fitch, George  THE BIG STRIKE AT SIWASH  NY 1909           60

Fitch, (William) Clyde  THE KNIGHTING OF THE TWINS +
                                          B (1891)         150

Fitts, Dudley  TWO POEMS  n-pl (1932) wraps (100 sgd)     125
```

Odette D'Antrevernes

A Study in Temperament

BY

ARTHUR FIRBANK

LONDON
ELKIN MATHEWS, VIGO STREET, W.

1905

SONNETS
TO AN
IMAGINARY
MADONNA

BY VARDIS FISHER

NEW YORK · HAROLD VINAL
MCMXXVII

Fitzgerald, Edward   see EUPHRANOR...

Fitzgerald, F(rancis) S(cott Key)   THIS SIDE OF PARADISE
            NY 1920 (Publ April 1920 and Scribner seal)   3,000
                        (four prev musical scores)

Fitzgerald, Robert (Stuart) POEMS NY (1935)   75

Fitzgerald, Zelda SAVE ME THE WALTZ NY 1932 (3010 cc)   600
                                      L (1953)   60

Fitzgibbon, Constantine THE ARIAN BIRD L 1949   50

FIVE YOUNG AMERICAN POETS N (1940) (John Berryman, et al)
            (800 cc) considered Berryman's first book as
            the five "books" were combined by publisher   200

Flaccus, Kimball IN PRAISE OF MARA Hanover 1932 wraps
                                      (100 cc)   100
                  AVALANCHE OF APRIL NY 1934   50

Flaherty, Robert MY ESKIMO FRIENDS NY 1924   300

Flanner, Janet THE CUBICAL CITY NY 1926   350

Flecker, James (Elroy) THE BEST MAN EIGHT'S WEEK L 1906
                                                   wraps   300
                        THE BRIDGE OF FIRE: POEMS L 1907
                        wr   i-no quote from Sunday Times   125

Fleming, Ian (Lancaster) KEMSLEY NEWPAPERS REFERENCE BOOK
                          L (1949) loose leaf folder   2,500
                          (mostly written by Fleming)
                          CASINO ROYALE L 1953   1,250
                                         NY 1954   300

Fleming, Oliver (Philip and Ronald MacDonald) AMBROTOX
                          AND LIMPING DICK L 1920   150

Fleming, Peter BRAZILIAN ADVENTURE L (1933)   75

Flender, Harold PARIS BLUES NY (1957)   30

Fletcher, J(oseph) S(mith) ANDREWLINA L 1889   50

Fletcher, John Gould FIRE AND WINE L (1913)   100
        (first or second book - there were five publ in 1913)

Flint, F.S. IN THE NET OF THE STARS L 1909   125

Flint, Timothy A SERMON, PREACHED... Newburyport 1808 wr   150

Flower, Robin ERIE + L (1910) wraps   60

Flynn, Robert NORTH TO YESTERDAY NY 1967   40

Follett, Ken EYE OF THE NEEDLE (NY 1978)   40

Foote, Horton HARRISON TEXAS: EIGHT TELEVISION PLAYS
                                   NY (1956)   60
               THE CHASE NY (1956) issued the same
                          day as the foregoing book   40

Foote, John Tintor BLISTER JONES Ind (1913)   50

Foote, Shelby THE MERCHANT OF BRISTOL (Greenville 1947)
                          wraps (260 sgd no. cc)   350

WEBSTER GENEALOGY.

Compiled and Printed

FOR

PRESENTATION ONLY

BY

NOAH WEBSTER

NEW HAVEN:

1836.

WITH

NOTES AND CORRECTIONS

BY

HIS GREAT-GRANDSON,

PAUL LEICESTER FORD.

BROOKLYN, N. Y.

PRIVATELY PRINTED.

1876.

```
                TOURNAMENT  NY 1949                            75

Forbes, Bryan   TRUTH LIES SLEEPING  L (1950)                  75

Ford, Charles Henry   THE YOUNG AND THE EVIL (with Parker
                      Tyler) P (1933) (first bk for both)
                                    wraps  50 no. cc          400
                                         regular edition      250
                      A PAMPHLET OF SONNETS  Majorca 1936
                                         (50 sgd cc)          250
                      THE GARDEN OF DISORDER +   L (1938)
                                    (30 sgd cc) (no dw)        250
                                         (460 unsgd cc)        100
                      N (1938) English ed in New Dir dw        100

Ford, Ford Madox  see Ford Madox Hueffer

Ford, Jesse Hill  MOUNTAINS OF GILEAD  B 1961                  40

Ford, Leslie (Mrs. Zenith Jones Brown)  see David Frome

Ford, Paul Leicester  WEBSTER GENEALOGY NEW HAVEN 1836
                      Brooklyn 1876 notes by Ford
                                         (250 cc)  wr          150
                      THE BEST LAID PLANS  Brooklyn 1889        50

Ford, Richard  A PIECE OF MY HEART  NY 1976                    35

Fordham, Mary Weston  MAGNOLIA LEAVES  Tuskegee (1897)
                      intro by Booker T. Washington           100

Forester, C.S.  A PAWN AMONG KINGS  L 1924                    750

Forrest, Felix C. (Paul Linebarger)  RIA  NY (1947)           75

Forster, E(dward) M(organ)  WHERE ANGELS FEAR TO TREAD
                            Edinburgh 1905
                      i -title not stated in ads
                                         (1050 cc)            500
                      ii -title in ads                        150

Forsyth, Frederick  THE BIAFRA STORY  (MDLSX 1969)  wr        75
                    THE DAY OF THE JACKAL  L (1971)            75
                                         NY 1971              35

Fort, Charles  THE OUTCAST MANUFACTURERS  NY 1909
                i -blue ribbed cloth ltr in gold             150
                ii -blue mesh cloth ltr in red               125

FORTRESS OF SORRENTO (THE) (Mordecai M. Noah) NY 1808 wr     300

Fowles, John  THE COLLECTOR  L 1963  i -dw flap w/o reviews   650
                                         B (1963)            100

Fox, John (William)  A CUMBERLAND VENDETTA  NY 1896           50

Fox, Paula  POOR GEORGE  NY (1967)                            50

Fox, William Price  SOUTHERN FRIED  Greenwich (1962) wraps    35

Fraenkel, Michael  see ANONYMOUS and WERTHER'S...

Frame, Janet  THE LAGOON  Christchurch 1951                  300

Francis, Dick (Richard Stanley)  SPORT OF QUEENS  L 1957     200
                                 DEAD CERT  L 1962           450
                                         NY 1962             150
```

Francis, Robert   STAND WITH ME HERE   NY 1936   60

Frank, Waldo   THE UNWELCOME MAN   B 1917   125

Frankau, Gilbert   ETON ECHOES   Eton 1901   wraps   100

Frankenberg, Lloyd   THE RED KITE   NY (1939)   40

FRANKENSTEIN (Mary Wollstonecraft Shelley)   L 1818 3 vol   15,000

Fraser, George MacDonald   FLASHMAN   L (1969)   60

Frazer, Sir James George   TOTEMISM   Edinburgh 1887   125

Frederick, Harold   SETH'S BROTHER'S WIFE   NY 1887
                             i - c 1886 & no ads   150

Freeling, Nicholas   LOVE IN AMSTERDAM   L 1962   60

Freeman, Gillian   THE LIBERTY MAN   L 1955   *   40

Freeman, John   TWENTY POEMS   L 1909   wraps   60

Freeman, Mary E. Wilkins   see Mary Wilkins

Freeman, R(ichard) Austin   TRAVELS AND LIFE IN ASHANTI AND
                                              JAPAN   L 1898   750
                        (also see Clifford Ashdown)

Freneau, Philip (Morin)   see A POEM, ON THE RISING GLORY...
                            THE AMERICAN VILLAGE   NY 1772   150

Freud, Sigmund   THE INTERPRETATION OF DREAMS   L 1913   150

Fried, Eric   THEY FIGHT IN THE DARK   (L 1944) wraps   75

Friedman, Bruce Jay   STERN   NY 1962 (prev. edited anthology)   50

Friedman, I. I.   THE LUCKY NUMBER   Ch 1896   75

Frome, David (Zenith Jones Brown)   THE MURDER OF AN OLD
                                           MAN   L 1929   75

Frost, A(rthur) B(urdette)   STUFF AND NONSENSE   NY (1884)
                             bds (also see Max Adeler)   100

Frost, Robert (Lee)   TWILIGHT (Lawrence, MA 1894)
                                2 known cc   40,000
                  A BOY'S WILL   L 1913   i -brown or
                  bronze cloth with lettering in
                             gilt, edges rough cut   1,250
                                            wraps   350
                  NY 1915   "aind" for "and" in last
                                line on p.14   350

Fruchter, Norman   COAT UPON A STICK   (L 1962)   50

Fry, Christopher   THE BOY WITH A CART... L 1939 wraps   75

Fry, Roger   GIOVANNI BELLINI   L 1899   75

Fuchs, Daniel   SUMMER IN WILLIAMSBURG   NY (1934)   200
                                         L (1935)   125

FUCK THE SYSTEM (Abbie Hoffman)   NY (1968) wraps   75

Fuentes, Carlos   WHERE THE AIR IS CLEAR   NY (1960)   30

Fugard, Athol   THE BLOOD KNOT   Johannesburg 1963 (issued
                                       without dw)   200

Fuller, Henry Black   see Stanton Page

Fuller, John   FAIRGROUND MUSIC   L 1961   25

Fuller, R(ichard) Buckminster   NINE CHAINS TO THE MOON
                                       Ph (1938)   150

Fuller, Roy (Broadbent)   POEMS   L (1939) (preceded by
                           privately printed book)   150

Fuller, Sarah Margaret   CONVERSATIONS WITH GOETHE   B 1839
                                (Trans by Fuller)   500
                         SUMMER ON THE LAKES ...
                                B/NY 1844   300
                                NY 1845 wraps   75

Furman, Garrit   RURAL HOURS   n-pl 1824 bds   125

Futrelle, Jacques   THE CHASE OF THE GOLDEN PLATE   NY 1906   200

Gaddis, Thomas E.   BIRDMAN OF ALCATRAZ   NY (1955)   35

Gaddis, William   THE RECOGNITIONS   NY (1955)   200

Gag, Wanda   MILLIONS OF CATS   NY 1928   250 sgd no. cc
                         with original engraving   350
                                Trade edition   125

Gaines, Charles   STAY HUNGRY   NY 1972   20

Gaines, Ernest J.   CATHERINE CARMIER   NY 1964   125

Gale, Zona   ROMANCE ISLAND   I (1906)   50

Gallagher, Tess   STEPPING OUTSIDE   Lisbon, Iowa (1974) wr   250

Gallant, Mavis   THE OTHER PARIS   B 1956   75

Gallico, Paul (William)   FAREWELL TO SPORT   NY 1938   150
                         THE ADVENTURES OF HIRAM HOLIDAY
                                       NY 1939   150

Gallup, George   A GUIDE TO PUBLIC OPINION POLLS   PR 1944   75

Galsworthy, John   see John Sinjohn

Garcia Lorca, Federico   BITTER OLEANDER   L 1935   150

Garcia-Marquez, Gabriel   NO ONE WRITES THE COLONEL   NY
                                       (1968)   125

Gardner, Erle Stanley   THE CASE OF THE VELVET CLAWS
                                       NY 1932   1,000

Gardner, Isabella (Stewart)   BIRTHDAYS FROM THE OCEAN
                                       C 1955   35

Gardner, John (English writer)   SPIN THE BOTTLE   L (1964)   75
                         THE LIQUIDATOR   L 1964   50

Gardner, John (Champlin)   THE FORMS OF FICTION   NY 1962
                         (with Lennis Dunlap) no dw   125
                         DRAGON, DRAGON + n-pl (Christmas 1962)
                         mimeographed pages in stiff boards   1,500
                         THE MILLER'S MULE + n-pl 1965 mimeo-
                         graphed pages in stiff boards   1,000

```
                THE COMPLETE WORKS OF THE GAWAIN POET
                        CH (1965) trans by Gardner        200
                THE RESURRECTION  (NY 1966)               450
                        (Ph.D dissertation prior to 1962)

Gardner, Leonard  FAT CITY  NY (1969)                      25

Garland, (Hannibal) Hamlin  UNDER THE WHEEL  B 1890  wr   250
                            MAIN TRAVELED ROADS  B 1891   100
                                     CH 1893 110 1pc       75

Garnett, David  THE KITCHEN GARDEN... L (1909)  wraps
        (trans. and adapted by DG from French work
          of Prof. Gressent) (also see Leda Burke)       150

Garnett, Richard  see PRIMULA

Garrett, George (Palmer)  KING OF THE MOUNTAIN  NY (1957)  50

Garrett, (Gordon) Randall  see Robert Randall

Garrigue, Jean  THE EGO AND THE CENTAUR  (N 1947)         35

Garson, Barbara  MACBIRD: Independent Socialist Club
                            (BE 1966)                     35

Garth, Will  (attributed to Henry Kuttner)  DR. CYCLOPS
                            NY 1940                       125

Garve, Andrew (Paul Winterton) NO TEARS FOR HILDA  L 1950  50

Gascoyne, David  ROMAN BALCONY +  L 1932                 750

Gaskell, Elizabeth C.  see MARY BARTON...

Gaskell, Jane  STRANGE EVIL  L 1957                       50

Gass, William H(oward)  OMENSETTER'S LUCK  (NY 1966)     125
                            L 1967                        75

Gasset, Jose Ortega  THE REVOLT OF THE MASSES  L (1932)  100
                            NY (1932)                     75

Gathorne-Hardy, Robert  LACEBURY MANOR  L 1930           100

Gault, William Campbell  DON'T CRY FOR ME  NY 1952        35

Gavin, Thomas  KING-KILL  NY 1977                         20

Geddes, Virgil  FORTY POEMS  P (1926) wraps              75

Gee, Maurice  THE BIG SEASON  L 1962                     60

Geismar, Maxwell  WRITERS IN CRISIS  B 1942              35

Gelber, Jack  THE CONNECTION  NY (1960)  wraps           35
                            L (1961)  cloth              30

Gellhorn, Martha (Ellis)  WHAT MAD PURSUIT NY 1934       125

Genet, Jean  OUR LADY OF THE FLOWERS  P (1949) (475 cc)  150
                imitation red morroco, issued w/o dw

GENIUS OF OBLIVION By a Lady of New Hampshire  (Sarah
                    Josepha Hale)  Concord 1823           125

Gent, Peter  NORTH DALLAS FORTY  NY 1973                 25
```

George, Henry OUR LAND AND LAND POLICY ... SF 1871
                         (map in black and red)   600

GEORGIA SCENES, CHARACTERS, INCIDENTS, ETC... (Augustine
                  Baldwin Longstreet) Augusta 1835   1,500
                         2nd ed NY 1840 illus   200

Gerhardi, William (Alexander) FUTILITY L (1922)   175
                                         NY (1922)   125

Gernsback, Hugo RALPH 124C41 + B 1925   600

Ghiselin, Brewster AGAINST THE CIRCLE NY 1946 (1250 cc)   50

GHOST IN THE BANK OF ENGLAND (THE) (Eden Phillpotts)
                                         L 1888   500

Gibbings, Robert   IORANA! A TAHITIAN JOURNAL B 1932
                         385 sgd no. cc   250
                         trade ed in slipcase   125
                                       L 1932   100

Gibbons, Euell STALKING THE WILD ASPARAGUS NY (1962)   35

Gibbons, Stella THE MOUNTAIN BEAST + L 1930 wraps   60

Gibbs, Barbara THE WELL Albuquerque (1941) wraps   150

Gibbs, Wolcott BIRD LIFE AT THE POLE   NY 1931   75

Gibran, Kahlil THE MADMAN: HIS PARABLES AND POEMS NY 1918   75

Gibson, Charles Dana DRAWINGS NY 1897   200

Gibson, Walter B. see Maxwell Grant

Gidlow, Elsa ON A GREY THREAD Ch 1923   50

Gilbert, Ruth LAZARUS + Wellington 1949 (65 sgd no. cc)   100

Gilbert, Michael (Francis) CLOSE QUARTERS L 1947   150

Gilbert W(illiam) S(chwenk) A NEW AND ORIGINAL EXTRAVA-
                   GANZA ENTITLED DULCAMARA...
                              L 1866 wraps   750

Gilbreth, Frank B(unker) CHEAPER BY THE DOZEN NY 1948
                              (with Carey)   25

Gilder, Richard Watson THE NEW DAY... NY 1876   50

Gilchrist, Ellen THE LAND SURVEYOR'S DAUGHTER (Fayette-
                              ville) 1979 wraps   75
                   IN THE LAND OF DREAMY DREAMS Fayette-
                              ville 1981 cloth   200
                              wraps (1000 cc)   75

Gill, Brendan DEATH IN APRIL + Windham, CT 1935 (160 cc)   150

Gill, Eric SERVING AT MASS Sussex 1916 wraps   1,200

Gillian, Strickland W. INCLUDING FINNIGAN (Ph 1908)   100

Gilmore, Millen SWEET MAN NY(1930)   75

Gilpin, Laura THE HOCUS-POCUS OF THE UNIVERSE GC 1977   35

Gingrich, Arnold CAST DOWN THE LAUREL (NY 1935)   25

```
Ginsberg, Allen  HOWL FOR CARL SOLOMON    SF 1955  wraps
                           (50 mineographed cc)    5,000
                SIESTA IN BALBA AND RETURN... Icy Cape,
                           Alaska  1956  wraps (56 cc)    3,000
                HOWL   SF (1956)  wr  (cover pr 75 cents)    300
                HOWL   SF 1971  275 sgd cc issued w/o dw    150

GINX'S BABY: HIS BIRTH AND OTHER MISFORTUNES (John Edward
                                Jenkins)  L 1870    250

Giorno, John  POEMS  NY 1967 (50 sgd no. cc) wraps    75

Giovanni, Nikki  BLACK FEELING, BLACK TALK  (Detroit)
                                1968  wraps    75

Gissing, George  WORKERS IN THE DAWN  L 1880  3 vol
                           (black end papers)    1,000

Gladstone, William (Ewart)  THE STATE IN ITS RELATIONS
                    WITH THE CHURCH  L 1038    300

Glasgow, Ellen  see THE DESCENDENT
                PHASES OF AN INFERIOR PLANET  NY 1898
                           with erratum slip    75

Glaspell, Susan  THE GLORY OF THE CONQUERED  NY (1909)    60

Glass, Montague (Marsden)  POTASH & PERLMUTTER  B (1910)    40

Glover, Mary Baker (Eddy)  SCIENCE AND HEALTH...  B 1875
                    i -errata slip w/o index    1,500

Gluck, Louise  FIRSTBORN: POEMS   NY 1968  cloth    75
                                       wraps    30
                    L 1969 (50 sgd cc)    125
                           trade in wraps    20

Godden, Rumer  THE CHINESE  PUZZLE  L (1936)    150

Godey, John  THE GUN & MRS. SMITH   NY (1947)    50

Godoy, Jose F.  WHO DID IT?  SF 1883  wraps    150

Godwin, Gail  THE PERFECTIONISTS  NY (1970)    75

Gogol, Nikolai  see HOMELIFE IN RUSSIA

Gogarty, Oliver St. John  see ALPHA AND OMEGA

Gold, H.L.  THE OLD DIE RICH +  NY (1955)    30

Gold, Herbert  BIRTH OF A HERO  NY 1951    50

GOLD-HUNTER'S ADVENTURE...(THE) (William Henry Thomes)
                                B 1864    250

Gold, Ivan  NICKEL MISERIES  NY (1963)    25
                                L 1964    25

Gold, Michael (Irving Granich)  JOHN BROWN   NY 1923    150

Goldberg, Gerald Jay  THE NATIONAL STANDARD  NY (1968)    30

Goldberg, R(ube)  FOOLISH QUESTIONS  B (1909)    100

Golden Cockerel Press  see A. E.  COPPARD

Golding, Louis  SORROW OF WAR  L (1919)    25
```

"A book all dog-lovers will delight in"

CHINESE PUZZLE

by

RUMER GODDEN

```
Golding, W(illiam) G(erald)  POEMS  L 1934              3,500
                        LORD OF THE FLIES  L (1954)      1,000
                                         NY (1954)         175

Goldman, Emma  ANARCHISM +  NY 1910                        125

Goldman, William  TEMPLE OF GOLD  NY 1957                  100

Goldring, Douglas  A COUNTRY BOY +  L 1910  wraps           50

Goldsmith, Oliver  see James Willington

Goodman, Paul  TEN LYRIC POEMS  (NY 1934)  wraps           200

Goodrich, Marcus  DELILAH  NY (1941)  only book             25

Goodrich, Samuel Griswold  see Peter Parley

Goodwin, Stephen  KIN  NY (1975)                            25

Goodwyn, Frank  THE MAGIC OF LIMPING JOHN...  NY (1944)     50

Goran, Lester  THE PARATROOPER OF MECHANIC AVENUE  B 1960   30

Gordon, Caroline  PENHALLY  NY 1931                        600

Gordon, Mary  FINAL PAYMENTS  NY (1978)                     25

Gordon, Mildred  THE LITTLE MAN WHO WASN'T THERE  GC 1946   35

Gordon, Taylor  BORN TO BE  NY 1929  (Covarrubias illus)    75

Gordimer, Nadine  FACE TO FACE  Johannesburg (1949)        400
                 THE SOFT VOICE OF THE SERPENT  NY 1952      75
                                         L (1953)           100

Gore-Booth, Eva  POEMS  L 1898                              35

Gores, Joe (Joseph N.)  A TIME OF PREDATORS  NY 1969       100

Gorey, Edward  THE UNSTRUNG HARP  NY (1953)                125

GORGEOUS POETRY  (J.B. (Beachcomber) Morton)  L 1920        60

Gosse, Edmund  MADRIGALS, SONGS AND SONNETS  L 1870
                      (with John A. Blaikie)               150

Gottschalk, Laura Riding  THE CLOSE CHAPLET  L 1926        600
                          NY (1926) tissue dw              450
                          ANATOLE FRANCE AT HOME by
                          Marcel Le Guff NY 1926
                          (trans by Gottschalk)            200

Gould, Gerald  LYRICS  L 1906  wraps                        35

Gould, Wallace  CHILDREN OF THE SUN...  B (1917)            35

Gover, (John) Robert  THE ONE HUNDRED DOLLAR MISUNDER-
                                   STANDING  L 1961         50
                                         NY 1962            35

Gowen, Emmett  MOUNTAIN BORN  I (1932)                      75

Goyen, (Charles) William  THE HOUSE OF BREATH  NY (1950)    75
                                         L 1951            50

Goytisolo, Juan  THE YOUNG ASSASSINS  NY 1958              25

Grady, James  SIX DAYS OF THE CONDOR  NY 1974              25
```

NOTES ON THE DISTRICT

OF MENTEITH

FOR TOURISTS AND OTHERS

BY

R. B. CUNNINGHAME GRAHAM

LONDON

ADAM & CHARLES BLACK

1895

Graham, John (David Graham Phillips)   THE GREAT GOD SUCCESS
                                          NY (1901)   60

Graham, R.B. Cunninghame   NOTES ON THE DISTRICT OF MENTIETH
                                          L 1895   wraps   150

Graham, Sheilah   GENTLEMEN-CROOK   L 1933   75

Graham, Tom (Sinclair Lewis)   HIKE AND THE AEROPLANE   NY
                              (1912) i -August 1912 c pg   200

Graham, W(illiam) S(ydney)   CAGE WITHOUT GRIEVANCE
                                       Glasgow (1942)   75

Grahame, Kenneth   PAGAN PAPERS   L 1894 (450 cc)   150
            (title page designed by Aubrey Beardsley)

Grainger, Francis Edward   see Headon Hill

Grant, Anne   POEMS OF VARIOUS SUBJECTS   Edinburgh 1803   50

Grant, J. C.   THE ROCK SHOOT   Edinburgh 1928   35

Grant, Maxwell (Walter B. Gibson)   THE LIVING SHADOW   NY
                 (1931) (first hardbound of Shadow)
                                       issued w/o dw   100

Grass, Gunter   THE TIN DRUM   NY 1962   40
                                L 1962   40

Grau, Shirley Ann   THE BLACK PRINCE   NY 1955   60

Graves, John   HOME PLACE   Ft. Worth 1958   wraps (200 cc)   400
               GOODBYE TO A RIVER   NY 1960   75

Graves, Robert (Ranke)   OVER THE BRAZIER   L 1916 wraps   1,000
                         L (1920) second edition   400

Gray, Francine du Plessix   DIVINE DISOBEDIENCE   NY 1970   30

Gray, John   SILVER POINTS   L 1893 (250 cc)   450

Gray, Simon   COLMAIN   L 1963   50

Greacen, Robert   THE BIRD   D 1941 (250 cc) stiff wraps   150

Green, Anna K(atherine Rohles)   THE LEAVENWORTH CASE
                                          NY 1878
                 i - "f" missing from "fresh" last
                                      line p.215   1,500

Green, Anne   THE SELBYS   NY 1930   40

Green, Ben K.   HORSE CONFORMATION...   (Ft. Worth 1963)   125

Green, Henry (Henry Vincent Yorke)   BLINDNESS   L 1926   1,500
                                     NY (1926)   250

Green, Julian   AVARICE HOUSE   NY 1917   30

Green, Paul   TRIFLES OF THOUGHT   NY 1917   50

Greenan, Russell H.   IT HAPPENED IN BOSTON?   NY (1968)   30

Greenaway, Kate   THE QUIVER OF LOVE   (with Walter Crane)
                                          (L 1876)   250
            UNDER THE WINDOW   L(1878) w/printer's imprint
            on back of title pg and "End of Contents" p14   150

THE MAN WITHIN

BY

GRAHAM GREENE

"There's another man within me
that's angry with me."

SIR THOMAS BROWNE.

LONDON : WILLIAM HEINEMANN LTD.

```
Greenberg, Joanne  THE KING'S PERSONS  NY (1963)            40
                                        L (1963)            35

Greene, A.C.  A PERSONAL COUNTRY  NY 1969                   50

Greene, Graham  BABBLING APRIL    L 1925                 2,500
                THE MAN WITHIN  L (1929)                 1,000
                                  GC 1929                  300

Greenleaf, Stephen  GRAVE ERROR  NY (1979)                 30

Gregor, Arthur  OCTAVIAN SHOOTING TARGETS  NY (1954)       40

Gregory, Horace  CHELSEA ROOMING HOUSE: POEMS  NY 1930    100
                 ROOMING HOUSE  L 1932 (new title)
                                        stiff wraps        75

Gresham, William Lindsay  NIGHTMARE ALLEY  NY (1946)       50

Gressent, Professor  see DAVID GARNETT

Grey, (P.) Zane  BETTY ZANE  NY (1903) (issued w/o dw)    400

Grieve, C(hristopher) M(urray)  ANNALS OF FIVE SENSES
                        Montrose (Scotland) 1923          350

Griffin, Howard  CRY CADENCE  NY 1947                      30

Griffin, John Howard  THE DEVIL RIDES OUTSIDE
                            Ft. Worth 1952                 75
                                      L 1953               60

Griffin, Jonathon  THE HIDDEN KING  L 1955                 75

Griffith, D. W.  THE RISE AND FALL OF FREE SPEECH IN
                            AMERICA  LA 1916              350

Griffith, (Jones) George  THE ANGEL OF THE REVOLUTION
                                      L 1893              150

Grigson, Geoffrey  SEVERAL OBSERVATIONS  L (1939)          75

Grile, Dod (Ambrose Bierce)  THE FIEND'S DELIGHT  L (1872)  600
                                      NY (1873)           400

Grimke, A(ngelina) E(mily)  APPEAL TO THE CHRISTIAN WOMEN
                      OF THE SOUTH  (NY 1836) wr          250

Grinnell, George B.  PAWNEE HERO...  NY 1889             150

Grossinger, Richard  THE STARMAKER  (Madison, Wisc 1968) wr   40

Grossman, Alfred  ACROBAT ADMITS  NY 1959                 30

Grosz, Georg  TWELVE REPRODUCTIONS...  Ch 1921  wraps
                      First American publication          150

Grubb, Davis  THE NIGHT OF THE HUNTER  (NY 1953) 1000 sgd   75
                                      regular trade        60
                                      L (1954)             40
Gruber, Frank  THE FRENCH KEY  NY (1940)                  100
          (This title lists PEACE MARSHALL as preceding
                      - not seen)

Grumbach, Doris  THE SPOIL OF THE FLOWERS  GC 1962        125

Guedalla, Philip  IGNES FATUI...  O/L 1911  wraps         100

Guest, Barbara  THE LOCATION OF THINGS  NY 1960 wraps
                                      (300 cc)             90
```

Guest, Edgar Albert HOME RHYMES Detroit 1909   50

Guest, Judith ORDINARY PEOPLE NY 1976   25

Guiney, Louis Imogen SONGS AT THE START B 1884   100
        (preceded by two pamphlets and a broadside)

Gunn, Thom(son William) (POEMS) Fantasy Press O 1953 wr   500
                FIGHTING TERMS (O 1954) wraps   175
                i -final "t" in "thought" omitted
                           on first line. Yellow
                             cloth issued w/o dw   400
                           NY 1958 stiff wraps
                i -w/o review label attached   50

Gunther, John THE RED PAVILION NY 1926   50

Gunthrie, Thomas Anstey see F. Anstey

Guthrie, A(lfred) B(ertram), Jr. MURDERS AT MOON DANCE
                                      NY 1943   400

Guthrie, Ramon TROBAR CLUS Northampton, MA 1923
                           (250 sgd cc)   75

Guthrie, Woody BOUND FOR GLORY NY 1945   150

Gysin, Brion TO MASTER, A LONG GOODNIGHT NY (1946)   60

H.D. see D., H. (Hilda Doolittle)

H. H. (Helen Hunt Jackson) BETHMENDI: A PERSIAN TALE
                            B 1867 trans by HH   200
                                 VERSES B 1870   150

Habberton, John HELEN'S BABIES B 1876 wraps
                         i - measures 1-3/16"   150

Hagedorn, Herman, Jr. THE SILVER BLADE Berlin 1907 wr   100
                  (prev broadside and colaboration)

Haggard, H(enry) Rider CETYWAYO... L 1882 (750 cc)   500

Hailey, Arthur FLIGHT INTO DANGER L 1958 (with
                                Joan Castle)   75
                THE FINAL DIAGNOSES NY 1959   50

Haines, John WINTER NEWS Middletown (1966)   30

Haines, William (William Heyen) WHAT HAPPENED IN FORT
                FORT LAUDERDALE NY (1958) wraps
                       (with William Taggard)   50

Halberstam, David THE NOBLEST ROMAN B 1961   35

Haldane, Charlotte MAN'S WORLD L 1926   125

Haldeman, Joe W. WAR YEAR NY 1972   30

Hale, Edward Everett see MARGARET PERCIVAL IN AMERICA

Hale, Nancy THE YOUNG DIE GOOD NY 1932   100

Hale, Sarah Josepha see THE GENIUS OF OBLIVION

Haley, Alex ROOTS NY 1976 500 sgd no. cc in slipcase   150
                                trade edition   35
            (also see Malcolm X)

CHICAGO SIDE-SHOW

BY

ALBERT HALPER

❦

NUMBER 6

PAMPHLET SERIES ONE

DRIFT

A NOVEL
by
JAMES HANLEY

ERIC PARTRIDGE, LTD.
THIRTY, MUSEUM STREET, LONDON
1930

CETYWAYO

AND

HIS WHITE NEIGHBOURS:

OR,

REMARKS ON RECENT EVENTS IN ZULULAND,
NATAL, AND THE TRANSVAAL.

BY

H. RIDER HAGGARD.

LONDON:
TRÜBNER & CO., LUDGATE HILL.
1882.
[All rights reserved.]

Haley, J. Evetts THE XIT RANCH OF TEXAS Ch 1929   500

Haliburton, Thomas Chandler see THE CLOCKMAKER

Hall, Adam see Mansell Black

Hall, Arthur Vine TABLE MOUNTAIN... Capetown (1896)   175

Hall, Austin PEOPLE OF THE COMET (LA 1948) first sci fi   25

Hall, Baynard Rush RIGHTEOUSNESS THE SAFE-GUARD...
                                      (IND 1827)   75

Hall, Donald (Andrew) THE HARVARD ADVOCATE ANTHOLOGY
                            NY (1950) (ed by DH)   35

                     (Poems) Fantasy Poets No. 4
                              O (1952) wraps   200

Hall, Henry THE TRIBUNE BOOK OF OPEN AIR SPORTS NY 1887
             (Hall edited this book believed to be the
              first printed from machine set type)   250

Hall, J. C. THE SUMMER DANCE + L 1951 (1st separate work)   60

Hall, James LETTERS FROM THE WEST... L 1828 (two previous
                                          pamphlets)   400

Hall, James B(yron) NOT BY THE DOOR NY (1954)   50

Hall, James Norman KITCHENER'S MOB B 1916   50

Hall, O(akley) MURDER CITY NY (1949) (not acknowledged)   40
                SO MANY DOORS NY (1950)   35

Hall, Marguerite Radclyffe 'TWIXT EARTH AND STARS L 1906   200

Halleck, Fitz-Greene see CROAKER and FANNY...

Halliday, Brett (Davis Dresser) see Asa Baker

Halper, Albert CHICAGO SIDE-SHOW NY 1932 (110 cc) wr   200
                UNION SQUARE NY 1933   75

Hamady, Walter THE DISILLUSIONED SOLIPSIST Mt. Horeb 1954
                (60 cc) (Also first Pershible Press) 2,000

Hamburger, Michael POEMS OF HOLDERLIN L 1943 (translation
                                   and 97 pg intro)   75
                    LATER HOGARTH L 1945   100

Hamilton, Clive (C. S. Lewis) SPIRITS IN BONDAGE
                                      L1919   250

Hamilton, Edmund THE HORROR ON THE ASTEROID L 1936   600

Hamilton, Gail (Mary Abigail Dodge) COUNTRY LIVING
                    AND COUNTRY THINKING B 1862   150

Hamilton, Gerald see Patrick Weston

Hamilton, George R. THE SEARCH FOR LOVELINESS + L 1910   60

Hammett, (Samuel) Dashiell RED HARVEST NY 1929   2,000
                i -no review on back panel of dw

Hamner, Earl, Jr. FIFTY ROADS TO TOWN NY (1953)   35

Handy, W.C. BLUES AN ANTHOLOGY NY 1926 edited by Handy   300

UNCLE REMUS

HIS SONGS AND HIS SAYINGS

THE FOLK-LORE OF THE OLD PLANTATION

By JOEL CHANDLER HARRIS

*WITH ILLUSTRATIONS BY FREDERICK S. CHURCH AND
JAMES H. MOSER*

NEW YORK
D. APPLETON AND COMPANY
1, 3, AND 5 BOND STREET
1881

```
Hanley, James  DRIFT  L 1930 (10 sgd cc)                    1,000
                      trade  (490 cc)                         150

Hannah, Barry  GERONIMO REX  NY (1972)                       100

Hansberry, Lorraine  A RAISIN IN THE SUN  NY 1959 wraps       50

Hansen, Joseph  see James Colton

Hanson, Pauline  THE FOREVER YOUNG +  Denver (1948) wraps     35

Hardwick, Elizabeth  THE GHOSTLY LOVER  NY (1945)            125

Hardy, Thomas  see DESPERATE REMEDIES

Hare, Cyril (Alfred Alexander Gordon Clark)  TENANT FOR
                                      DEATH  L 1937           60

Hare, David  SLAG  L (1971)  wraps                            40

Harland, Henry  see Sidney Luska

Harper, Frances E(llen) W(atkins)  IOLA LEROY, OR SHADOWS
                                  UPLIFTED  Ph 1892          300

Harrigan, Stephen  ARKANSAS  NY 1980                          25

Harrington, Alan  THE REVELATIONS OF DR. MODESTO  NY 1955     40
                              (L 1957) Len Deighton dw         50

Harrington, Donald  THE CHERRY PIT  NY (1965)                 30

Harrington, William  WHICH THE JUSTICE...  L (1963)           35

Harris, Bertha  CATCHING SARADOVE  NY (1969)                  40

Harris, Frank  ELDER CONKLIN +  NY 1894                       75
                              L 1895                          50

Harris, Joel Chandler  UNCLE REMUS: HIS SONGS AND SAYINGS
               NY 1881      i -"presumtive" for
               "presumptuous" last line p.9 & no
               mention of this bk in ads at back            350
               UNCLE REMUS AND HIS LEGENDS OF THE
               OLD PLANTATION  L 1881 (new title)           250

Harris, Mark  TRUMPET THE WORLD  NY (1946)                    50

Harris, Timothy  KRONSKI/McSMASH  GC 1969                     35

Harris, Wilson  PALACE OF THE PEACOCK  L (1960)               60

Harrison, Jim (James Thomas)  PLAIN SONG  NY (1965)          125

Harrison, Tom  LETTER TO OXFORD (1933)  wraps                 40

Harrison, William  THE THEOLOGIAN  NY(1965)                   40

Hart, Joseph C.  see MIRIAM COFFIN...

Hart, William S. and Mary  PINTO BEN +  NY (1919)             25

Harte, (Francis) Bret OUTCROPPINGS  SF 1866 (ed anon by BH)  250
                      CONDENSED NOVELS +  NY 1867  1st book   250
                      THE LOST GALLEON  SF 1867  1st verse   300

Hartley, L(eslie) P(oles)  NIGHT FEARS +  L 1924            200

Hartley, Marsden  TWENTY-FIVE  (P 1923) wraps               400
```

Harwell, Meade   POEMS FROM SEVERAL WILDERNESS   DV 1946
                                    wraps   (250 cc)   50

THE HASHEESH EATER (Fitz-Hugh Ludlow)   NY 1857   200

Hass, Robert   FIELD GUIDE   NH 1973   35

Hauser, Marianne   DARK DOMINION   NY (1947)   40

Hawkes, J(ohn) C(lendinnin) B(urne)   FIASCO HALL   C 1943
                                    wraps   (100 cc - 60 des) 750

Hawthorne, Julian   BRESSANT   NY 1873   100

Hawthorne, Nathaniel   see FANSHAW: A TALE
                          TWICE-TOLD TALES   B 1837   1,500

Hay, John   JIM BLUDSO OF THE PRAIRIE BELLE...   B 1871
                 (orange wraps) (previous pamphlets)   100

Hayakawa, S. J.   LANGUAGE IN THOUGHT AND ACTION   Madison
                                    1939   wraps   150

Hayes, Joseph   AND CAME THE SPRING   NY (1942) wraps
                                    (with M. Hayes)   50

Haywarde, Richard (Frederick Swarthout Cozzens)
                          PRISMATICS   NY 1853   150

Hazel, Robert   POEMS 1951 - 1961   Morehead (1961)   30

Hazlitt, W. Carew   THE HISTORY OF THE ORIGIN AND RISE OF
                 THE REPUBLIC OF VENICE   L 1858   2 vol   100
Hazo, Samuel   DISCOVERY +   NY (1959)   wraps   25

Hazzard, Shirley   CLIFFS OF FALL +   L 1963   60

Heaney, Seamus   ELEVEN POEMS   Belfast (1965)
              i -creme wraps, cvr device in purple   600
             ii -wove paper, cvr device in black purple   300
            iii -grey paper in stiff green wraps   150
                 DEATH OF A NATURALIST   L (1966)   350
                 NY 1966 (English sheets)   250

Hearn, Lafcadio   ONE OF CLEOPATRA'S NIGHTS by T. Gautier
                 NY 1882 trans by LK   i - publ name in
                                    capitals on spine   200
                 STRAY LEAVES FROM STRANGE LITERATURE
                 B 1884   i -has J.R. & O. on sp   250

Hearon, Shelby   AT HOME AFTER 1840...   Austin 1966
                          100 sgd no. cc   125
              (Text by SH, drawings by Peggy Goldstein)
                          regular ed - 1000 cc   60

Hecht, Anthony (Evan)   A SUMMONING OF STONES   NY (1954)   100

Hecht, Ben (see Maxwell Bodenheim)   THE HERO OF SANTA MARIA
                 NY (1920) wraps (with Frank Shay)   200
                 ERIK DORN   NY 1921
                 i -yellow lettering on cover   125

Hedge, Frederic Henry   A SERMON PREACHED...   B 1834 wraps 100

Hedley, Leslie Woolf   THE EDGE OF INSANITY   LA 1949 wraps 60

Hegen, Alice Caldwell   MRS. WIGGS OF THE CABBAGE PATCH
                 NY 1901 (gold sky on front cvr)   40

```
Heggen, Thomas   MISTER ROBERTS   B 1946                          50
                                  L 1948                          50

Heinemann, Larry   CLOSE QUARTERS   NY (1977)                     25

Heinlein, Robert (Anson)   ROCKET SHIP GALILEO   NY (1947)       300

Heller, Joseph   CATCH-22   NY 1961   (dw price $5.95)           350
                                      L (1962)                   100

Hellman, Lillian   THE CHILDREN'S HOUR   NY 1934                 250
                                  L (1962) wraps & dw             75

Helprin, Mark   A DOVE OF THE EAST +   NY 1975                    40

Helps, Sir Arthur   see THOUGHTS IN THE CLOISTER...

Hemans, Felicia Dorothea   POEMS   L 1808                        200

Hemingway, Ernest   THREE STORIES AND TEN POEMS (P 1923)
                                      (300 cc)   wraps         5,000
                    IN OUR TIME   P 1924   (170 cc)           4,000
                                           NY 1925           1,000
                                           L 1926              500
                                           NY 1930             300

Hemingway, Leicester   THE SOUND OF THE TRUMPET   NY (1953)       35

Henderson, Elliot Blaine   PLANTATION ECHOES   Columbia 1904     125

Henderson, George Wylie   OLLIE MISS   NY 1935                    75

Henley, Beth   AM I BLUE   (NY 1982) wraps                        40

Henley, William Ernest   A BOOK OF VERSES   L 1888   75 lpc
                                      in white tissue dw         600
                             regular edition, stiff wraps        100

Henri, Adrian   TONIGHT AT NOON   L (1968) 26 sgd ltr cc          60
                                  100 sgd no. cc                  30

Henry, Arthur   NICHOLAS BLOOD, CANDIDATE   NY (1890)             75

Henry, O. (Wm. Sidney (later Sydney) Porter)   CABBAGES AND
        KINGS   NY 1904   i -McClure, Phillips & Co. on spine    150

Henty, G(eorge) A(lfred)   A SEARCH FOR A SECRET   L 1867
                                      3 vols                   3,000

Herbert, Sir A(lfred) P(atrick)   POOR POEMS AND ROTTEN
                    RHYMES   Winchester, Eng 1910   wraps        175

Herbert, Frank (Patrick)   SURVIVAL AND THE ATOM (Santa
                    Rosa 1950)   wr   an off-print              400

Herbert, Henry William   see THE BROTHERS...

Herbst, Josephine   NOTHING IS SACRED   NY 1928                  125

Herford, Oliver   ARTFUL ANTICKS   NY 1888                       125

Hergesheimer, Joseph   THE LAY ANTHONY   NY 1914                  75

Herlihy, James Leo   BLUE DENIM   NY 1958 (with Wm Noble)         40
                    THE SLEEP OF BABY FILBERTSON   NY 1959        50
                                            L 1959               30

Herr, Michael   DISPATCHES   NY 1977                              75
```

THREE STORIES

Up In Michigan

Out of Season

My Old Man

& TEN POEMS

Mitraigliatrice

Oklahoma

Oily Weather

Roosevelt

Captives

Champs d'Honneur

Riparto d'Assalto

Montparnasse

Along With Youth

Chapter Heading

ERNEST HEMINGWAY

Published by
Contact Publishing Co

114

Herriot, James ALL CREATURES GREAT AND SMALL   NY (1972)   30

Herrmann, John WHAT HAPPENS (P 1926) wraps   150

Herron, Stella Wynne BOWERY PARADE + NY (1936) glassine dw 50

Hersey, John (Richard) MEN ON BATAAN NY 1942   125

Hesse, Hermann DEMIAN NY 1923 (1st Eng trans)   300

Hewlett, Maurice EARTHWORK OUT OF TUSCANY L 1895 (500 cc) 125

Heyen, William see William Haines
                DEPTH OF FIELD Baton Rouge 1970   25

Heyer, Georgette (Mrs. George Ronald Rougier)
                THE BLACK MOTH   B 1921   100

Heyward, DuBose CAROLINE CHANSONS NY 1922 (with H. Allen) 100
                SKYLINES AND HORIZONS NY 1924   100

Heyward, Jane Screven BROWN JACKETS Columbia 1923   60

Hickmott, Allerton Cushman FABRIC OF DREAMS (Hartford 1925)
                           11 cc on Kelmscott   200
                                    100 cc   100

Higgins, Colin HAROLD AND MAUDE Ph (1971)   30

Higgins, Dick WHAT ARE LEGENDS? Caleis, Maine 1960 wraps 25

Higgins, F. R. ISLAND BLOOD + L 1925   75

Higgins, George V(incent) THE FRIENDS OF EDDIE COYLE NY
                           1972 i -green cloth (priority
                                          assumed)   35
                           ii -blue cloth   25
                                          L (1972)   35

Highsmith (Mary) Patricia (Ploughman) STRANGERS ON A
                           TRAIN NY 1950   350
                                    L 1950   300

Hildreth, Richard see THE SLAVE...

Hill, Headon (Francis Edward Grainger) CLUE'S FROM A
                           DETECTIVE'S CAMERA L 1893   50

Hill, Susan THE ENCLOSURE L 1961   50

Hillyer, Robert S(illman) SONNETS + C 1917   50

Hilton, James CATHERINE HERSELF L (1920)   400

Himes, Chester (Bomar) IF HE HOLLERS LET HIM GO GC 1945 150

Hine, Daryl FIVE POEMS T (1955) wr   150

Hinton, S.E. THE OUTSIDERS NY (1967)   75
             (also catalogued in a library binding w/o dw)

Hirsch, Sidney THE FIRE REGAINED NY 1913 considered
                           the first "Fugitive book"   150

Hirschman, Jack FRAGMENTS (NY 1952) (priv publ) wraps   250
                A CORRESPONDENCE OF AMERICANS Bloomington
                           1960 (glassine dw)   60

```
Hoover, Herbert C.  PRINCIPLES OF MINING  NY 1909
                    (with Lou Henry Hoover)              150

Hope, Bob  THEY GOT ME COVERED  Hollywood 1941  wr       35

Hopkins, Gerard Manley  POEMS  L (1918)                 400

Horan, Robert  A BEGINNING  NH 1948 (1014 cc)            50

Horgan, Paul  VILLANELLE OF EVENING  n-pl 1926 wr (200 cc)  1,000
              LAMB OF GOD  Roswell 1927 wr (60 cc)       1,500
              MEN OF ARMS  Ph (1931)(Juvenile) (500 cc bd)   600
              THE FAULT OF ANGELS  NY (1933)             125

Hornung, E(rnest) W(illiam)  UNDER TWO SKIES  L 1892     50

Hoskins, Katherine  A PENETENTIAL PRIMER  Cummington 1945
                              (350 cc)  wraps            60

Houdini, Harry (Ehrich Weiss)  THE RIGHT WAY TO DO WRONG
                              B 1906  wraps             150

Hough, Emerson  THE SINGING MOUSE STORIES  NY 1895     150
                (cover by Will Bradley)

Hough, Lindy  THE VIBRATING SERPENT  Madison  (1968)    30

Houghton, Claude (C. H. Oldfield)  THE PHANTOM HOST +
                              L 1917  wraps              50

Hours Press  PERONNIK THE FOOL by George Moore  Chapelle-
              Reanville  1928  (200 sgd cc) (2 prev
              pamphlets published for the authors)      200

Household, Geoffrey (Edward West)  THE TERROR OF VILLE-
                              DONGA  L (1936)           150
                    THE THIRD HOUR  L 1937               75
                                    B 1938               60

Housman, A.E.  A SHROPSHIRE LAD  L 1896 (350 cc)
               "Shropshire" on label 33 millimeters wide  1,500
                              NY 1897 (150 cc)          750

Housman, Clemence  THE WERE-WOLF  L/Ch 1896            125

Housman, Laurence  A FARM IN FAIRYLAND  L 1894         200

Hovenden, Robert M.  EPHEMERIDES...  L 1844            100

Hovey, Richard  POEMS  W 1880  cloth                   500
                               wraps                   250

Howard, Brian  GOD SAVE THE KING  Hours Press  P (1930)
                              (150 cc)                 250

Howard, Elizabeth Jane  THE BEAUTIFUL VISIT  L (1950)   75

Howard, H. R.  THE HISTORY OF VIRGIL A. STEWART...  NY 1836  250

Howard, (James) H. W.  BOND AND FREE  Harrisburg 1886
                    portrait of author opposite title  300

Howard, Maureen  NOT A WORD ABOUT NIGHTINGALES  NY (1962)  35

Howard, Richard  THE VOYEUR by A. Robbe-Grillet  NY 1958
                    translated by RH    wraps           25
                QUANTITIES  Middletown (1962) wraps     25
                (6 prev translations)
```

HISTORY OF A SIX WEEK TOUR THROUGH A PART OF FRANCE ...
(Mary W. & Percy B. Shelley)   L 1817   1,500

Hjortsberg, William ALP NY (1969)   50
                          L (1970)   35

Hoagland, Edward CAT MAN B 1956   60

Hoagland, Kathleen FIDDLER IN THE SKY NY (1944)   35

Hobson, Laura Z. DRY GULCH ADAMS NY 1934 (with T. Hobson) 250
                 A DOG OF HIS OWN NY 1941   150

Hochman, Sandra VOYAGE HOME (P 1960) wraps   50

Hodgson, Ralph THE LAST BLACKBIRD + L 1907 i -edges uncut 75
                                      teg NY 1907   50

Hodgson, William Hope THE BOATS OF THE "GLENCARRIG" L 1907 500
              THE HOUSE ON THE BORDERLAND   L 1908   450
                                    SC 1946   250

Hoff, H(arry) S(ommerfield) TRINA L 1934   75

Hoffer, Eric THE TRUE BELIEVER NY (1951)   20

Hoffman, Abbie see FUCK THE SYSTEM

Hoffman, Charles Fenno see A WINTER IN THE WEST

Hoffman, Daniel (Gerard) PAUL BUNYAN... Ph 1952   40
              AN ARMADA OF THIRTY WHALES NY 1954   35

Hogarth Press TWO STORIES by V & L Woolf Richmond (Eng)
                          1917 wraps (150 cc)   5,000

Hogg, James SCOTTISH PASTORALS... Edinburgh 1801   500

Holcombe, W(illiam) H(enry) A MYSTERY OF NEW ORLEANS
                                 Ph 1890   60

Hollander, John A CRACKLING OF THORNS (fwd Auden) NY 1958   50

Hollo, Anselm (Paul Alexis) SATEIDEN VALILLA Helsinki
                                    1956   100
         ST. TEXT AND FIN POEMS Birmingham (Eng) 1961   125

Holmes, John A. THE GREEN DOOR... n-pl 1934   50

Holmes, John Clellon GO NY 1952   300

Holmes, Mary J(ane) TEMPEST AND SUNSHINE... NY 1854
              i -ads "new copyright works..."   50

Holmes, Oliver Wendell POEMS B 1836 (Boston imprint only) 250

Holmes, Justice Oliver Wendell THE COMMON LAW B 1881   300

Holst, Spencer THIRTEEN ESSAYS NY(1960) wr   60

Holtby, Winifred ANDERBY WOLD L 1923   75

HOME LIFE IN RUSSIA (Nikolai Gogol) L 1854 2 vol   750

Honig, Edwin GARCIA LORCA N (1944)   40
                           L (1945)   35

Hooker, Richard (H. Richard Hornberger) M.A.S.H. NY (1968)   60

Howard, Robert E. A GENT FROM BEAR CREEK L (1937) (most
                                    destroyed)   3,500

Howe, E(dgar) (W(atson) THE STORY OF A COUNTRY TOWN
                         Atchison, Kansas 1882
         i -no lettering on spine base and "D. Caldwell,
         manufacturer, Atchison Kan" rubber-stamped
                                    inside cover   100

Howe, Irving SHERWOOD ANDERSON (NY 1951)   35

Howe, Julia Ward see PASSION FLOWERS

Howe, Mark A(thony) DeWolfe RARI NANTES... B 1893 (80 cc)
                                          wraps   150

Howells, William Dean see POEMS OF TWO FRIENDS
                       LIVES AND SPEECHES OF ABRAHAM
                       LINCOLN AND HANNIBAL HAMLIN
                       Columbus 1860 (w J.L. Hayes)
                       wraps   i -pp 95-96 blank   300
                       VENETIAN LIFE... L (1866)   500
                                      NY 1866   400

Howes, Barbara THE UNDERSEA FARMER Banyon Press
                       Pawlet 1948 (250 cc)   100

Hoyem, Andrew THE WAKE SF 1963 35 deluxe cc   100
                         wraps (750 cc)   30

Hoyningen-Huene, George AFRICAN MIRAGE NY 1938   150

Hubbard L(afayette) Ron BUCKSKIN BRIGADES NY 1937   1,500

Hudson, W. H. THE PURPLE LAND THAT ENGLAND LOST L 1885
               2 vol   i -Oct ads in 2nd vol   1,500

Hueffer, Ford Madox (Ford) THE BROWN OWL L 1892
                       (actually 1891)   600

Hughes, Daniel WAKING IN A TREE NY (1963)   25

Hughes, Dorothy B(elle Flannagan) THE SO BLUE MARBLE
                                   NY (1940)   175

Hughes, Glenn SOULS + SF 1917   60

Hughes, Langston THE WEARY BLUES NY 1926   600

Hughes, Hatcher HELL-BENT FOR HEAVEN NY 1924 (Pulitzer)   75

Hughes, Richard (Arthur Warren) GIPSY-NIGHT + Berkshire
                              (1922) (750 cc)   150
                       Chicago 1922 (63 sgd cc)   150

Hughes, Rupert THE LAKERIM ATHLETIC CLUB NY 1898   75

Hughes, Ted THE HAWK IN THE RAIN L (1957)(preceded NY
                         edition by five days)   150
                                    NY (1957)   150

Hughes, Thomas see TOM BROWN'S SCHOOL DAYS

Hugo, Richard F. POEMS (Portland 1959) wraps   100
                  A RUN OF JACKS Minn (1961)   75

Huie, William Bradford MUD ON THE STARS NY (1942)   50

118

Hulme, Keri THE BONE PEOPLE Baton Rouge (1985) (2500 cc)   30

Hulme, T. E. AN INTRODUCTION TO METAPHYSICS L 1913 trans
                  and intro by Hulme of Henri Bergson's work   100

Hume, Cyril WIFE OF THE CENTAUR NY (1923)   125

Hume, David see A TREATISE OF HUMAN NATURE

Hume, Fergus THE MYSTERY OF THE HANSON CAB Melbourne 1886
                                 (4 known copies) 1,000
                                 L 1887 wraps   500

Humphries, Rolph A LITTLE ANTHOLOGY OF VERY SHORT POEMS...
                                 (Ch 1922) ed by RH   50
                  EUROPA + NY 1928 (350 cc)   75

Humphrey, William THE LAST HUSBAND + NY 1953   150
                                       L 1953   100

Huncke, Herbert HUNCKE'S JOURNAL NY 1965 wr   30

Huneker, James G(ibbons) MEZZOTINTS IN MODERN MUSIC
                                 NY 1899   100

Hunt, E. Howard EAST OF FAREWELL NY 1942 sgd tipped-in pg 75
                                   regular edition   40

Hunt, Gill (John Brunner) GALACTIC STORM L (1952) wr 100

Hunt, (Leigh) H. L. JUVENILIA: OR, COLLECTION OF POEMS
                                 L 1801   750

Hunt, Robert THE EARLY WORLD + Santa Fe (1936)   40

Hunt, Violet THE MAIDEN'S PROGRESS L 1894   250
                                     NY 1894   200

Hunter, Dard see RIP VAN WINKLE

Hunter, Evan FIND THE FEATHERED SERPENT Ph (1952)   50

Hunter, Kristen GOD BLESS THE CHILD NY (1964)   75

Huntley, Lydia (Lydia Huntley Sigourney) MORAL PIECES...
                                 Hartford 1815   150

Hurston, Zora Neale JONAH'S GOURD VINE Ph 1934   400

Hutchins, Maude (Phelps) DIAGRAMMATICS NY (1932) (with
                                 M.J. Adler)
                  i -7 1/8" x 9 3/16" October 1932
                                 (250 cc)   100
                  ii -9 1/4" x 12 1/4" December
                                 1932 (250 cc) boxed   75
                  GEORGIANA (NY 1948)   35

Hutton, Laurence PLAYS AND PLAYERS NY 1875   75

Huxley, Aldous THE BURNING WHEEL O 1916 wraps   750

Huxley, Elspeth MURDER AT GOVERNMENT HOUSE L 1937   125

Huxley, Julian THE INDIVIDUAL IN THE ANIMAL KINGDOM
                       Cambridge 1912 (preceded by
                       Newdigate Prize Poem)   75

Hyman, Mac   NO TIME FOR SERGEANTS   NY (1954)   35

Hyman, Stanley Edgar   THE ARMED VISION   NY 1948   40

Ignatow, David   POEMS   Prairie City, Il (1948)   300

Imbs, Bravig   EDEN: EXIT THIS WAY +   P 1926 wraps   150

INCIDENTAL NUMBERS (Elinor Wylie)   L 1912 (65cc)   5,000

INEZ: A TALE OF THE ALAMO (Augusta Jane Evans Wilson)
                                        NY 1855   150

Inge, William   COME BACK, LITTLE SHEBA   NY (1950)   60

Ingersoll, Robert G.   AN ORATION DELIVERED...AT ROUSE'S
                HALL, PEORIA, ILL...   Peoria 1869
                        wraps (first publ work)   100

Ingraham, Joseph Holt   see THE SOUTHWEST...

Inman, Col. Henry   STORIES OF THE OLD SANTE FE TRAIL
                                        KC 1881   150

Innes, Michael (John Innes MacIntosh Stewart)
            DEATH AT THE PRESIDENT'S LODGING   L 1936   400
            SEVEN SUSPECTS   (new title)   NY 1936   150

INSUBORDINATION...(T. S. Arthur)   NY 1841   300

Iris, Scharmel   LYRICS OF A LAD   CH 1914   75

Iron, Ralph (Olive Schreiner)   THE STORY OF AN AFRICAN
                                FARM   L 1883 2 vols   750

Irving, John   SETTING FREE THE BEARS   NY (1968)   250

Irving, Washington   see Launcelot Langstaff and Diedrich
                Knickerbocker

Irwin, Russell (Peter Russell)   PICNIC TO THE MOON L (1944)   100

Irwin, Wallace   THE LOVE SONNETS OF A HOODLUM   SF 1902 wr   20

Isherwood, Christopher   ALL THE CONSPIRATORS   L 1928   1,000

ITALIAN SKETCH BOOK (THE) (Henry T. Tuckerman) Ph 1835   125

Jackson, Charles   THE LOST WEEKEND   NY (1944)   60

Jackson, Daniel, Jr.   see Isaac Mitchell

Jackson, Shirley   THE ROAD THROUGH THE WALL   NY 1948   125

Jacobi, Carl   REVELATIONS IN BLACK   SC 1947   60

Jacobs, W. W.   MANY CARGOES   L 1896   125

Jacobsen, Josephine   LET EACH MAN REMEMBER   Dallas (1940)   100

Jacobson, Dan   THE TRAP   NY (1955)   25

Jaffe, Sherril   YOUNG LUST & OTHERS   SB 1973 wraps   15
                SCARS MAKE YOUR BODY MORE INTERESTING
                SB 1974 26 sgd ltr cc in acetate dw   60
                     200 sgd no. cc in acetate dw   25

Jakes, John   THE TEXANS RIDE NORTH...   Ph (1952)   30

120

James, C(yril) L(ionel) R(obert) THE LIFE OF CAPTAIN
                 CIPRIANI Nelson (Eng) 1932 wraps   175

James, Henry, Jr. A PASSIONATE PILGRIM + B 1875
              i -J.R. Osgood & Co. on spine   850
             ii -Houghton Osgood & Co.   400
            iii -Houghton, Mifflin & Co.   300

James, M(ontague) R(hodes) GHOST STORIES OF AN ANTIQUARY
                                        L 1904   200

James, Norah C. SLEEVELESS ERRAND P 1929 first bk publ
                      by J. Kahane 50 sgd cc   400
                             450 unsigned   100

James, P(hyllis) D(orothy) COVER HER FACE L 1962   300
                                      NY 1962   75

James, Will(iam Roderick) COWBOYS NORTH AND SOUTH
                                      NY 1924   150

James, William PRINCIPLES OF PSYCHOLOGY NY 1890   750

Jameson, Storm THE POT BOILS L 1919   75

Janeway, Elizabeth THE WALSH GIRLS GC 1943   30

Janvier, Thomas Allbone COLOR STUDIES NY 1885 (1000 cc) 125
                 (preceded by WOMAN'S DARING Annisquam
                          MA 1872 2 pp wraps)

Jarrell, Randall BLOOD FOR A STRANGER NY (1942)   350
                 (also see FIVE YOUNG AMERICAN POETS)

Jeffers, John Robinson FLAGONS & APPLES LA 1912 (500 cc) 750
                 CALIFORNIANS NY 1916 1st commer-
                                    cial book   175

Jefferson, Thomas NOTES ON THE STATE OF VIRGINIA...
                                        L 1787   2,500

Jenkins, John Edward see GINX'S BABY

Jennings, Elizabeth (POEMS) Fantasy Poets No. 1
                         O (1953)   wraps   75
                 A WAY OF LOOKING L 1955   50

Jepson, Edgar (Alfred) THE DICTATOR'S DAUGHTER L 1902   75

Jerome, Jerome K. ON STAGE AND OFF L 1885   200
                 THE IDLE THOUGHTS OF AN IDLE FELLOW
                                        L 1886   150

Jessup, Richard THE CINCINNATI KID B (1963)   30

Jewett, Sarah Orne DEEPHAVEN B 1877
                 i -"was" vs "so" p.65:16   200
                 ii -"so" vs "was"   75

Jhabvala, R(uth) Prawer TO WHOM SHE WILL L (1955)   125

Johns, Orrick ASPHALT + NY 1917   60

Johnson, B.S. TRAVELING PEOPLE L (1963)   150

Johnson, Ben see Mr. LeGrand

DEEPHAVEN.

BY

SARAH O. JEWETT.

BOSTON:
JAMES R. OSGOOD AND COMPANY,
Late Ticknor & Fields, and Fields, Osgood, & Co.
1877.

Johnson, Benj. F. (James Whitcomb Riley) THE OLD SWIMMING
                              HOLE + I 1883 wraps   600
                         (facsimile in 1909 lacks
                         "W" in "Williams" p.41)   25

Johnson, Diane FAIR GAME NY 1965   60

Johnson, James Weldon see THE AUTOBIOGRAPHY...

Johnson, Josephine (Winslow) NOW IN NOVEMBER NY 1934   40

Johnson, Lionel THE ART OF THOMAS HARDY L 1894 (150 cc) 500
                              trade edition   150
                 POEMS L/B 1895 25 sgd no. cc   1,000
                 regular edition (750 cc)   750

Johnson, Merle (DeVore) A BIBLIOGRAPHY OF MARK TWAIN
                              NY 1910 (500 cc)   150

Johnson, Pamela Hansford SYMPHONY FOR FULL ORCHESTRA
                              L 1934 wraps   125

Johnson, Ronald A LINE OF POETRY, A ROW OF TREES
                 Highlands 1964 50 sgd no. cc   200
                              stiff wraps (500 cc)   75

Johnson, Samuel see FATHER JEROME LOBO

Johnson, Uwe SPECULATIONS NY (1963)   25

Johnston, Mary PRISONER OF HOPE B 1898   50

Jolas, Eugene CINEMA : POEMS NY 1926   200

Jolly, Andrew LIE DOWN IN ME NY (1970)   50

Jones, David (Michael) IN PARENTHESIS L (1937)   500
                 L (1961) 70 sgd no. cc (Jones & Eliot) 900
                 NY (1961)
                 i -Eliot intro not listed
                              on contents page   75
                 ii -Eliot intro listed   35

Jones, Edith Newbold (Edith Wharton) VERSES Newport RI
                              1878 wr   25,000

Jones, Edward Smyth THE SYLVAN CABIN + B 1911   50
                 SF 1915 wraps (first
                              separate edition)   150

Jones, Gayl CORREGIDORA NY (1975)   40

Jones, Glyn THE BLUE BED + L (1937)   50

Jones, Howard Mumford A LITTLE BOOK OF LOCAL VERSE
                              LaCross 1915 wraps   60

Jones, James FROM HERE TO ETERNITY NY 1951 Presentation
                 ed w/sgd no. tipped-in pg (about 1500 cc) 225
                              regular trade edition   125
                              L 1952   75

Jones, James Athearn see Matthew Murgatroyd

Jones, Joshua Henry BY SANCTION OF LAW B 1924   75

```
Jones, (Everatt) Leroi (Immamu Amiri Baraka)  CUBA LIBRE
                                     NY 1961  wr        200
                PREFACE TO A TWENTY VOLUME SUICIDE NOTE
                                     NY (1961) wraps
                i -ads in bold cap                      35
                ii -ads not in bold caps                25
                (3 Intervening broadsides)

Jones, Madison Percy  THE INNOCENT  NY (1957)           60

Jong, Erica  FRUITS AND VEGETABLES  NY (1971) cloth     35
                                            wraps        15

Jonson, Ben(jamin)  EVERY MAN OUT OF HIS HUMOUR  L 1600  2,500

Jordon, June  WHO LOOK AT ME  NY 1969                   30

Josephson, Matthew  GALIMATHIAS  NY (1923) stiff wraps
                                     (250 no. cc)       125

Joyce, James  TWO ESSAYS  Dublin(1901) wraps (with F.J.C.
                Skellington) (contains "Day of the
                                     Rabblement")       5,000
                THE HOLY OFFICE (Pola 1904 or 1905)
                                     Broadside          8,000

                CHAMBER MUSIC  L 1907
                i -thick laid ep -horizontal chain lines,
                   Poems in signature C - well centered  6,000
                ii -thick wove ep, signature C - poorly
                                           centered     1,250
                iii -thin wove transparent ep, signature
                           C is poorly centered         1,250
                                 L 1918 wraps             250
                        B (1918) unauthorized ed          200
                                 NY 1918                  200
                L 1923  Egoist Press (107 cc)            200
                        Jonathan Cape (393 cc)           100

Judah, Samuel B(enjamin) H(erbert)  THE MOUNTAIN
                TORRENT... NY 1820  wraps               200

Just, Ward  TO WHAT END  B 1968                         30

Justice, Donald  THE OLD BACHELOR + Miami 1951 wr (240 cc)  250
                THE SUMMER ANNIVERSARIES  Middletown CT
                                     (1960)  cloth       50
                                            wraps        20

K.,R.A. (Ronald Knox)  SIGNA SEVERA  Eton College 1906 wr  250

Kael, Pauline  I LOST IT AT THE MOVIES  B (1965)        40

Kafka, Franz  THE CASTLE  L 1930 (1st Engtrans)         250
                                 NY 1930                150

Kahane, Jack  TWO PLAYS  Manchester (Eng) 1912  wraps   150

Kahn, Roger  THE PASSIONATE PEOPLE... NY (1968)         35

Kain, Saul (Siegfried Sassoon)  THE DAFFODIL MURDERER (L)
                          1913 wraps  (1000 cc)         250
              previous priv pr books (also see Sassoon)

Kaler, James Otis  see James Otis

Kallman, Chester  ELEGY  NY(1951)  wraps  (500 cc)      50
```

124

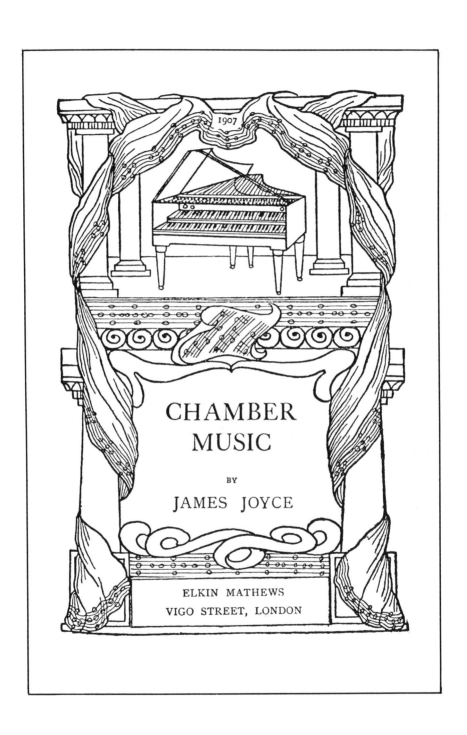

1907

CHAMBER
MUSIC

BY

JAMES JOYCE

ELKIN MATHEWS
VIGO STREET, LONDON

```
Kaltenborn, H.V.  KALTENBORN EDITS THE NEWS  NY (1937)
            (ghostwritten by Mary McCarthy)   cloth dw          125
                                              wraps dw           50

Kandel, Lenore  A PASSING DRAGON  Studio City, CA 1959
                                              wraps             30


Kantor, McKinley  DIVERSAY  NY 1928 also first book by
             Coward McCann  i  -no reviews on dw               125

Karp, David  THE BIG FEELING  NY(1952)  wraps                  35
             ONE  NY (1953) (first hardback - sixth book)       35

Karp, Ivan  DOOBIE DOO  GC (1965) Warhol + Lichtenstein dw      30

Katz, Steven  THE LESTRIAN  Leece 1962 (300 cc) wraps         100

Kaufman, George S.  DULCY  NY (1921) with Marc Connelly       200

Kavan, Anna  see Helen Ferguson

Kavanagh, Dan (Julian Barnes)  DUFFY  L (1980)                 40

Kavanagh, Patrick  PLOUGHMAN +  L 1936  wraps                  75

Kaye, Philip B.  TAFFY  NY 1950                                75

Kaye-Smith, Sheila  THE TRAMPING METHODIST  L 1908            125

Kazan, Elia  AMERICA AMERICA  NY (1962)                        30

Kazin, Alfred  ON NATIVE GROUND  NY (1942)                     75
                                  L (1943)                      50

Keating, H.R.F.  DEATH AND THE VISITING FIREMAN  L 1959        40

Keats, John  POEMS  L 1817                                  8,000

KEEP COOL (John Neal)  Baltimore 1817  2 vol                  300

Kees, Weldon  THE LAST MAN  SF 1943 bds w/o dw (300 cc)       200

Keillor, Garrison  HAPPY TO BE HERE  NY 1982                   30

Keller, David H(enry)  THE THOUGHT PROJECTOR  NY (1929) wr     60

Kelley, Edith Summers  WEEDS  NY (1923)                       125
                              L 1924                           100

Kelley, William Melvin  A DIFFERENT DRUMMER  GC 1962           75

Kellogg, Marjorie  TELL ME THAT YOU LOVE ME, JUNIE MOON
                                              NY 1968          30

Kelly, Robert  ARMED DESCENT  (NY 1961)  stiff wr             50

Kelly, Walt  POGO  NY (1961)  wraps                            50

Kemelman, Harry  FRIDAY THE RABBI SLEPT LATE  NY (1964)        35

Keneally, Thomas  THE PLACE AT WHITTON  L (1964)              100

Kennan, George  TENT LIFE IN SIBERIA  NY 1870                100

Kennan, George F.  AMERICAN DIPLOMACY 1900-1950  Ch (1951)     40
```

```
Kennedy, Edward   THE FRUITFUL BOUGH   Priv pr 1965
                  (tribute to father collected by EMK        100
                  DECISIONS FOR A DECADE  NY 1968             40

Kennedy, John F(itzgerald)  WHY ENGLAND SLEPT  NY 1940       400
                                  '           L (1940)        150

Kennedy, John Pendleton  see SWALLOW BARN

Kennedy, Mark  THE PECKING ORDER  NY (1953)                   30

Kennedy, Robert  THE ENEMY WITHIN  NY (1960)                  40

Kennedy, Thomas  POEMS  W 1816                               100

Kennedy, William  THE INK TRUCK  NY 1969                     175

Kennedy, X.J. (Joseph Charles Kennedy)  NUDE DESCENDING
                              A STAIRCASE  NY (1961)          50

Kenner, Hugh  PARADOX IN CHESTERTON  L 1948                 125

Kent, Rockwell  see ARCHITEC-TONICS
                 THE SEVEN AGES OF MAN  NY 1918 1st
                              collected illustrations        150
                 WILDERNESS... NY 1920
                 i -cover in grey                            250
                 ii -cover in tan                            150

Kernahan, (John) Coulson  A BOOK OF STRANGE SINS  L 1893      40

Kerouac, John (Jack) (Jean Louis)  THE TOWN AND THE CITY
                                        NY (1950)            300
                                        L 1951              200

Kerrigan, Anthony  LEAR IN THE TROPIC OF PARIS  Barcelona
                         1953  wraps (100 cc)                 60

Kersh, Gerald  JEWS WITHOUT JEHOVAH  L 1934                 125

Kesey, Ken (Elton)  ONE FLEW OVER THE CUCKOO'S NEST
                                        NY 1962            300
                                        L 1962              75

Keyes, Frances Parkinson  DINNER AT ANTOINE'S  NY 1948       40

Keyes, Sidney  THE IRON LAUREL  L 1942  stiff wraps & dw      40

Kiely, Benedict  COUNTIES OF CONTENTION  Cork 1945           75

Killens, John O.  YOUNGBLOOD  NY 1954                        75

Kilmer, Aline  CANDLES THAT BURN  NY (1919)                  30

Kilmer, (Alfred) Joyce  SUMMER OF LOVE  NY 1911 Baker &
                        Taylor foot of spine (glassine dw)   250

Kincaid, Jamaica  AT THE BOTTOM OF THE RIVER  NY (1983)       35

King, Francis  TO THE DARK TOWER  (L) 1946                  100

King, Grace (Elizabeth)  MONSIEUR MOTTE  NY 1888             75

King, Larry L.  THE ONE-EYED MAN  NY (1966)                  50

King, Martin Luther, Jr.  STRIDE TOWARD FREEDOM  NY 1958    100
                                              L 1959         50
```

```
King, Rufus (Frederick)  MYSTERY DELUXE  NY (1927)              35

King, Stephen  CARRIE  GC 1974                                175

Kingsley, Charles  THE SAINT'S TRAGEDY...  L 1848            200

Kingsley, Henry  THE RECOLLECTIONS OF GEOFFREY HAMLYN
                                  C 1859  3 vol              300

Kingsmilll, Hugh  see Hugh Lunn

Kingston, Maxine Hong  THE WOMAN WARRIOR  NY 1976             50

Kinnell, Galway  BITTER VICTORY  by Rene Hardy (translated
                              by GK)  GC 1956                125
                 WHAT A KINGDOM IT WAS  B 1960               125

Kinsella, Thomas  THE STARLIT EYE  D 1952                    100

Kinsella, W(illiam) P(atrick)  DANCE ME OUTSIDE  Ottawa
                              1977  cloth                    250
                                    wraps                     40

Kipling, Rudyard  SCHOOLBOY LYRICS  Lahore 1881 wraps (50
                  cc) white presumed  to precede brown    12,000

Kirkup, James (Falconer)  INDICATIONS  L 1942 (with J.
                          Ormond and J. Bayliss)            125
                          COSMIC SHAPE   L (1946) (500
                          no. cc (with Ross Nichols)          75
                          THE DROWNED SAILOR +  L 1947        60

Kirkwood, James  THERE MUST BE A PONY  B (1960)              40

Kirsch, Robert R.  IN THE WRONG RAIN  B (1959)               40

Kirst, Hans Helmut  THE REVOLT OF GUNNER ASCH  B (1955)      40

Kirstein, Lincoln  FLESH IS HEIR  NY 1932                    75

Kissinger, Henry A.  A WORLD RESTORED...  B 1957             75

Kitchin, C(lifford) H(enry) B(enn)  CURTAINS  O 1919 wraps   75

Kizer, Carolyn   POEMS  Portland (1959)  wraps             100
                 THE UNGRATEFUL GARDEN  Bloomington
                              (1961)  cloth                  75
                                      wraps                  20

Klane, Robert  THE HORSE IS DEAD  NY 1968                    50

Kneale, Nigel  TOMATO CAIN +  L 1949                         40

Knickerbocker, Diedrich (Washington Irving)   A HISTORY OF
                  NEW YORK FROM THE BEGINNING OF THE
                  WORLD...  NY 1809  2 vol with
                              268 pp in vol 1             1,000

Knowles, John   A SEPARATE PEACE  L 1959                    400
                NY 1960  i -pictorial dw                    150
                         ii -printed dw                      75

Knowlton, Charles  ELEMENTS OF MODERN MATERIALISM...
                              Adams, MA 1829                 750

Knox, Ronald A(rbuthnott)  see R.A.K.
```

Kober, Arthur   THUNDER OVER THE BRONX   NY 1935   35

Koch, Kenneth   POEMS (w Nell Blain's PRINTS)   NY 1953
                              stiff wraps (300 cc)   400

Koestler, Arthur   see A. Costler
                SPANISH TESTAMENT   L 1937 cloth   250
                      wraps (Left Book Club)   75

Kohler, Wolfgang   THE MENTALITY OF APES   NY 1925   100

Korda, Michael   MALE CHAUVINISM! HOW IT WORKS   NY (1973) 40

Kosinski, Jerzy (Nikodem)   see Joseph Novak
                THE PAINTED BIRD   B 1965 (third
                      book--first under his name)
                i -extraneous line top of p.270   200

Kotzwinkle, William   THE FIREMAN   NY 1969 (juvenile)   75

Kovacs, Ernie   ZOOMAR   NY 1957   35

Kreymborg, Alfred   LOVE AND LIFE +   NY (1908) (500 cc)   75

Krim, Seymour   VIEWS OF A NEARSIGHTED CANNONEER   NY (1961)
                                             wraps   20

Kroll, Harry Harrison   THE CABIN IN THE COTTON   NY 1931   35

Kromer, Tom   WAITING FOR NOTHING   NY 1935   125

Kronenberger, Louis   THE GRAND MANNER   NY 1929   40

Krutch, Joseph Wood   COMEDY AND CONSCIENCE...   NY 1924 wr 100

Kumin, Maxine W.   SEBASTIAN AND THE DRAGON   NY 1960
                                     (Juvenile)   50
                      HALFWAY   NY (1961)   50

Kunitz, Stanley (Jasspon)   INTELLECTUAL THINGS   GC 1930 125

Kuttner, Henry   see Will Garth also see Lewis Padgett

Kyd, Thomas (Alfred Bennett Harbage)   BLOOD IS A BEGGAR
                                     Ph/NY (1946)   35

Kyger, Joanne   THE TAPESTRY AND THE WEB   SF 1965
                      27 sgd no. cc   125
                              cloth   50
                              wraps   15

L., E.V. (Edward Verrall Lucas)   SPARKS FROM A FLINT
                                     L 1890   60

LaFarge, Christopher   HOXIE SELLS HIS ACRES   NY 1934   25

LaFarge, Oliver (Hazard Perry)   LAUGHING BOY   B 1929 pc   75

Laing, Alexander   THE CADAVER OF GIDEON WYCK...   NY 1934 60

Lamantia, Philip   EROTIC POEMS   (BE) 1946   200

Lamar, Mirabeu B.   VERSE MEMORIALS   NY 1857   1,500

Lamkin, Speed   TIGER IN THE GARDEN   B 1950   40

Lamming, George (Eric)   IN THE CASTLE OF MY SKIN   L (1953) 50

```
Lampman, Archibald   AMONG THE MILLET +   Ottawa 1888
                     i -double rule above & below title on
                                               spine        175

L'Amour, Louis  SMOKE FROM THIS ALTAR  Okla City (1939)      150

Lamson, David  WE WHO ARE ABOUT TO DIE  NY 1936               50

Lang, Andrew  BALLADS AND LYRICS OF OLD FRANCE +  L 1872      60

Lang, V. R.  THE PITCH  NY 1962 (Edw. Gorey illus) wraps      60

Lange, John (Michael Crichton)  ODDS ON  NY 1966              30

Langstaff, Launcelot (Washington Irving, Wm. Irving and
              J.K. Paulding)  SALMAGUNDI... NY 1807/8
                             20 parts in wraps             2,500
                                     2 volumes               750

Lanham, Edwin  SAILORS DON'T CARE  P 1929 wraps              400
                                   NY 1930                   125

Lanier, Sidney  TIGER-LILIES  NY 1867
                i -title page on stub                       100

Larcom, Lucy  SIMILITUDES  B 1854                            75

Lardner, Ring(old Wilmer)  BIB BALLADS   Ch (1915)
                                (500 cc) boxed              125

Lardner, Ring, Jr.  THE YOUNG IMMIGRUNTS   I (1920)         150
                    JUNE MOON  NY 1930 with Geo. S.
                                            Kaufman         150
                    THE ECSTASY OF OWEN MUIR  L (1954)       40
                                             NY (1954)       35

Larkin, Philip  THE NORTH SHIP  L (1945)                    600

Larner, Jeremy  DRIVE, HE SAID  NY (1964)  i -wraps          15
                                          ii -hardback       25

Lathen, Emma (Mary Jane Latsis & Martha Henissart)
                BANKING ON DEATH  NY 1961                   200

Latimer, Jonathan (Wyatt)  MURDER IN THE MADHOUSE  GC 1935  200

Latimer, Margery  WE ARE INCREDIBLE  NY (1928)             175

Lattimore, Richard (Alexander)  HANOVER POEMS  NY 1927
                                (with A.K. Laing)            60

Laughlin, James  THE RIVER   Norfolk 1938  wr              150
                 SOME NATURAL THINGS Norfolk  1945           75

Laurence, Margaret  A TREE FOR POVERTY  Nairobi 1954        150
                    (Somali anthology edited by Laurence)
                    THIS SIDE OF JORDAN  T 1960             150
                                         NY 1960             35

Laurents, Arthur  HOME OF THE BRAVE  NY (1946)              75

Laver, James  CERVANTES... O (1921) wraps                   50

Lavin, Mary  TALES FROM BECTIVE BRIDGE  B 1942 (999 cc)     125
                                        L 1943              125

Lawrence, D(avid) H(erbert)  THE WHITE PEACOCK  NY 1911
                                                (c 1910)   7,000
```

```
                          NY 1911 (c 1911)
                     (precedes Eng one day)      2,500
                                L 1911
           i -publ windmill device on back cover;
                       p 227-230 tipped in          750
          ii -same as i but pp 227-230 integral     400

Lawrence, T(homas) E(dward) (T.E.Shaw)  CARCHEMISH  L 1914
                               (with C.L. Woolley)   500
                     THE WILDERNESS OF ZIN (L 1915)
                               (with C.L. Woolley)   300
                     SEVEN PILLARS OF WISDOM
                     (L) 1926 inscribed "complete"
                        and sgd "T.E.S."  (170 cc) 12,000
                              L (1935) (750 cc)      750
                              NY 1935 (750 cc)       600

Lawson, John Howard  ROGER BLOOMER  NY 1923             35

LAYTON COURT MYSTERY (THE) by "?" (Anthony Berkeley,
                     pseudonym of A.B. Cox)  L 1925    400

Layton, Irving  HERE AND NOW  Montreal 1945 wraps     500

Lazarus, Emma  POEMS AND TRANSLATIONS  NY 1866        150

Lea, Homer  THE VERMILLION PENCIL  NY 1908             60

Lea, Tom  RANDADO  (El Paso, TX 1941) stiff wraps
                              (100 sgd cc)          3,500

Leacock, Stephen (Butler)  ELEMENTS OF POLITICAL SCIENCE
                                      B 1906          100
                     LITERARY LAPSES +  Montreal
                                      1910           150

Lear, Edward  VIEWS IN ROME AND ITS ENVIRONS  L 1841 folio  2,000
              see DERRY, DERRY DOWN

LEATHER STOCKING AND SILK (John Esten Cooke)  NY 1854    200

LEAVES OF GRASS  (Walt Whitman)  Brooklyn 1855
              i -marbled endpapers, frontis on plain
                         paper, no press notices   7,500
             ii -yellow endpapers, frontis on plain
                    India paper, 8 pages of notices  2,500

Leavis, F.R.  MASS CIVILIZATION AND MINORITY CULTURE
                              C 1930 wraps            50

LeBlanc, Maurice (Marie Emile)  THE EXPLOITS OF ARSENE
                              LUPIN  NY 1907          50

LeCarre, John (David John Moore Cornwell)  CALL FOR THE
                              DEAD  L 1960          1,250
                              NY 1962                200

Lee, Andrew (Louis Auchincloss) THE INDIFFERENT CHILDREN
                              NY (1947)              150

Lee, Dennis  THE KINGDOM OF ABSENCE  T (1967) 300 no. cc
                              wraps                  125

Lee, Manfred Bennington  see Ellery Queen

Lee, Gypsy Rose  THE G-STRING MURDERS  NY 1941        125
```

THE
NORTH
SHIP

Poems

by

PHILIP LARKIN

THE FORTUNE PRESS
15 BELGRAVE ROAD, LONDON, S.W.1

The

White Peacock

By

D. H. Lawrence

London
William Heinemann
1911

```
Lee, Harper  TO KILL A MOCKINGBIRD  Ph 1960
           i -dw photo of author by Truman Capote      250
                              L 1960                    75

Lee, Laurie  THE SUN MY MONUMENT  L 1944               75
                              GC 1947                   25

Lee, William (William Burroughs)  JUNKIE (Ace Doublebook)
                              NY (1953)  wraps         175

LeFanu, Joseph Sheridan  THE COCK AND ANCHOR  D 1845   350

LeGallienne, Richard  MY LADIES'S SONNETS  (Liverpool Eng)
                         1887 (250 cc sgd)            300
                              trade edition           100
              VOLUMES IN FOLIO  L 1889  53 lpc        250
                         250 regular cc               100
                    (also first book publ by Elkin
                              Mathews)

Legman, G(ershon)  LOVE & DEATH  (NY) 1949  red cloth  150
                              wraps                     50

LeGrande, Mr.  A VOYAGE TO ABYSSINIA BY FATHER JEROME
              LOBO  L 1735 (trans by Johnson)        1,500

LeGuin, Ursula  ROCANNON'S WORLD  NY(1966) wraps       60
     bound dos-a-dos with a novel by A. Davidson

Lehmann, John  A GARDEN REVISITED +  L 1931 (400 cc)
                    (1928 Broadsheets preceded)        125

Lehmann, Rosamond (Nina)  DUSTY ANSWER  L 1927         125

Leiber, Fritz (Reuter)  NIGHT'S BLACK AGENTS  SC 1947  125

Leigh-Fermor, Patrick  THE TRAVELLER'S TREE  L 1950    50

Leland, Charles (Godfrey)  MEISTER KARL'S SKETCH BOOK
                              Ph 1855                  100

LeMay, Alan  PAINTED PONIES  NY (1927)                100

Lengel, Frances (Alexander Trocchi)  THE CARNAL DAYS OF
                    HELEN SEFERIS  P 1954 wraps        175

Lengyel, Cornell  THIRTY PIECES  LA 1933  Also first   40
              book printed by Richard Hoffman

Lennon, John  IN HIS OWN WRITE  L 1964 (issued w/o dw) 60

Leonard, Elmore  THE BOUNTY HUNTERS  Houghton-Mifflin
                              B 1954                  300
                    Ballantine NY 1954 wraps           75

Leonard, George  SHOULDER THE SKY  NY (1959)           30

Leonard, John  THE NAKED MARTINI  NY (1964)            35

Leonard, Jonathan  BACK TO STAY  NY 1929               35
              (preceded by 100 cc pr by author under
                              Box Bush Press)

Leonard, William Ellery  SONNETS AND POEMS  B 1906     75

Leroux, Gaston  THE MYSTERY OF THE YELLOW ROOM  L 1908 50
```

```
Leslie, (Sir John Randolph) Shane  SONGS OF ARIEL  D 1908      100

Lessing, Doris (May)  THE GRASS IS SINGING  L (1950)           150
                                            NY 1950             75

Lester, Julius  TO BE A SLAVE  NY 1968                          35

LETTER FROM AN AMERICAN FARMER (Michel Crevecoeur)
                              L 1793  wraps                  1,000

Lever, Charles  see THE CONFESSIONS OF HARRY LORREQUER

Levertoff, Denise (Levertov)  THE DOUBLE IMAGE  L 1946         175

Levi, Peter (Chad Tiger)  EARTHLY PARADISE (priv printed
                                                1958)         100
                          THE GRAVEL PONDS  L 1960             75

Levin, Harry  THE BROKEN COLUMN... Cambridge (MA) 1931         75

Levin, Ira  A KISS BEFORE DYING  NY (1953) issued w/o
                                           endpapers           35

Levin, Meyer  REPORTER  NY (1929) (withdrawn by publ)          75

Levine, Philip  ON THE EDGE  Iowa City (1963) (220 no. cc)    250

Lewis, Alfred Henry  WOLFVILLE  NY (1897)
                     i -"Moore" in perfect type p.19:18       100

Lewis, C.S.  see Clive Hamilton

Lewis, David  END AND BEGINNING  Johannesburg 1945 wraps
                                   50 sgd no. cc               75
                                  450 unsigned                 25

Lewis, Ethelreda  THE HARP  NY (1925)                          75

Lewis, Janet  THE INDIANS IN THE WOODS  (Bonn Germany
                                         1922)  wraps         400

Lewis, Grace Hegger  HALF A LOAF  NY (1931)
                     (Sinclair's wife)                         60

Lewis, Matthew Gregory  THE MONK  L 1796                      750

Lewis, Norman  SAMARA  L 1949                                  75

Lewis (Harry) Sinclair  see Tom Graham  OUR MR. WRENN  NY
                        1914 first under own name              75

Lewis, Wyndham  TIMON OF ATHENS  (L 1913) 16 plates in
                                  large portfolio           2,000
                THE IDEAL GIANT  L (1917) (200 cc)            600
                TARR  NY 1918 red cloth                       250
                      blue cloth                              150
                      L 1918                                  100

Lhomond, M.  ELEMENT OF FRENCH GRAMMAR  see Henry Wadsworth
                                              Longfellow

Lieber, Joel  HOW THE FISHES LIVE  NY 1967                     30

Lieberman, M.M.  MAGGOT AND WORM  West Branch 1968             40

Liebling, A.J.  THEY ALL SANG... NY 1934                      125
                BACK WHERE I CAME FROM... NY (1938)           200
```

THE
DOUBLE
IMAGE

by

DENISE LEVERTOFF

THE CRESSET PRESS
LONDON

```
Lifshin, Lyn (Diane)  WHY IS THE HOUSE DISSOLVING?  SF 1968
                                              wraps      40

Lima, Frank  INVENTORY  (NY 1964)  wraps                40

Lin, Frank (Gertrude Franklin Atherton)
        WHAT DREAMS MAY COME  Ch (1888) wraps           300
                                        cloth           150
                                     L 1889             100

Lincoln, Joseph (Crosby)  CAPE COD BALLADS  Trenton NJ
                                             1902       125

Lindbergh, Anne Morrow  NORTH TO THE ORIENT  NY 1935     35

Lindbergh, Charles A.  WE +  NY 1927  (1000 sgd cc boxed)  800
                                 1st trade edition       100

Lindsay, David  A VOYAGE TO ARCTURUS  L (1920) (red cloth,
                              8 page catalog at rear)  1,000
Lindsay, Jack  FAUNS AND LADIES  Sydney 1923            500

Lindsay, (Nicholas) Vachel  THE TREE OF LAUGHING BELLS
                                (NY 1905) wraps        2,000
                            A MEMORIAL OF LINCOLN...
                                (Springfield, IL 1908/1909)  500
                            THE TRAMP'S EXCUSE +
                                (Springfield, IL 1909) wraps  1,500
                            GENERAL WM BOOTH ENTERS INTO
                                     HEAVEN +  NY 1913    75

Lindsay, Norman  BOOK NUMBER ONE  Sydney 1912 wraps    600

Linebarger, Paul  see Felix C. Forrest

LINES ON LEAVING THE BEDFORD STREET SCHOOLHOUSE (George
                Santayana) (B 1880) 4 pages wraps      750

Lippard, George  ADRIAN, THE NEOPHYTE... Ph 1843 wraps  75

Lippman, Walter  A PREFACE TO POLITICS  NY 1913         50
                    (prev translations)

Litvinoff, Emanuel  CONSCRIPTS  L 1941 wraps            75

Livingstone, David  see A NARRATIVE...

Llewellyn, Richard  (R.D.V.L. Lloyd) HOW GREEN WAS MY
        VALLEY  L 1939  200 sgd no. cc in slipcase      250
                                        trade           100
                                     NY 1940             75

Llosa, Mario Vargas  THE TIME OF THE HERO  NY 1966      35

Lobo, Father Jerome  see Mr. LeGrande

Locke, David Ross  see PETROLEUM V. NASBY

Lockridge, Richard  MR. AND MRS. NORTH  NY 1936         75
        Richard and Frances  THE NORTHS MEET MURDER
                                     NY 1940            150

Lockridge, Ross  RAINTREE COUNTRY  B 1948               75
                                 L (1949)               50

Lodge, George Cabot  THE SONG OF THE WAVE  NY 1898      50

Loeb, Harold (Albert)  DOODAB  NY 1925                 125
```

THE SON OF THE WOLF

Tales of the Far North

BY

JACK LONDON

BOSTON AND NEW YORK
HOUGHTON, MIFFLIN AND COMPANY
The Riverside Press, Cambridge
1900

Loewinsohn, Ron(ald William) WATERMELONS NY 1959
                              wraps (1000 cc)   35

Lofting, Hugh THE STORY OF DOCTOR DOOLITTLE NY 1920   200

Lofts, Norah I MET A GYPSY NY 1936 (250 no. cc in
                              dw & slipcase)   40

Logan, John CYCLE FOR MOTHER CABRINI NY (1955)
             30 sgd no. cc with sgd wood block   200
                              250 sgd no cc   125
                              trade (wraps)   30

Logue, Christopher WAND AND QUADRANT P 1953 wraps
                              300 no. cc   125
                              300 unno. cc   75

Long, Haniel POEMS NY 1920   500

London, Jack (John Griffith) THE SON OF THE WOLF B 1909
                              (belt stamped in silver
                              on cover)
             i -8 preliminary unnumbered pages (i-viii)   500
             ii -6 preliminary unnumbered pages (i-vi)   400

Long, Frank Belnap A MAN FROM GENOA + ATHOL 1926   750

Longfellow, Henry Wadsworth ELEMENTS OF FRENCH GRAMMAR
                              by M. Lhomond Portland
                              1830 (HWL translated
                              anonymously)   250
                           FRENCH EXERCISES by M. Lhomond
                              Portland 1830 (HWL trans)   250
                           EXERCISES AND ELEMENTS...
                              bound as one volume in 1830
                              represents first book to
                              bear HWL's name)   350
                           also see OUTRE-MER

Longfellow, Samuel THE WORD PREACHED... NY 1853 wr   75

Longstreet, Augustus Baldwin AN ORATION... (Augusta
                              1831) wraps   3,500
                           also see GEORGIA SCENES...

Loos, Anita HOW TO WRITE PHOTOPLAYS NY 1920 (with W.J.
                              Emerson)   200
             BREAKING INTO THE MOVIES NY(1921) (with W.
                              J. Emerson)   200
             GENTLEMEN PREFER BLONDES NY 1925
             i -incorrect spelling on Contents page,
                Chapter 4 "Divine" for "Devine"   175

Lorca, Federico BITTER OLEANDER L 1935   150

Lorde, Audre THE FIRST CITIES NY (1968) wraps   20

Lothrop, Harriet (Mulford Stone) see Margaret Sidney

LOVE EPISTLES OF ARISTAENETUS (THE) (Richard Sheridan)
                              L 1771   600

Lovecraft, H.P. THE SHUNNED HOUSE Athol MA 1928 (bound
                              by Paul Cook)   3,500
             unbound folded signatures (Derleth sold
                about 50) (rest used on Arkham House ed) 1,500
             various bindings of sheets between 1928-1963 1,500
             Arkham House 1963 (100 cc) in plain brown dw 1,250
                (at least four pamphlets/off-prints precede)

138

```
Lovell, Robert   see Robert Southey

Lovesey, Peter  WOBBLE TO DEATH  L 1970                        40

Lowell, Amy  see DREAM DROPS BY A DREAMER
             A DOME OF MANY-COLORED GLASS  B 1912             300

Lowell, James Russell  see CLASS POEM
             A YEAR'S LIFE  B 1841 with or
                           without errata                    225

Lowell, Robert  THE LAND OF UNLIKENESS  (Cunningham MA)
                           1944  26 sgd no.  cc            7,500
                                     224 cc                3,000
             LORD WEARY'S CASTLE  NY (1946)                   300

Lowenfels, Walter  EPISODES AND EPISTLES  NY 1925            125

Lowndes, Marie Belloc  THE PHILOSOPHY OF THE MARQUISE
                                            L 1899            75

Lowry, Malcolm  ULTRAMARINE  L 1933                        5,000
                  Revised Ed NY 1962                          75
                           L (1963)                           50
                           T (1963)                           50

Lowry, Robert  HUTTON STREET  CI 1940                        150
             THE JOURNEY OUT (Bari, Italy June 1945) wr
                           (350 cc)  250 sgd cc              150
                                     100 unsgd               100

Loy, Mina  SONGS TO JOANNES  NY 1917 WRAPS  (April issue
                                     of Others mag)          300
             LUNAR BAEDECKER  (P 1923)  wraps                750

Lucas, E. V.  see E.V.L.

Lucie-Smith, (John) Edward (McKenzie) (POEMS) Fantasy Press
                           Oxford  1954  wraps              125

Ludlow, Fitz-Hugh  see THE HASHEESH EATER

Ludlum, Robert  THE SCARLATTI INHERITANCE  NY (1971)         75
                                            L (1971)         60

Luhan, Mabel Dodge  LORENZO IN TAOS  NY 1932                 200

Lumpkin, Grace  THE MAKE MY BREAD  NY (1932)                 75

Lunn, Hugh (Hugh Kingsmill)  THE WILL TO LOVE  L 1919        40

Lurie, Alison  V. R. LANG  Munich (1959) (300 cc) wraps
                           (Edw. Gorey cover)               175

Luska, Sidney (Henry Harland)  AS IT IS WRITTEN  NY (1885)  150

Lustgarten, Edgar (Marcus)  A CASE TO ANSWER  L 1947         35
                  ONE MORE UNFORTUNATE  NY 1947
                                     (new title)             25

Lyon, Harris Merton  SARDONICS: SIXTEEN SKETCHES  NY 1909   125

Lyons, Arthur  THE SECOND COMING: SATANISM IN AMERICA
                                     NY (1970)               50

Lytle, Andrew (Nelson)  BEDFORD FORREST AND HIS CRITTER
                  COMPANY  NY 1931 -Minton Balch            350
                           NY (1931) -Putnam                125
```

Lytton, David THE GODDAM WHITE MAN L 1960   30

Lytton, Edward (George Earle) Bulwer ISMAEL: AN ORIENTAL
                                           TALE L 1820   350

Lytton, Edward Robert see CLYTEMNESTRA

M., E.H.W. (E.H.W. Meyerstein) THE DOOR O/L 1911 wraps   40

Maas, Willard FIRE TESTAMENT NY 1935 wr 135 sgd no. cc   75

Mabie, Hamilton Wright NORSE STORIES RETOLD... B 1882   75

Macaulay, Rose ABBOTS VERNEY L 1906   100

Macaulay, Thomas Babington POMPEII, A POEM... (C 1819)   250

MacBeth, George A FORM OF WORDS Oxford 1954 (150 cc)   125

MacCarthy, Desmond THE COURT THEATRE 1904-1907 L 1907   100

MacDonagh, Donagh VETERANS + Cuala Press D 1941 (270 cc) 250

MacDonald, George WITHIN AND WITHOUT + L 1855   300

MacDonald, John D(ann) THE BRASS CUPCAKE NY 1950 wraps   50
                        WINE OF THE DREAMER NY (1951)
                                      first hardback   100

MacDonald, Philip see Oliver Fleming

MacDonald, Ross see Kenneth Millar

MacFall, Haldane THE WOOINGS OF JEZABEL PETTYFER L 1898
                  i -picture of Jezabel front cover   150
                  THE HOUSE OF THE SORCERER B 1900
                                      (new title)   100

MacGrath, Harold ARMS AND THE WOMAN NY 1899   40

MacHarg, William (Briggs) THE ACHIEVEMENTS OF LUTHER TRANT
                        B (1910) (with E. Balmer)   100

Machen, Arthur ELEUSINIA Hereford 1881 wraps
                        (1 known copy)   10,000?
                 also see Leolinus Siluriensis

MacInnes, Colin TO THE VICTOR THE SPOILS L (1950)   100

MacInnes, Helen ABOVE SUSPICION B 1941   50
                 (two prev. trans)

MacKaye, Percy (Wallace) JOHNNY CRIMSON B 1895 wraps
                                      (50 cc)   300

MacKenzie, (Montague) Compton POEMS O 1907 wraps   150

MacLaine, Christopher THE CRAZY BIRD (SF) 1951 bds
                                      (100 no. cc)   75

MacLaren, Ross J. THE STUFF TO GIVE THE TROOPS L 1944   75

MacLean, Alistair H.M.S. ULYSSES L 1955   40

MacLeish, Archibald CLASS POEM (NH) 1915 (4 pg leaflet) 2,500
                     SONGS FOR A SUMMER DAY (NH) 1915 wr   500
                     TOWER OF IVORY NH 1917 (750 cc)   150

THE WOOINGS OF JEZEBEL PETTYFER

Being the personal history of **Jehu Sennacherib Dyle,** commonly called Masheen Dyle ; together with an account of certain things that chanced in the **House of the Sorcerer ;** here set down

by

HALDANE MACFALL

LONDON

GRANT RICHARDS

9 HENRIETTA STREET, COVENT GARDEN, W.C.

1898

```
MacLeod, Fiona  (William Sharp)  PHARAIS  Derby 1894
                              (75 sgd no cc)            200

MacLeod, Joseph (Todd Gordon)  BEAUTY AND THE BEAST  L 1927    75
                              THE ECLIPTIC  L 1930  wraps      50

MacLeod, Norman  HORIZONS OF DEATH  NY 1934 wraps
                    100 signed numbered copies              125
                              263 no. cc                     50

MacNeice, (Frederick) Louis  BLIND FIREWORKS  L 1929        400

MacNamara, Brinsley  THE VALLEY OF THE SQUINTING WINDOWS
                              Dublin 1918                     75

MacSweeney, Barry  THE BOY FROM THE GREEN CABERET...
                              Sussex 1967 (100 cc)            40

Madden, David  THE BEAUTIFUL GREED  NY (1961)               50

Madge, Charles  THE DISAPPEARING CASTLE  L (1957)          40

Magee, David  JAM TOMORROW  B 1941                         60

Magowan, Robin  IN THE WASH  Mallorca 1958  wraps          35

Mahan, A. T.  THE NAVY IN THE CIVIL WAR  NY 1883          125

Mailer, Norman  THE NAKED AND THE DEAD  NY (1948)        250
                              L (1949) (240 cc)             400
                              L 1949  trade                 150
             preceded by THE FOUNDATION (priv pr)
                      (mimeographed sheets)

Maitland, Margaret (Margaret Oliphant) PASSAGES IN THE
                      LIFE OF...  L 1849 3 vols             350

Malamud, Bernard  THE NATURAL  NY (1952)  red, blue or
                    grey cloth  (priority uncertain)        250
                      L 1963 (Glossary added)               75

Malanga, Gerard  3 POEMS FOR BENEDETTA BARZINI  (NY 1967)
                              wraps (500 cc)                 75

Malcolm X  THE AUTOBIOGRAPHY OF MALCOLM X  NY (1965)
                              (with Alex Haley)              75

Malraux, Andre  THE CONQUERORS  L 1929                      75

Maltz, Albert  BLACK PIT  NY 1935                          100
             THE WAY THINGS ARE +  NY (1938)                75
      (two plays written with George Sklar preceded)

Mamet, David  AMERICAN BUFFALO  NY (1977)  wraps            40
                              NY (1978)  cloth               50

Manchester, William  DISTURBER OF THE PEACE  NY (1951)      40
                    THE SAGE OF BALTIMORE   L (1952)         35

Manfred, Frederick (Feikema)  see Feike Feikema

Manhood, H. A.  NIGHTSEED  L 1928                           50

Mann, Horace  LECTURES ON EDUCATION  B 1845               300
             (preceded by a number of pamphlets)

Mann, Thomas  ROYAL HIGHNESS  NY 1916 (first Eng tr)       75
```

Mannes, Myra MESSAGE FROM A STRANGER L 1948   25

Manning, Frederic THE VIGIL OF BRUNHILD L 1907   75

Mano, D. Keith BISHOP'S PROGRESS B 1968   40

Mansfield, Katherine IN A GERMAN PENSION L (1911)   500

March, Joseph Mancure THE SET-UP NY 1928 (275 cc)   60

March, William (Wm. Edw. March Campbell) COMPANY K NY 1933
                    issued in clear dw w/pr paper flaps   300

Marcus, Frank THE KILLING OF SISTER GEORGE L 1965   60

MARGARET PERCIVAL IN AMERICA (Edw. Everett Hale) B 1850   100

Marjoram, J. (Ralph H. Mottram) REPOSE + L 1907 wraps   125

Markfield, Wallace (Arthur) TO AN EARLY GRAVE NY 1964   40

Markham, (Charles) Edwin THE MAN WITH THE HOE appeared
                    as supp to SF Examiner 4 pp   250
                              SF 1899 wraps   125
                         NY 1899 i -"fruitless"
                              p.35:5 (2nd ed)   75

Markson, David EPITAPH FOR A TRAMP (NY 1959) wraps   20
                    (edited two books previously)

Markus, Julia LA MORA Wash (1976) wraps (1000 cc)   25

Marlowe, Derek A DANDY IN ASPIC NY (1966)   25

Marquand, John Philips see Charles E. Clark
                    THE UNSPEAKABLE GENTLEMEN NY 1922
                    i -Scribner's seal on c page   150

Marquez, Gabriel Garcia NO ONE WRITES THE COLONEL NY
                                        (1968)   125

Marquis, Don(ald) Robert Perry) DANNY'S OWN STORY GC 1912 75

Marryat, Frederick A CODE OF SIGNALS FOR USE OF VESSELS...
                                        L 1818   250
                    THE NAVAL OFFICER... L 1829 3 vols   300

Marsh, (Dame Edith) Ngaio A MAN LAY DEAD L 1934   250

Marsh, Patrick BREAKDOWN NY 1953   25

Marsh, Willard WEEK WITH NO FRIDAY NY (1965)   40

Marshall, Paule BROWN GIRL, BROWNSTONES NY 1959   150

Marston, Philip SONG TIDE + L 1871   100

Marvel, Ik (Donald Grant Mitchell) FRESH GLEANINGS...
                    NY 1847 2 vol wr   100
                         1 vol cloth   50

Marx, Groucho BEDS NY 1930   125

MARY BARTON: A TALE OF MANCHESTER LIFE (Elizabeth C.
                    Gaskell) L 1848 2 vol   500

```
Masefield, John   SALT WATER BALLADS   L 1902
                i -"Grant Richards" on t p              500
               ii -"Elkin Mathews" on t p              350

Mason, Alfred Edward   A ROMANCE OF THE WASTELAND   L (1895)     75

Mason, A(lfred) E(dward) W(oodley)   BLANCHE DE MALETROIT
                                             L 1894     40

Mason, Bobbie Ann   NABOKOV'S GARDEN   Ann Arbor (1974)     100
                (precedes THE GIRL SLEUTH)

Mason, (Francis) Van Wyck   THE VESPER SERVICE MURDERS
                                          NY 1931     100

Massey, T. Gerald   VOICE OF FREEDOM AND LYRICS OF LOVE
                                             L 1851     125

Masters, Anthony   A POCKETFUL OF RYE   L 1964              35

Masters, Edgar Lee   A BOOK OF VERSES   Ch 1898            200

Masters, Hilary   THE COMMON PASTURE   NY (1967)            35

Masters, John   COMPLEAT INDIAN ANGLER   L 1938           100
                NIGHTRUNNERS OF BENGAL   NY 1951            50

Mather, Increase   THE MYSTERY OF ISRAEL'S SALVATION
                                      (L) 1669         3,000

Matheson, Richard   SOMEONE IS BLEEDING   NY (1953) wraps    100
                BORN OF MAN AND WOMAN   Ph 1954   (first
                                hardback - third book)     150

Mathews, Elkin, Publisher   see Richard LeGallienne
```

LIZA
OF LAMBETH

BY

William Somerset Maugham

LONDON

T. FISHER UNWIN

Paternoster Square

1897

Mathews, Harry   THE CONVERSIONS   NY (1962)   60

Mathews, Jack (John Harold)   BITTER KNOWLEDGE   NY (1964)   35

Matthiessen, Peter   RACE ROCK   NY (1954)   100
                                 L 1954   100

Maugham, Robin   THE 1946 MS   L 1943   125

Maugham, W(illiam) Somerset   LIZA OF LAMBETH   L 1897
                                            (2000 cc)   600

Mauldin, Bill (William Henry)   STAR SPANGLED BANTER   San
                                Antonio, TX 1941   wr   125

Maurois, Andre   THE SILENCE OF COLONEL BRAMBLE   L 1919   40
                                                  NY 1920   150

Maxwell, Gavin   HARPOON AT A VENTURE   L 1952   60

Maxwell, Gilbert   LOOK TO THE LIGHTNING   NY 1933   50

Maxwell, William   BRIGHT CENTER OF HEAVEN   NY 1934   250

Mayer, Tom   BUBBLE GUM AND KIPLING   NY 1964   35

Mayfield, Julian   THE HIT   NY (1957)   40

Mayo, E(dward) L(eslie)   THE DIVER   Minn (1947)   50

McAlmon, Robert   EXPLORATIONS   L 1921   750

McCiag, Norman   FAR CRY   (L 1943)   wraps   75

McCarthy, Cormac   THE ORCHARD KEEPER   NY (1965)   75
                                        (L 1966)   50

McCarthy, Mary (Therese)   see H. V. Kaltenborn
                           THE COMPANY SHE KEEPS   (NY) 1942   125
                                                   L 1943   75

McClanahan, Ed   THE NATURAL MAN   NY 1983   20

McClure, James   THE STEAM PIG   L 1971   30
                                 NY (1971)   25

McClure, Michael   PASSAGE   Big Sur 1956 stiff wr (200 cc)   450

McCord, David (Thompson Watson)   ODDLY ENOUGH   C 1926   40

McCord, Howard   PRECISE FRAGMENTS   D 1963 wraps   (250 cc)   40

McCoy, Horace THEY SHOOT HORSES,DON'T THEY   NY 1935   300

McCullers, (Lula) Carson   THE HEART IS A LONELY HUNTER
                                            B 1940   350
                                            L 1943   200

McCullough, Colleen   TIM   NY (1974)   50

McCutcheon, George Barr   GRAUSTARK   CH 1901   i -"Noble"
                           for "Lorry" p.150:6   75

MacDonald, Gregory   RUNNING SCARED   NY (1964)   60

McElroy, Joseph   A SMUGGLER'S BIBLE   NY (1960)   150

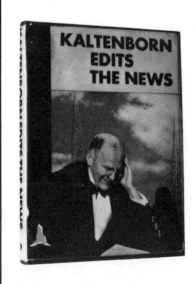
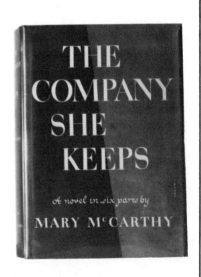

McKenna, Richard THE SAND PEBBLES NY (1962)   25

McKenna, Stephen THE RELUCTANT LOVER L 1913   100

McKinley, Georgia THE MIGHTY DISTANCE B 1965   40

McKuen, Rod AND AUTUMN CAME NY (1954)   90

McLuhan, (Herbert) Marshall THE MECHANICAL BRIDE NY (1951)
                    Reprinted in "Ltd Ed" according to dw but
                    book itself does not indicate (differ-
                    ences between 1st and "Ltd Ed"-$4.50 vs
                    $12.50, white endpaper vs yellow, white
                                cover lettering vs gold)   75

McManus, Kay LISTEN AND I'LL TALK (L 1969)   25

McMurtrie, Douglas C. THE DISABLED SOLDIER NY 1919   40
                       (previous pamphlets)

McMurtry, Larry (Jeff) HORSEMAN, PASS BY NY (1961)   500

McNeile, H(erman) C(yril) (SAPPER) THE LIEUTENANT AND
                                    OTHERS L 1915   100

McPhee, John A SENSE OF WHERE YOU ARE NY (1965)   150

McPherson, James A. HUE AND CRY B (1969)   40

Mead, Harold THE BRIGHT PHOENIX (NY 1956)   cloth   75
                                              wraps   15

Meade, L(illie) T(homas) (Elisabeth Thomasina Meade Smith)
                       THE MEDICINE LADY L 1892   125

Meagher, Maud WHITE JADE B 1930   50

Melanter (R.D. Blackmore) POEMS L 1854   600

Meltzer, David POEMS (SF 1957) (with D. Schenker)
                            25 sgd cloth   150
                     5 sgd cloth, blood stained cc   250
                               wraps (470 cc)   75
                RAGAS SF 1959 wraps (1500 cc)   30

Melville, Herman NARRATIVE OF A FOUR MONTH... L 1846
                i -"Pomarea" on p.19:1 -2 vols in wr   5,000
                            1 vol - red cloth   2,000
                ii -"Pomare" on page 19, line 1   1,000
                   TYPEE: A PEEP AT POLYNESIAN LIFE NY
                            1846 2 vols in wraps   3,000
                            1 vol - blue or brown cloth   1,500

Mencken, H(enry) L(ouis) VENTURES INTO VERSE Balt 1903
                       two issues, bound in boards &
                          in wraps (100 cc in total)   4,000
                       GEORGE BERNARD SHAW B 1903
                       (noted at 7 3/4" tall & & 7/8"
                                  priority unknown)   175

Menen, (Salvator) Aubrey THE PREVALENCE OF WITCHES
                                     L 1947   50

Meredith, George POEMS L (1851) half title & errata at
                            end, purple cloth   750
                               green cloth   400

NARRATIVE

OF A

FOUR MONTHS' RESIDENCE

AMONG THE NATIVES OF A VALLEY OF

THE MARQUESAS ISLANDS;

OR,

A PEEP AT POLYNESIAN LIFE.

By HERMAN MELVILLE.

LONDON:

JOHN MURRAY, ALBEMARLE STREET.

1846.

Meredith, William (Morris)   LOVE LETTERS FROM AN IMPOSSIBLE
                                              LAND   NH 1944   125

Merriam, Eve   FAMILY CIRCLE   NH 1946   25

Merril, Judith   SHADOW ON THE HEARTH   GC 1950   25

Merrill, James (Ingram)   JIM'S BOOK   NY (priv print) 1942   3,500
                          THE BLACK SWAN +   ATHENS 1946
                                          wraps (100 cc)   1,500
                          FIRST POEMS   NY 1951 (990 cc)
                                          (1st reg pub bk)   175

Merritt, A(braham)   THE MOON POOL   NY (1919)   cloth
                     i -no ad on p.(434), sheets bulk
                                           3.2 cm   75

Merton, Thomas   THIRTY POEMS   N (1944) boards   150
                                          wraps   60

Merwin, W(illiam) S(tanley)   A MASK FOR JANUS   NH 1952   300

Metcalf, Paul   WILL WEST   Asheville 1956   wraps (500 cc)   75

Metcalf, John   THE SMOKING LEG   L 1925   100

Mew, Charlotte   THE FARMER'S BRIDE   L 1916 wraps   125

Mewshaw, Michael   MAN IN MOTION   NY (1970)   30

Meyer, Thomas   THE BANG BOOK   Jargon n-pl 1971   cloth in
                                          acetate dw   60
                              wraps in acetate dw   30

Meyerstein, Edward Henry W. see E.H.W.M.

Meynell, Alice   see A. C. Thompson

Mezey, Robert   THE WANDERING JEW   Mt. Vernon 1960 wr 350 cc   60
                     (prev collected appearance in 1957)

Michaels, Leonard   GOING PLACES   NY (1969)   30

Micheaux, Oscar (or Micheaud) see THE CONQUEST

Micheline, Jack   RIVER OF RED WINE +   NY (1958) wraps   40

Michener, James A(lbert)   TALES OF THE SOUTH PACIFIC
                                              NY 1947   225
                          NY 1950   1500 sgd cc,
                          special ABA ed w/o dw   100
                     (one prev non-fic collaboration)

Middleton, Christopher   POEMS   L (1944)   75

Middleton, Richard   THE GHOST SHIP +   L 1912   100

Middleton, Stanley   A SHORT ANSWER   L 1958   60

Midwood, Barton   BODKIN   NY (1967)   25

Miles, Josephine   LINES AT THE INTERSECTION   NY 1939   50

Millar, Kenneth (Ross MacDonald)   DARK TUNNEL   NY 1944   2,000

Millar, Margaret (Mrs. Kenneth Millar)   THE INVISIBLE WORM
                                              GC 1941   250

```
Millay, Edna St. Vincent  RENASCENSE + NY 1917
                     i -15 cc on Japanese vellum sgd   4,000
                    ii -Glaslan watermark pp (2 blank
                                  precede half-title)     125
                   iii -not on Glaslan watermark pp
                                   (no blank leaves)       50
                       (previous Vassar material)

Millen, Gilmore  SWEET MAN  NY 1930                      100

Miller, Alice  see Alice Duer

Miller, Arthur  SITUATION NORMAL  NY (1944)              150

Miller, Caroline  LAMB IN HIS BOSOM  NY 1933 (only book
                                      - Pulitzer)        100

Miller, Heather Ross  THE EDGE OF THE WOODS  NY 1964      50

Miller, Henry (Valentine)  TROPIC OF CANCER  P (1934)
                                     decorated wraps
                 i -has "first publ Sept 1934"
                    on c pg and a wrap-around band      3,000
                ii -w/o notice                           750
                     THE COSMOLOGICAL EYE  N 1939
                                     (1st U.S. publ)
                 i -eye on cover, dw price $2.50         125

Miller, Joaquin (Cincinnatus Hiner Miller)  see SPECIMENS
```

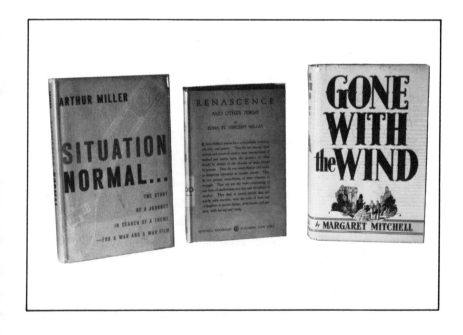

Miller, Jason NOBODY HEARS A BROKEN DRUM NY (1971) wraps   25

Miller, Merle ISLAND 49 NY (1945)   35

Miller, Patrick THE NATURAL MAN L 1924   100

Miller, Vassar ADAM'S FOOTPRINT   New Orleans 1956 wraps   60

Miller, Walter M., Jr. A CANTICLE FOR LEIBOWITZ Ph/NY 1960   400
                                              L (1960)   150

Miller, Warren THE SLEEP OF REASON L 1956   100
               (also see Amanda Vail)

Mills, James PANIC IN NEEDLE PARK NY (1966)   35

Milne, A(lan) A(lexander) LOVERS IN LONDON L 1905   100

Milton, Ernest TO KILL A CROCODILE NY 1928   50

Minot, Stephen CHILL OF DUCK GC 1964   35

Mirabeau, Honore Gabriel Riquetti see ESSAI

MIRIAM COFFIN: OR, THE WHALE FISHERMAN (Joseph C. Hart)
                                    NY 1834 2 vol   250

Mishima, Yukio (Hiraoka Kimitake) THE SOUND OF WAVES NY
                            1956 (first Eng trans)   50

MR. DOOLEY IN PEACE AND WAR (Finley Peter Dunne) B 1898   50

Mitchell, Donald G(rant) THE DIGNITY OF LEARNING NY 1841 wr 200
               (also see Ik Marvel)

Mitchell, Isaac THE ASYLUM: OR, ALONSO AND MELISSA Pough-
               keepsie 1811 2 v (many later eds credited
                            to Daniel Jackson, Jr.)   500

Mitchell, Joseph MY EARS ARE BENT NY (1938)   40

Mitchell, Julian IMAGINARY TOYS L 1961   40

Mitchell, Margaret GONE WITH THE WIND NY 1936 "May
                            1936" on c page   850

Mitchell, S(ilas) Weir see E.W.S.
               THE WONDERFUL STORIES OF... Ph 1867
                               (170 lpc)   750
                                  trade   200
               (a number of biological and natural science
                            pamphlets preceded)

Mitchell, W. O. WHO HAS SEEN THE WIND B 1947   40

Mitford, Mary Russell POEMS L 1810
               i -leaf of "alterations"   400

Mittelholzer, Edgar (Austin) CREOLE CHIPS British Guiana
                                          1937   125
                            CORENTYNE THUNDER L 1941   100

Mo, Timothy THE MONKEY KING (L 1978)   35

Moffett, Cleveland (Langston) THROUGH THE WALL NY 1909   100

Molloy, Robert PRIDE'S WAY NY 1945   40

POEMS

BY MARIANNE MOORE

LONDON

THE EGOIST PRESS

2 *Robert Street, Adelphi, W.C.*

1921

```
Momaday, N(atachee) Scott   THE COMPLETE POEMS OF FREDERICK
                            GODDARD TUCKERMAN  NY 1965
                                  (edited by Momaday)        50
                            THE JOURNEY OF TAI-ME  SB (1968)
                                        (100 cc) Boxed      500
                            HOUSE MADE OF DAWN  NY 1968       75

Monk, Maria  AWFUL DISCLOSURES... NY 1836                    400

Monroe, Harriet  VALERIA +  Ch 1891 subscribers ed (300 cc)  200
                            Ch 1892 regular ed                75

Montague, C(harles) E(dward)  A HIND LET LOOSE  L (1910)
                                        (150 cc)             150
                                      regular ed              75

Montague, John  FORMS OF EXILE  O (1958)  wr                  75
                (preceded by POEMS on mimeographed sheets, about 1955)

Montgomery, L(ucy) M(aude)  ANNE OF GREEN GABLES  NY 1908    175

Moody, William Vaughn  THE MASQUE OF JUDGEMENT  B 1900
                              boards (150 cc)               150
                              regular edition                50

Moon, William Least Heat  BLUE HIGHWAYS  B (1982)            40

Moorcock, Michael  see Desmond Reid  THE STEALER OF SOULS
                                            L (1963)
                            i -orange boards                 75
                            ii -green boards                 60

Moore, Brian  WREATH FOR A REDHEAD  Winnipeg 1951 wraps     200
              JUDITH HEARNE  L 1955 (first hardback)        125
              THE LONELY PASSION OF JUDITH HEARNE  B 1955   100

Moore, Catherine Lucile  see Lewis Padgett

Moore, Clement C(larke)  see OBSERVATIONS UPON CERTAIN
                                            PASSAGES...
                         see A NEW TRANSLATION...

Moore, Edward (Edwin Muir)  WE MODERNS +  L (1918)          200

Moore, George  FLOWERS OF PASSION  L 1878                   250

Moore, Marianne  POEMS  L 1921  wraps                       500

Moore, Merrill  THE NOISE THAT TIME MAKES... NY (1929)      125

Moore, Nicholas  THE ISLAND AND THE CATTLE  L (1941)        75

Moore, T(homas) Sturge  THE VINEDRESSER +  L 1899          100
                (prev privately printed pamphlet preceded)

Moore, Thomas  ODES OF ANACREON  L 1800 (tr & notes)       250

Morand, Paul  OPEN ALL NIGHT  NY 1923 (1st Eng tr)          40

Moravia, Alberto (Alberto Pincherle) THE INDIFFERENT ONES
                                            NY (1932)        75

Morecamp, Arthur (Thomas Pilgrim)  THE LIVE BOYS... B (1878) 200

Morgan, Charles (Langbridge)  THE GUNROOM  L 1919   (blue-
                              grained or blue-ribbed cloth
                              -priority uncertain)          75
```

Morison, Samuel Eliot HARRISON GRAY OTIS B 1913   150

Morley, Christopher (Darlington) THE EIGHTH SIN O/L 1912
                                    wraps (250 cc) 1,000
                        PARNASSUS ON WHEELS GC 1917
                        i -space between "y" and "e" p.4:8   150

Morrell, David FIRST BLOOD NY (1972)   40
                      L (1972)   35

Morris, Julian (Morris West) MOON IN MY POCKET Sidney
                                    (1948)   100

Morris, William THE DEFENSE OF GUENEVERE + L 1858
                              (250 cc sold)   600

Morris, Willie NORTH TOWARD HOME B 1967   50

Morris, Wright MY UNCLE DUDLEY NY (1942)   1,000

Morrison, Arthur THE SHADOWS AROUND US... L 1891   250
                MARTIN HEWITT, INVESTIGATOR L 1894   1,000
                (third book, first mystery)

Morrison, James Douglas THE LORDS LA 1969 (100 cc)   100

Morrison, Theodore THE SERPENT IN THE CLOUD B 1931   40

Morrison, Toni THE BLUEST EYE NY (1970)   300
                        L 1979   40

Morse, Samuel French TIME OF YEAR (Cummington) 1943
                              (275 cc)   75

Morton, David SHIPS IN HARBOR NY 1921   60

Morton, J.B. see GORGEOUS POETRY

Morton, Sarah Wentworth OUABI: OR THE VIRTUES OF NATURE
                              B 1790   100

MORTON OF MORTON'S HOPE... (John Lothrop Motley) L 1839
                              3 vols   300

MORTON'S HOPE...(John Lothrop Motley) NY 1839 2 Vols   250

Moses, Robert THE CIVIL SERVICE OF GREAT BRITAIN NY
                              1914 wraps   50

Moss, Howard THE WOUND AND THE WEATHER NY (1946)   75

Motley, John Lothrop see MORTON...and MORTON'S HOPE

Motley, Willard KNOCK ON ANY DOOR NY (1947)   50

Mottram, Ralph Hale see J. Marjoram

Mowat, Farley PEOPLE OF THE DEER B 1952   75

Moynahan, Julian SISTERS AND BROTHERS NY (1960)   25

Muir, Edwin see Edward Moore
              WE MODERNS NY 1920 includes Mencken intro 150

Muir, Emily SMALL POTATOES NY 1940   35

Muir, John THE MOUNTAINS OF CALIFORNIA NY 1894   250
              (previous off-prints and edited books)

```
Mulford, Clarence Edward  BAR-20 (Hopalong Cassidy) NY 1907
                       i -"Blazing Star" in list of illus     125
                      ii -without "Blazing Star" in list       60

Mumey, Nolie  A STUDY OF RARE BOOKS  Denver 1930
                      (1000 signed cc)                        150

Mumford, Lewis  THE STORY OF UTOPIAS  NY (1922)              200

Mundy, Talbot (William Lancaster Gribbon)  RUNG HO!  NY 1914  100

Munro, Alice  DANCE OF THE HAPPY SHADES  T (1968)           125

Munro, H(ector) H(ugh)(Saki)  THE RISE OF THE RUSSIAN EMPIRE
                      L 1900 (also see Saki)                 200

Munro, Neil  THE LOST PIBROCK +  Edinburgh 1896              75

Munroe, Kirk  WAKULLA +  NY 1886                             50

Munson, Gorham  WALDO FRANK A STUDY  NY (1923) (Stieglitz
                      frontis photo) (500 no. cc)           300

Murdoch, (Jean) Iris  SARTRE: ROMANTIC RATIONALIST
                      NH (1953)                             150

Murgatroyd, Captain Matthew (James Athearn Jones)
                      THE REFUGEE  NY 1823  2 vol           400

Murphy, Audie  TO HELL AND BACK  NY (1949)                  60

Murphy, Richard  SAILING TO AN ISLAND  L 1963               75

Murray, Albert  THE OMNI-AMERICANS...  NY (1970)            40

Murray, M(argaret) A.  EGYPTIAN POEMS  L (1920)             75

Murray, Pauli  PROUD SHOES  NY (1956)                       60

Myrer, Anton  EVIL UNDER THE SUN  NY 1951                   35

Nabokoff, Vladimir (Nabokov)  LAUGHTER IN THE DARK  I (1938)  400
                      (1st publ in US) green cloth is said to be 1st
                      issue, also in red and brown cloths (revised
                      version of CAMERA OBSCURA)

Nabokoff-Sirin (Nabokov), Vladimir CAMERA OBSCURA  L (1936)
                      (1st book trans into Eng) 1,500

Nabokov, Vladimir  see two entries above

Naipaul, V(idiadhar) S.  THE MYSTIC MASSEUR  L 1957         250
                      NY (1959)                             75

Naipaul, Shiva  FIREFLIES  L 1970                           75
                      NY 1971                               35

Nardi, Marci  POEMS  Denver (1956)                          50

NARRATIVE OF DR. LIVINGSTON'S DISCOVERIES IN CENTRAL AFRICA
                      (David Livingstone)  L 1857           400

Nasby, Petroleum V. (David Ross Locke)  THE NASBY PAPERS
            I 1864 wraps  i -"Indianapolic" front cover     150
                         ii -spelled correctly              100

Nash, Ogden  THE CRICKET OF CARADOR  GC 1925 (with J. Alger)  250
             HARD LINES  NY 1931                            250
```

L 1932   150

Nast, Thomas   THE FIGHT AT DAME EUROPA'S SCHOOL NY (1871)   100

Nathan, George Jean   THE ETERNAL MYSTERY NY 1913   60

Nathan, Robert (Gruntal)   PETER KINDRED NY 1919   60

NATURE (Ralph Waldo Emerson)   B 1836
               i -page 94 numbered 92   750
               ii -page 94 correctly numbered   350

Naylor, Gloria   THE WOMEN OF BREWSTER PLACE   NY 1982   50

Neagoe, Peter   STORM P 1932 publ by New Review wraps   150
               (1 cc noted in cloth) (preceded Obelisk ed)

Neal, John see KEEP COOL

Negro Pioneer, A see THE CONQUEST

Neihardt, John G(neisenau)   THE DIVINE ENCHANTMENT +   NY
               1900 (supposedly he burned
                                    most cc)   650

Neilson, Shaw   HEART OF SPRING   Sydney 1919   350
               (two prev pamphlets)

Nemerov, Howard   THE IMAGE AND THE LAW   (NY 1947)   100

Nesbit, E(dith)   LAYS AND LEGENDS   L 1886   200
               (preceded by edited anthology
                -SPRING SONGS AND SKETCHES)

NEW BATH GUIDE, OR, MEMOIRS...(THE) (Christopher Anstey)
                                    L 1766   100

(New Directions)   PIANOS OF SYMPATHY   N 1936 wr written
               by Montague O'Reilly - First book of
                                    the press   300

NEW DIRECTIONS IN PROSE AND POETRY   N 1936 (1st in series)
                         cloth -issued w/o dw   200
                                         wraps   100

NEW TRANSLATION WITH NOTES OF THE THIRD SATIRE OF JUVENAL
               (Clement Moore and John Duer) NY 1806
               i -"additional errata" leaf   250

Newbolt, Sir Henry see A FAIR DEATH

Newby, Eric   THE LAST GRAIN RACE   L 1956   50

Newby, P(ercy) H(oward)   A JOURNEY TO THE INTERIOR   L 1945   60

Newell, Peter see TOPSYS AND TURVEYS

Newhouse, Edward   YOU CAN'T SLEEP HERE   NY (1934)   100

Newlove, John   GRAVE SIRS   Vancouver 1962 stiff wraps   200

Newton, A(lfred) Edward   THE AMENITIES OF BOOK COLLECTING
                                    B 1918
               i -w/o index, p.268:3 has "Piccadilly"   60
               ii -has index   25

Nichols, John   THE STERILE CUCKOO   NY (1965)   50

158

ANAÏS NIN

D. H. LAWRENCE

An unprofessional Study

With two facsimile manuscript pages out of
Lady Chatterley's Lover

Paris 1932

EDWARD W. TITUS
at the sign of the black manikin
4, RUE DELAMBRE, MONTPARNASSE

THE STORY OF THE
IRISH CITIZEN ARMY

By P. O CATHASAIGH

The first account that has been given of the
formation of the Irish Citizen Army during the
Dublin strike of 1913-14, and the part played
by it in the subsequent history of Ireland. The
author, who was himself a leading figure in the
movement, writes with vigour and conviction
upon the role of labour in Ireland, and ex-
pressing a very definite opinion as to the relations
of the workers to the National movement. The
book contains original character sketches of
Larkin, Connolly, Captain White, and Madame
Markiewicz, and some facts bearing on the
relations between the Citizen Army and the
Volunteers now emerge for the first time.

MAUNSEL & CO., LTD.

ONE SHILLING NET

159

Nichols, Robert INVOCATION... L 1915 i -blue wraps   75

Nicholson, Norman FIVE RIVERS (L 1944)   60

Nicolson, Harold VERLAINE L (1921)   250

Niedecker, Lorine NEW GOOSE Prairie City (1946)   800

NILE NOTES OF A HOWADJI (George William Curtis) NY 1851
                                            wraps   200
                                            cloth   100

Nims, John Frederick THE IRON PASTORAL NY(1947)   35

Nin, Anais D.H. LAWRENCE: AN UNPROFESSIONAL STUDY
                        P 1932 (550 no. cc)   250

Nixon, Richard THE CHALLENGES WE FACE NY 1960   75

Noah, Mordecai Manuel see THE FORTRESS...

Noguchi, Yone SEEN & UNSEEN SF 1896   75

Nordhoff, Charles Bernard THE FLEDGLING B 1919   40

Nordhoff, Charles B. & Hall, James N. THE LAFAYETTE FLYING
                        CORPS B 1920 2 vol   600

Norman, Charles TRAGIC BEACHES NY 1925 (100 sgd cc)   100

Norman, Marc BIKE RIDING IN LOS ANGELES NY 1972   20

Normyx (Norman Douglas) UNPROFESSIONAL TALES L 1901
                        (750 cc)(8 were sold by
                        author; about 600 pulped)   650
                (preceded by a number of pamphlets)

Norris, (Benjamin) Frank(lin) YVERNELLE + Ph 1892
                        (actually 1891)   1,000

Norris, Kathleen MOTHER A STORY NY 1911   60

Norse, Harold THE UNDERSEA MOUNTAIN Denver 1953   40

North, Sterling THE PEDRO GORINO B 1929 (with Capt.
                                    Harry Dean)   125
                PLOWING ON SUNDAY NY 1934   75

Norton, Andre (Alice Mary Norton) THE PRINCE COMMANDS...
                                            NY 1934   600

Norton, Charles Eliot see CONSIDERATIONS...

Nott, Kathleen MILE END Hogarth L 1938   75

Nourse, Alan Edward TROUBLE ON TITAN Ph (1954)   40

Nova, Craig TURKEY HASH NY (1972)   35

Novak, Joseph (Jerzy Kosinski) THE FUTURE IS OURS,
                        COMRADE GC 1960   250

Noyes, Alfred THE LOOM OF YEARS L 1902   50

Noyes, John H(umphrey) THE BEREAN... Putney 1847   200

Nutt, Howard SPECIAL LAUGHTER... Prairie City (1940)   125

160

```
Nye, Edgar Wilson  A HOWL IN ROME  Ch (1880) wr          100
                   BILL NYE AND BOOMERANG... Ch 1881        75

Nye, Hermes  FORTUNE IS A WOMAN (NY 1958) wraps             30

Nye, Robert  JUVENILIA 1  (Northwood 1961) 25 sgd no.  cc  75

Oates, Joyce Carol  BY THE NORTH GATE  NY (1963)          100

OBITER DICTA (Augustine Birrell)  L 1884                   50

O'Brien, Edna  THE COUNTRY GIRLS  L 1960                   50

O'Brien, Edward J.  THE FLOWING OF THE TIDE  NY 1910       50

O'Brien, Fitz-James  POEMS AND STORIES  B 1881            175

O'Brien, Flann (Brian O'Nolan) AT SWIM-TWO-BIRDS  L (1939)
               i  -black cloth                          2,000
              ii  -grey-green cloth (issued in 1941 or 1942  800
                           NY (1951) (1939 stated)         100

O'Brien, Kate  DISTINGUISHED VILLA  L 1926               125

O'Brien, Tim  IF I DIE IN A COMBAT ZONE  NY (1973)       250
                                         L (1973)          50

OBSERVATION UPON CERTAIN PASSAGES in Mr. Jefferson's "Notes
              on Virginia" (Clement C. Moore possible
                   author)  NY 1804  wraps               300

O'Casey, Sean  see next entry

O'Cathasaigh, P. (Sean O'Casey)  THE STORY OF THE IRISH
                                  ARMY  D 1919 wr
                            i -grey wraps                 100
                           ii -tan wraps                   75

O'Connor, Edwin  THE ORACLE  NY (1951)                    25

O'Connor, (Mary) Flannery  WISE BLOOD  NY (1952)         650
                                       L (1955)          250

O'Connor, Frank (Michael O'Donovan)  GUESTS OF THE NATION
                                         L 1931          250

O'Connor, Jack  CONQUEST  NY 1930                        125

O'Connor, Philip F.  OLD MORALS, SMALL CONTINENTS...
                          Iowa City (1971)                25

Odets, Clifford  THREE PLAYS  NY (1935)                   60

O'Donnell, Peter  MODESTY BLAISE  (L 1965)                75
                                  NY 1965                 35

O'Duffy, Eimhar  A LAY OF THE LIFFEY +  D 1918 wraps      60

O'Faolain, Sean MIDSUMMER NIGHT MADNESS +  L (1932)      250
                                           NY 1932       125

Offord, Carl Ruthaven  THE WHITE FACE  NY (1943)         100

O'Flaherty, Liam  THY NEIGHBOR'S WIFE  L (1923)          175

Ogawa, Florence  see AI
```

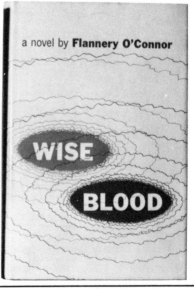

OGILVIES (THE) (Dinah Craik) L 1849 3 vols   300

O'Gorman, Ned (Edward Charles) THE NIGHT OF THE HAMMER
                                         NY 1959   20

O'Hara, Frank (Francis Russell) A CITY WINTER + NY 1951
                                 (Larry Rivers illus)
                                      20 sgd cloth   1,500
                                     130 no. cc wraps   500

O'Hara, John APPOINTMENT IN SAMARRA NY (1934)
              i -back panel of dw has ads for
                             "Recent Fiction"   600
                                  L (1935)   250
         (preceded by REMINISCENCES: FROM "KUNGSHOLM" written
              anonymously for Swedish American line)

OLD LIBRARIAN'S ALMANACK (THE) (Edmund L. Pearson)
                                 Woodstock, VT 1909   75

Oliphant, Margaret see Margaret Maitland

Oliver, Chad MISTS OF DAWN Ph (1952)   30

Ollivant, Alfred BOB, SON OF BATTLE NY 1898   75

Olsen, Tillie TELL ME A RIDDLE Ph 1961 cloth   150
                                 L 1964 wraps   30

Olson, Charles CALL ME ISHMAEL NY (1947)   250
                                 L 1962 wraps   35

Olson, Elder THING OF SORROW NY 1934   25

Olympia Press AMOROUS EXPLOITS OF A YOUNG RAKEHELL P 1953
                       (R. Seaver's trans of APOLLINAIRE
                        - first book of Press) wraps   50

O'Neill, Eugene G(ladstone) THIRST + B (1914) (1000 cc) 250

O'Neill, Rose Cecil THE LOVES OF EDWY B (1904)   40

Onions, Oliver THE COMPLEAT BACHELOR L 1900   60

Oppen, George DISCRETE SERIES... NY 1934   300

Oppenheim, E(dward) Phillips EXPIATION L 1887   50

Oppenheimer, Joel (Lester) FOUR POEMS TO SPRING (Black
                             Mountain 1951) wraps   250
                        THE DANCER Highlands, NC 1952
                                   (Jargon 2)   500

Optic, Oliver see William Taylor Adams

Orage, A.R. FRIEDRICH NIETZCHE... L 1906   50

Orcutt, WilliamDana ROBERT CAVALIER Ch 1904   60

Orczy, Baroness (Emmuska) THE EMPEROR'S CANDLESTICKS
                                  L 1899   150

Orlovitz, Gil CONCERNING MAN Banyan Press NY 1947
              (350 no. cc) (also first of press)   75

Orton, Joe ENTERTAINING MR. SLOANE L 1964   75

Orwell, George (Eric Arthur Blair) DOWN AND OUT IN PARIS
                                 AND LONDON   L 1933   3,000
                                             NY 1933   850

Osborn, John Jay, Jr. THE PAPER CHASE B 1971   35

Osborn, Laughton see SIXTY YEARS...

Osbourne, John LOOK BACK IN ANGER L 1957 wraps   100
    (Evans Bros edition preceded Faber edition)
                                             NY 1957   40

O'Shaughnessy, Arthur W. E. AN EPIC OF WOMEN + L 1870
                 i -pictorial title precedes title   200

O'Sheel, Shaemus THE BLOSSOMY BOUGH NY 1911   35

Ostenso, Maria A FAR LAND NY 1924   50

Ostroff, Anthony IMPERATIVES NY (1962)   25

O'Sullivan, Seumas (James Sullivan Starkey)   THE TWILIGHT
                                 PEOPLE D 1905 wraps   125

Otis, James (Otis Kaler) TOBY TYLER OR TEN WEEKS WITH
                                 A CIRCUS NY 1881   150

Oursler, Fulton see Anthony Abbott

OUTCROPPINGS... see Bret Harte

OUTRE-MER: A PILGRIMAGE BEYOND THE SEA (Henry Wadsworth
    Longfellow) B 1833-4 2 vols (Vol I wr, Vol II bds)   1,500
    (five Spanish translations between French
                          grammars and this)

Owen, Robert A NEW VIEW OF HUMAN SOCIETY... L 1813/14
                          (four parts in one)   1,200

Owen, Robert Dale MORAL PHYSIOLOGY... NY 1831   750

Owen, Wilfred POEMS   L 1920   600
                       NY (1921)   350

Owens, Rochelle NOT BE ESSENCE THAT CANNOT BE NY (1961)
                                                 wraps   50

OWL CREEK LETTERS (THE) (Wm. C. Prime) NY 1848   125

Ozick, Cynthia TRUST NY (1966)   100

Padgett, Lewis (H. Kuttner) THE BRASS RING NY 1946 (with
                          C.L. Moore, her first bk)   100

Padgett, Ron IN ADVANCE OF THE BROKEN ARM NY 1964
                          wraps (200 no. cc)   50

Page, Stanton (Henry Blake Fuller) THE CHEVALIER OF
                    PENSIERIVABU B (1800) wraps   200
                                         cloth   75

Page, Thomas Nelson IN OLE VIRGINIA... NY 1887
                    i -has ads headed "Popular Books...
                                 OLD CREOLE DAYS..."   60

Paine, Albert Bigelow RHYMES BY TWO FRIENDS Fort Scott
                    (1893) (with W.A. White) (500 cc)   75

```
Painter, Charlotte   THE FORTUNES OF LAURIE BREAUX   B 1961        40

Paley, Grace   THE LITTLE DISTURBANCES OF MAN   GC 1959            75
                                                 L 1960            35

Palmer, (Charles) Stuart   THE ACE OF JADES   NY 1931            300
                           THE PENGUIN POOL MURDERS   NY 1931    250

Pancake, Breece D'J   THE STORIES OF BREECE...   B (1983)         30

Parker, Dorothy   MEN I'M NOT MARRIED TO   GC 1922
                  (dos-a-dos) (previous collaborations)          200

Parker, Robert B(rown)   THE GODWULF MANUSCRIPT   B 1974         150

Parker, Theodore   THE PREVIOUS QUESTION...   B 1840 wraps       100

Parkinson, C. Northcote   EDWARD PELLEW...   L (1934)            125

Parkman, Francis   THE CALIFORNIA AND OREGON TRAIL   NY 1849
                                      2 vols in wraps    8,500
                                      1 vol in cloth     1,000
                       i -terminal catalog inserted not integral

Parks, Gordon   THE LEARNING TREE   NY (1963)                     35

Parley, Peter (S.G. Goodrich)   THE TALES OF PETER PARLEY
                                ABOUT AMERICA   B 1827    3,500

Parrish, Anne   A POCKETFUL OF POSES   NY (1923)                  75

Parrish, Maxfield   see L. Frank Baum

Parton, James   THE LIFE OF HORACE GREELEY...   NY 1855          75

PASSAGES FROM THE DIARY OF A LATE PHYSICIAN   (Samuel
                      Warren)   NY 1831 (pirated)               350
                                L 1832   2 vols                 150

PASSION FLOWERS   (Julia Ward Howe)   B 1854                    125

Pastan, Linda   A PERFECT CIRCLE OF SUN   Ch (1971)              40

Patchen, Kenneth   BEFORE THE BRAVE   NY (1936)                 250

Pater, Walter   STUDIES IN THE HISTORY OF THE RENAISSANCE
                                                 L 1873         75

Patmore, Coventry   POEMS   L 1844                             750

Paton, Alan (Stewart)   MEDITATION FOR A YOUNG BOY
                         CONFIRMED   L 1944                     200
                CRY THE BELOVED COUNTRY   L 1948                100
                                         NY 1948                 50

Patrick, Q. (Richard Wilson Webb et al)   COTTAGE SINISTER
                                            L 1931             100

Paul, Eliot   INDELIBLE, A STORY OF LOVE...   B 1922           200

Paul, Louis   THE PUMPKIN COACH   NY 1935                       25

Paulding, J(ames) K(irke)   see Launcelot Langstaff
                            also see Hector Bull-us

PAULINE: A FRAGMENT OF A CONFESSION (Robert Browning)
                                     L 1833         25,000
                       (also see Browning)
```

SYMBOL AS NEED

WALKER PERCY

Reprinted from
THOUGHT
FORDHAM UNIVERSITY QUARTERLY
Vol. XXIX, No. 114, Autumn, 1954

Pavey, L.A. MR. LINE L 1931   40

Payton, Lew DID ADAM SIN? LA (1937) wraps   50

Peabody, Elizabeth Palmer see FIRST LESSONS...

Peake, Mervyn CAPTAIN SLAUGHTERBOARD DROPS ANCHOR
                                 L 1939   2,000
                                 L 1945   250

Pearce, Donn COOL HAND LUKE NY (1965)   50

Pearson, Edmund L. see THE OLD LIBRARIAN'S ALMANACK

Peattie, Donald Culross BLOWN LEAVES (Ch) 1916 wraps   1,000

Peck, George (Wilbur) ADVENTURES OF ONE TERRENCE
                      McGRANT... NY 1871   150
                 PECK'S BAD BOY AND HIS PA Ch 1883   250

Pelieu, Claude AUTOMATIC PILOT NY/SF (1964) wraps   35

Pemberton, Sir Max DIARY OF A SCOUNDREL L 1891   150
                    JEWEL MYSTERIES I HAVE KNOWN... L 1894   100

Pendleton, Tom THE IRON ORCHARD NY (1966)   40

Pennington, Patience (Elizabeth Pringle) A WOMAN RICE
                                 PLANTER NY 1913   60

Pentecost, Hugh (Judson Pentecost Philips) CANCELLED IN
                                 RED NY 1939   40

PENTLAND RISING (THE) (Robert Louis Stevenson) Edinburgh
                                 1866 wraps   1,750

Perchik, Simon THE BOMBER MOON (NY 1950) wraps   50

Percy, Walker SYMBOL AS NEED Fordham Univ NY (1954)
                      an offprint in stapled wraps   500
               THE MOVIEGOER NY 1961   600
                             L 1963   200

Percy, William Alexander SAPHO IN LEVKAS + NY 1915   75

Perelman, S(idney) J(oseph) DAWN GINSBURG'S REVENGE
                                 NY (1929)
                      i -apple green binding   600
                      ii -silver binding   250

Perishable Press see Walter Hamady

Perkoff, Stuart Z. THE SUICIDE ROOM Karlsruhe 1956 wr
                                 (200 cc)   50

Perles, Alfred SENTIMENTS LIMITROPHES P 1935 wr   125

Perry, Charles PORTRAIT OF A YOUNG MAN DROWNING NY 1962   40

Perry, George S. WALLS RISE UP NY 1939   60

Perse, St. J(ohn) (Alexis St. Leger) ANABASIS L 1930
                      (trans by T.S. Eliot) (350 cc sgd by
                                 Eliot) boxed   500
                      trade ed, top edge green, white dw   150

Peterkin, Julia GREEN THURSDAY NY 1924 (2000 no. cc)   125

Peters, Curtis Arnoux see Peter Arno

Petrakis, Harry Mark LION AT MY HEART B 1959   60
                                       L 1959   40

Petry, Ann (Lane) THE STREET B 1946   75

Pharr, Robert Dean THE BOOK OF NUMBERS GC 1969   50

Phillips, David Graham see John Graham

Phillips, Jayne Anne SWEETHEARTS Carrboro 1976 (400 cc)
                                            wraps   125
                     St. Paul 1978 wraps (600 cc)   30
                   (preceded by two related broadsides)

Phillips, Stephen ORESTES + L 1884 wraps   150

Phillpotts, Eden see THE GHOST IN THE BANK OF ENGLAND
                 MY ADVENTURES IN THE FLYING SCOTSMAN
                            L 1888 stiff wraps   1,000

Phoutrides, Aristides LIGHTS AT DAWN B 1917   30

Piatt, John J. see POEMS OF TWO FRIENDS

Pickard, Tom HIGH ON THE WALLS L 1967 (50 sgd cc)   60
                                trade edition   20

Picthall, Marmaduke SAID THE FISHERMAN L 1903   75

Piercy, Marge BREAKING CAMP Middletown (1968) cloth   50
                                            wraps   15

Pierpont, John THE PORTRAIT B 1812   35

PIGS IS PIGS (Ellis Parker Butler) CH 1905 (author's
                        name on first page of text   200

Pike, Albert PROSE SKETCHES AND POEMS... B 1834   1,250

Pilgrim, Thomas see Arthur Morecamp

Pillin, William POEMS Prairie City 1939 wraps   40

Pim, Herbert Moore SELECTED POEMS D 1917 wraps   60

Pinchot, Gifford BILTMORE FOREST Ch 1893   75

Pinckney, Josephine SEA-DRINKING CITIES NY 1927
                          225 sgd no. cc   250
                                trade   125

Pinkerton, Allan TESTS ON PASSENGER CONDUCTORS   CH 1867
                                            wraps   200

Pinter, Harold THE BIRTHDAY PARTY L 1959 (Encore Publ)
                                            wraps   175

Pirsig, Robert M. ZEN AND THE ART OF MOTORCYCLE
                    MAINTENANCE NY (1974)   50
                                L (1974)   40

Pitter, Ruth FIRST POEMS L 1920 stiff wraps   75

Plaidy, Jean BEYOND THE BLUE MOUNTAINS NY (1947)   50

```
Plante, David  THE GHOST OF HENRY JAMES  L 1970 w/o errata      100
                                              with errata        75
                                                 B 1970          50

Plath, Sylvia  see A WINTER SHIP
               THE COLOSSUS +  L (1960)                         850
                               NY (1962)                        125

Plimpton, George  THE RABBIT'S UMBRELLA  NY 1955                 50

Plomer, William (Charles Franklyn)  TURBOT WOLFE  L 1925        200

Plowman, Max  FIRST POEMS  L 1913                               50

Plunkett, James  THE TRUSTING AND THE MAIMED +  L 1959          35

Plunkett, Joseph Mary  THE CIRCLE AND THE SWORD  D 1911 wr     200

Poe, Edgar Allan  see TAMERLANE
                  TAMERLANE +  L 1884 vellum (100 cc)        1,250

POEM AND VALEDICTORY ORATION... (Edw. R. Sill) NY 1861 wr      150

POEM ON THE RISING GLORY OF AMERICA   (Hugh Henry
        Brackenridge and Philip Freneau)  Ph 1772              200
```

One hundred copies only printed.

TAMERLANE

AND OTHER POEMS

BY

EDGAR ALLAN POE

FIRST PUBLISHED AT BOSTON IN 1827 AND NOW
FIRST REPUBLISHED FROM A UNIQUE COPY
OF THE ORIGINAL EDITION
WITH A PREFACE

BY

RICHARD HERNE SHEPHERD

LONDON
GEORGE REDWAY
MDCCCLXXXIV.

```
POEMS  (Siegfried Sassoon)  (L 1906) (50 cc)  wraps            2,500
                (also see KAIN)
POEMS BY TWO BROTHERS  (Charles Alfred and Frederick
                Tennyson)  L (1827) boards 1pc                 1,500
        (Alfred's first book)  small paper copy                 750

POEMS OF TWO FRIENDS  (William Dean Howells and John
                J. Piatt)  Columbus, Ohio 1860                   800

Pohl, Frederik  THE SPACE MERCHANTS  NY (1953) (with C.M.
        Kornbluth) (prev edited anthologies)
                                        cloth                   100
                                        wraps                    15
        ALTERNATING CURRENTS  NY 1956 cloth                     500
                (first separate book) wraps                      25

Polite, Carlene Hatcher  THE FLAGELLANTS  NY (1967)             25
        (French edition - 1966, preceded)

Politi Leo  LITTLE PANCHO  NY 1938                              75

Pollini, Francis  NIGHT  P (1960)  wraps and dw                50

Pollock, Channing  BEHOLD THE MAN  Washington 1901             75

Ponicsan, Darryl  THE LAST DETAIL  NY 1970                     35

Poole, Ernest  KATHERINE BRESHOVSKY... CH 1905 pic wraps      100

Porter, Alan  THE SIGNATURE OF PAIN +  NY 1931                 50

Porter, Gene (Stratton)  THE SONG OF THE CARDINAL  I (1903)   125

Porter, Katherine Anne  see M.T.F.
        OUTLINE OF MEXICAN POPULAR ARTS AND CRAFTS
                        (La) 1922 wraps                        500

Porter, Katherine Anne Herwig Shaw  see Kathleen Winsor

Porter, William Sidney  see O. Henry

Porterfield, Nolan  A WAY OF KNOWING  NY (1971)                40

Portis, Charles  NORWOOD  NY (1966)                            40

Posner, David  THE DOUBLE VISION  P 1948 wr                    75

Post, Melville Davisson  THE STRANGE SCHEMES OF RANDOLPH
                        MASON  NY 1896 wraps                   350
                                cloth                          300

Postgate, Raymond (William)  VERDICT OF TWELVE  L (1940)      100
                                NY 1940                         40

Potter, Beatrix  THE TALE OF PETER RABBIT  L (1901)
                (priv pr) Dec 1901  (250 cc)                 3,000
                        Feb 1902  (200 cc)                   2,000
                Oct 1902 -(1st trade (bds and cl)
                i -holly leaf end pp; "wept" for
                                "shed" p.51                    750

Potter, Dennis  THE GLITTERING COFFIN  L 1960                 35

Pottle, Frederick A.  STRETCHERS  NH 1929                     75

Pound, Ezra (Loomis)  A LUME SPENTO (Venice Italy) 1908
                        wraps (150 cc)                      20,000
                PERSONEA  L 1909 (1000 cc) (3rd bk)           300
```

170

```
Powell, Adam Clayton, Jr.  MARCHING BLACKS  NY 1945          40

Powell, Anthony (Dymoke)  AFTERNOON MEN  L 1931             750
                               NY (1932)                   350

Powell, Lawrence Clark AN INTRODUCTION TO ROBINSON JEFFERS
                1932 (225 cc - 85 for presentation)        300
                ROBINSON JEFFERS THE MAN AND HIS
                          WORKS  La 1934 (750 cc)          200

Powell, Padgett  EDISTO  NY (1984)                          20

Powers, J(ames) F(arl)  PRINCE OF DARKNESS  GC 1947         75
                                      L 1948                60

Powys, John Cowper  CORINTH  (O 1891) - cover states
                "English Verse"     Powys' name
                appears at the end of text    wr           750
                ODES +  L 1896                             600

Powys, Llewelyn  CONFESSIONS OF TWO BROTHERS  Rochester
                         1916  (with J. C. Powys)           50
                THIRTEEN WORTHIES  L 1923                  125

Powys, Philippa  DRIFTWOOD  L 1930                         125

Powys, T(heodore) F(rancis)  AN INTERPRETATION OF GENESIS
                          L 1907 (100 cc)                  400
                THE SOLILOQUY OF A HERMIT  NY 1916          60
                SOLILOQUIES OF A HERMIT  L 1918
                i -light blue bds                           40
                ii -dark blue bds                           35

Prather, Richard S(cott)  CASE OF THE VANISHING BEAUTY
                          NY (1950) wraps                   20

Pratt, E.J.  RACHEL: A SEA-STORY OF NEWFOUNDLAND  NY 1917
                                      wraps             3,000

Pratt, Fletcher  THE HEROIC YEARS... 1801 - 1815  NY 1934   60

PRECAUTION: A NOVEL (James Fenimore Cooper)  NY 1920
                2 vols  i -errata slip                  2,000

Prewett, Frank  POEMS  Richmond (Eng) (1921) wraps         60

Price, Emerson  INN OF THAT JOURNEY  Caldwell 1939          40

Price, (Edward) Reynolds ONE SUNDAY IN LATE JULY (priv pr)
                          1960 (50 cc) wraps            2,500
                A LONG AND HAPPY LIFE  NY 1962
                i -dw blurbs in light green               100
                          L 1962                           75

Price, Richard  THE WANDERERS  B 1974                      35
                          L 1975                           35

Priestly, J(ohn) B(oynton)  THE CHAPMAN OF RHYMES  L 1918
                                      wraps               400

Prime, William Cowper  see THE OWL CREEK LETTERS...

PRIMULA... (Richard Garnett)  L 1858                       200

Prince, F(rank) T(empleton)  POEMS  L (1938)               75
                          (N1941)                          60

Pringle, Elizabeth Waties Allston  see Patience Pennington
```

Don't Call Me By My Right Name

AND OTHER STORIES

by James Purdy

WITH ILLUSTRATIONS BY THE AUTHOR

THE WILLIAM-FREDERICK PRESS

NEW YORK   1956

```
Pritchett, V(ictor) S(awdon)  MARCHING SPAIN  L 1928 cloth      250
                              wraps (Left Book Club)             75

Prokosch, Frederick  THREE MYSTERIES  NH 1932                   250
                     THE ASIATICS  NY 1935
                     (1st novel, 10th bk)                       75
                                       L 1935                   75

Prose, Francine  JUDAH THE PIOUS  NY 1973                        30

PROTEUS, SONNETS AND SONGS (Wilfred Scawen Blunt)  L 1875       200

Purdy, Al  THE ENCHANTED ECHO  Vancouver 1944                  600

Purdy, James  DON'T CALL ME BY MY RIGHT NAME +  NY 1956 wr
              noted in both gray and white (variant)           125

Putnam, Howard Phelps  TRINC  NY (1927)                         75

Putnam, Samuel  EVAPORATION...Winchester 1923 (with Mark
                                            Turbyfill)         100
                FRANCOIS RABELAIS...  NY (1929)                 50

Puzo, Mario  THE DARK ARENA  NY (1955)                          60

Pyle, Howard  YANKEE DOODLE  NY 1881  1st illus                500
              THE MERRY ADVENTURES OF ROBIN HOOD  NY 1883      400
                                                   L 1883      300

Pym, Barbara  SOME TAME GAZELLE  L 1950                        125

Pynchon, Thomas  V  Ph (1963)                                  350
                    L (1963)                                   200

Q (Sir Arthur Quiller-Couch)  DEAD MAN'S ROCK  L 1887         250

Queen, Ellery (Frederic Dannay & Manfred B. Lee)
              ROMAN HAT MYSTERY  NY 1929                     1,000

Quennell, Peter  MASQUES AND POEMS  Berkshire (1922)          125

Quiller-Couch, Sir Arthur  see Q

Quinn, Arthur Hobson  PENNSYLVANIA STORIES  Ph 1899            75

Quinn, Seabury (Grandin)  ROADS  1938  wraps (reprinted
                                  from Weird Tales)            150
                                         SC 1948               75

R.,C.G. (Christina G. Rossetti)  VERSES  L 1847             4,000

Radcliffe, Ann (Ward)  THE MYSTERIES OF UDOLPHO  L 1794
                                         (4 vols)             500

Rago, Henry  THE PHILOSOPHY OF ESTHETIC INDIVIDUALISM
                          Notre Dame  1941  wraps              75

Raine, Kathleen (Jessie)  STONE AND FLOWER, POEMS
                                         L (1943)              90

Raine, William MacLeod  A DAUGHTER OF RAASAY  NY (1902)       150

Rakosi, Carl  TWO POEMS  (NY 1932)  wr                        150

Ramal, Walter (Walter De La Mare)  SONGS OF CHILDHOOD
                                         L 1902              400
```

```
Rand, Ayn   WE THE LIVING   L (1936)                          1,000
                             NY 1936                             750
            NIGHT OF JANUARY 16TH   NY (1936)   wraps            250

Randall, Julia   THE SOLSTICE TREE   BA 1952                     50

Randall, Robert (Randall Garrett and Robert Silverberg)
            THE SHROUDED PLANET   NY 1957                        35

Random House   CANDIDE   NY 1928 (ltd to 1470 cc sgd by
                             Rockwell Kent)                     150

Ransom, Arthur   THE SOULS OF THE STREET +   L 1904             60

Ransom, John Crowe   POEMS ABOUT GOD   NY 1919                 500

Ransom Press (Will)   OPEN SHUTTERS (Oliver Jenkins)
                             Ch 1922 (245 cc)                   150

Raphael, Frederic   OBBLIGATO   L 1956                          50

Rattigan, Terrence (Mervyn)   FRENCH WITHOUT TEARS   L 1937     75

Rattray, Simon   see Mansell Black

Raven, Simon   THE FEATHERS OF DEATH   L 1959                   50

Rawlings, Marjorie Kinnan   SOUTH MOON UNDER    NY 1933        150

Raworth, Tom   THE RELATION SHIP   (L 1966) 50 sgd no. cc   wr   50
                                          450 cc.   wr          30

Rawson, Clayton   DEATH FROM A TOP HAT   NY 1938              250

Reach, Angus B(ethune)   CLEMENT LORIMER... L(1849)           400

Read, Herbert   SONGS OF CHAOS   L (1915)                     200
                NAKED WARRIORS   L 1919 (1st commercial)       100

Read, Piers Paul   GAME IN HEAVEN WITH TUSSY MARX   L 1966     50
                                          NY 1966              25

Read, Thomas Buchanan   PAUL REDDING...   B 1845             125

Reade, Charles   PEG WOFFINGTON   L 1853                      100

Reaney, James   THE RED HEART   T 1949                        300

Reavey, George   FAUST'S METAMORPHOSES...   Seine (1932) wr   100

Rechy, John   CITY OF THE NIGHT   NY (1963)                    30

Reddings, J(ay) Saunders   NO DAY OF TRIUMPH   NY (1942)       50

Redgrove, Peter (William)   THE COLLECTOR +   L 1960           40

Redman, Ben Ray   MASQUERADE   NY 1923                        25

Reed, Henry   A MAP OF VERONA +   L (1946)                    75

Reed, Ishmael   THE FREELANCE PALLBEARERS   GC 1967            60

Reed, John Silas   SANGAR, TO LINCOLN STEFFENS   Riverside,
                             CT 1913   wraps   (500 cc boxed)  100
                THE DAY IN BOHEMIA   NY 1913 stiff wr
```

174

```
                500 cc boxed (priority uncertain)        100

Reed, Kit   MOTHER ISN'T DEAD SHE'S ONLY SLEEPING  B 1961     35

Reese, Lizette Woodworth  A BRANCH OF MAY  BA 1887        250

Reeve, Arthur B(enjamin)  THE SILENT BULLET  NY 1912      100
                          THE BLACK HAND  L 1912           100

Reeves, James  THE NATURAL NEED  Oeya/L (1935)           125

Reeves, Robert  DEAD AND DONE FOR  NY 1939                35

Reid, Alastair  TO LIGHTEN MY HOUSE  Scarsdale (1953)     40
                (prev priv. printed pamphlet)

Reid, Desmond (Michael Moorcock and Jim Cawthorn)
                CARIBBEAN CRISIS  L (1962) wraps           75

Reid, Forrest  THE KINGDOM OF TWILIGHT  L 1904           125

Reid, (Thomas) Mayne  THE WHITE CHIEF... L 1855  3 vols   500

Reid, Victor S.  NEW DAY  NY 1949                         75

Reiser, Anton  ALBERT EINSTEIN: A BIOGRAPHICAL PORTRAIT  NY
               1931 (trans anonymously by Louis Zukofsky)  600
                                            L (1931)       400

Remarque, Erich Maria  ALL QUIET ON THE WESTERN FRONT
                                  L (1929)                125
                                  B 1929                   75

Remington, Frederick (Sack Rider)  PONY TRACKS  NY 1895
                                        suede           1,000
                                        cloth             250

Renault, Mary (Mary Challans)  PURPOSES OF LOVE  L 1939   125
                  PROMISE OF LOVE  NY 1940 (new title)     75

Renek, Morris  THE BIG HELLO  NY 1961                     30

Repplier, Agnes  BOOKS AND MEN  B 1888                    50

Rexroth, Kenneth  IN WHAT HOUR  NY 1940                  200

Reynolds, Tim  RYOANJI  NY 1964                           35
               (preceded by a self-published item)

Reznikoff, Charles  RHYTHMS  Brooklyn (priv. printed 1918)
                                          wraps  1,000

Rhode, John (Major Cecil John Charles Street)  A,S.F.
          THE STORY OF A GREAT CONSPIRACY  L (1924)      150
          THE WHITE MENACE  NY (1926) new title          100

Rhodes, Eugene Manlove  GOOD MEN AND TRUE  NY 1910       100

Rhodes, W(illiam) H(enry)  CAXTON'S BOOK  SF 1876        250

Rhys, Ernest  A LONDON ROSE +  L 1894                     75

Rhys, Jean  LEFT BANK +  NY (1927)                       400

RHYMES OF IRONQUILL (Eugene Fitch Ware)  Topeka 1885      75

Rice, Alice (Caldwell) Hegen  MRS. WIGGS OF THE CABBAGE
                                PATCH  NY 1901            40
```

PONY
TRACKS

WRITTEN AND
ILLUSTRATED BY

FREDERIC REMINGTON

NEW YORK

HARPER & BROTHERS PUBLISHERS

FRANKLIN SQUARE

1895

```
Rice, Anne  INTERVIEW WITH THE VAMPIRE  NY 1976          50

Rice, Craig (Georgiana Ann Randolph) 8 FACES AT 3 NY 1939  150

Rich, Adrienne Cecile  ARIADNE: A PLAY IN THREE ACTS
                              (BA) 1939 wraps      2,000
                        NOT I, BUT DEATH  BA 1941 wraps    1,500
                        A CHANGE OF WORLD  NY 1951            350

Richards, I. A.  THE FOUNDATION OF AESTHETICS  L (1922)
                        with C.K. Ogden and James Wood       100
                 THE MEANING OF MEANING  NY 1923 with
                                       C. K. Ogden           100
                 PRINCIPLES OF LITERARY CRITICISM  NY 1924   100
                                             L 1925           75

Richardson, Dorothy  POINTED ROOFS  L 1915               150

Richler, Mordecai  THE ACROBATS  T 1954                 250
                                 L 1954                  200
                                 NY 1954                 100

Richter, Conrad  BROTHERS OF NO KIN +  NY (1924) white dw  500
                                             orange dw       300

Rickword, Edgell  BEHIND THE EYES  L 1921                 30

Ridge, Lola  THE GHETTO +  NY 1918                        40

Riding, Laura  see Laura Riding Gottschalk

Ridler, Anne (Barbara)  SHAKESPEARE CRITICISM, 1919-1935
                                    by Ridler)  L 1936     60
                        POEMS  L 1939 (most destroyed in
                                            blitz)         100

Riley, James Whitcomb  see Benj. F. Johnson

Rinehart, Mary Roberts  THE CIRCULAR STAIRCASE  I (1908)
                                    (Sept copyright)       75

RIP VAN WINKLE (W. Irving)  Roycrofters' (East Aurora 1905)
                        initials and title page by  Dard Hunter
                               (his first book contribution)  100

Rives, Amelia  A BROTHER TO DRAGONS  NY 1888              75

Roark, Garland  WAKE OF THE RED WITCH  B 1946             30


Robbins, Harold (Harold Ruben) NEVER LOVE A STRANGER
                                        NY 1948            30

Robbins,  Tom  ANOTHER ROADSIDE ATTRACTION  GC 1971      150

Roberts, B(righam) H(enry)  THE LIFE OF JOHN TAYLOR
                                    Salt Lake 1892        150

Roberts, Elilzabeth Madox  IN THE GREAT STEEP'S GARDEN
                        (Colo Springs 1915)  wraps      3,500
                        UNDER THE TREE  NY 1922            150

Roberts, Kenneth L(ewis)  PANATELA... (Ithaca) 1907 (song
                        book) wraps (with R. Berry)       300
                        EUROPE'S MORNING AFTER
                                    NY (1921)              200

Roberts, Morley  THE WESTERN AVERNUS...  L 1887          150
```

Robertson, E. (Earle Birney) CONVERSATIONS WITH TROTSKY
                                          L 1936   1,500

Robeson, Paul HERE I STAND NY (1958) wraps   100

Robinson, Edwin Arlington THE TORRENT AND THE NIGHT BEFORE
                                     C 1896 wraps 2,000
                        THE CHILDREN OF THE NIGHT B 1897
                                     50 cc vellum 1,500
                                  500 cc lain/paper   400

Robinson, Marilynne HOUSEKEEPING NY 1980   20

Robinson, Rowland Evans see AWAHSOOSE, THE BEAR
                        UNCLE 'LISHA'S SHOP   NY 1887   50

Robison, Mary DAYS NY 1979   25

Rodd (James) Rennell SONGS TO THE SOUTH L 1881
             (prev 1880 Newdigate prize poem)   125

Rodgers, W. R. AWAKE + L 1941   40

Roditi, Edouard (Herbert) POEMS FOR F P (1935) wraps 175

Rodker, John POEMS L (1914) boards 50 sgd no. cc   600
                                              wraps   150

Rodman, Seldon MORTAL TRIUMPH + NY (1932)   60

Roe, Edward Payson BARRIERS BURNED AWAY NY 1872   50

Roethke, Theodore OPEN HOUSE NY 1941 (1000 cc)   600

Rogers, Will(iam Penn Adair) THE COWBOY PHILOSOPHER ON
                         PROHIBITION NY (1919)   50

Rogin, Gilbert THE FENCING MASTER + NY 1965   25

Rohmer, Sax (Arthur Henry Sarsfield Ward) PAUSE! L 1910   200
         DR. FU-MANCHU L (1913)   250
         THE INSIDIOUS DR. FU-MANCHU NY 1913
                              (new title)   75

Rolfe, Edwin TO MY CONTEMPORARIES NY 1936 1000 no. cc   40

Rolfe, Frederick William see Baron Corvo

Rolvaag, O. E. GIANTS IN THE EARTH NY 1927   100

Rook, Alan SONGS FROM A CHERRY TREE O 1938 wraps   50

Rooke, Leon LAST ONE HOME SLEEPS IN THE YELLOW BED
                         Baton Rouge (1968)   25

Rooney, Andy AIR GUNNER NY (1944) with Bud Hutton   40

Roosevelt, Eleanor IT'S UP TO THE WOMEN NY 1933   75

Roosevelt, Franklin D. WHITHER BOUND? B 1926   200

Roosevelt, Theodore THE SUMMER BIRDS OF THE ADIRONDACKS
                    (Salem 1877) wr (with H.D. Minot)   400
                    THE NAVAL WAR OF 1812... NY 1882   200

Root, E. Merrill LOST EDEN NY 1927   50

Ros, Amanda M'Kitrrick IRENE IDDESLEIGH Belfast 1897 75

GOODBYE,

COLUMBUS

AND FIVE SHORT STORIES

BY PHILIP ROTH

1959

HOUGHTON MIFFLIN COMPANY BOSTON

The Riverside Press Cambridge

Poems

Karl Jay Shapiro

*Two hundred copies of this
book have been printed, of
which this is No. 188...*

Karl Jay Shapiro

Baltimore, Maryland
1935

```
Rosenbach, A.S.W.  SAMUEL JOHNSON'S PROLOGUE... NY 1902
                                      (100 cc)        350
                THE UNPUBLISHABLE MEMOIRS  NY 1917
                            (1st regularly publ)      35

Rosenberg, Isaac  NIGHT AND DAY  (L 1912) wraps      6,000
                  YOUTH  L 1915  wraps                 600

Rosenfeld, Isaac  PASSAGE FROM HOME  NY (1946)         60

Ross, Alan  THE DERELICT DAY  L 1947                   60

Rossetti, Christina  see C.G.R.
                GOBLIN MARKET  L 1862 (16 page
                              catalog at rear)        400

Rossetti, Dante  SIR HUGO THE HERON  L 1843         1,500

Rossetti, William Michael  SWINBURNE'S POEMS & BALLADS
                                        L 1886         75

Rossner, Judith  WHAT KIND OF FEET DOES A BEAR HAVE?
                                   Ind 1963            75
                TO THE PRECIPICE  NY (1966)            50

Rosten, Norman  RETURN AGAIN, TRAVELLER  NH 1940      40

Roth, Henry  CALL IT SLEEP  NY 1934                 1,500
                             L 1963                    50

Roth, Philip (Milton)  GOODBYE, COLUMBUS +  B 1959   175
                       L 1959 (title story only)     100

Roth, Samuel  FIRST OFFERING  NY 1917 (500 cc)        50

Rothenberg, Jerome  see David Antin entry
                NEW YOUNG GERMAN POETS  SF 1959 wraps
                                   (edited/trans)      35
                WHITE SUN BLACK SUN  (NY 1960)  wraps  60

Rowan, Carl T.  SOUTH OF FREEDOM  NY 1952             40

Royall, Ann (Newport)  see SKETCHES OF HISTORY...

Royde-Smith, Naomi  UNA AND THE RED CROSS...  L 1905  60

Ruark, Robert  GRENADINE ETCHING  NY 1947            60

Rubens, Bernice  SET ON EDGE  L 1960                 40

Rukeyser, Muriel  THEORY OF FLIGHT  NY 1935         250

Rule, Jane  THE DESERT OF THE HEART  T 1964          60

Rumaker, Michael  EXIT 3 +  NY 1958                  40

Runyon, Damon  THE TENTS OF TROUBLE  NY (1911) flex cover  75

Rushdie, Salman  GRIMUS  L 1975                     100
                         NY (1979)                   35

Ruskin, John  SALSETTE AND ELEPHANTA...  O 1839 wraps  600

Russell, Bertrand  GERMAN SOCIAL DEMOCRACY  L 1896  1,500

Russell, Charles (Marion)  STUDIES OF WESTERN LIFE
                        Cascade Montana (1890)      4,500
```

```
                           NY 1890  i -no text on "War"        2,000
                                    ii -text on "War"          1,750

Russell, Eric Frank  SINISTER BARRIER  Surrey (1943)            200
                     Reading 1948  (500 sgd no. cc)             125
                                    trade edition                50

Russell, George  see A.E.

Russell, Peter see Russell Irwin

Russell, Saunders  THE CHEMICAL IMAGE (SF 1947) wraps           50

Russell, William  see Waters

Russell, William Clark  FRA ANGELO  L 1865 wraps             2,500
                        THE HUNCHBACK'S CHARGE  L 1867  3 vols  2,000

Rutledge, Archibald   UNDER THE PINES + n-pl 1906               75

Ryan, Abram Joseph  FATHER RYAN'S POEMS  Mobile 1879           125
                                         BA 1880                75

Ryan, Don  ANGEL'S FLIGHT  NY 1927                             75

Ryan, Richard  LEDGES  (O 1970) wraps                         30

S., E.W. & S.W.M. (E.W. Sherman & S. Weir Mitchell)
                THE CHILDREN'S HOUR  PH 1864                   300

S., I. (Isidor Schneider)  DOCTOR TRANSIT  NY 1925            125

S., S.H. (Stephen Spender)  NINE EXPERIMENTS  O 1928         6,000

Sabatini, Rafael  THE TAVERN KNIGHT  L 1914                    60

Sackler, Howard  WANT MY SHEPHERD: POEMS  NY 1954             40
                 THE GREAT WHITE HOPE  NY 1968                40

Sackville-West, Edward  PIANO QUINTET  L 1925                  75

Sackville-West, V(ictoria Mary)  CHATTERTON  Seven Oaks
                                    1909  wraps               3,500
                                 CONSTANTINOPLE  L 1915
                                            wraps             450

Sadler, Michael (Thomas Harvey)  HYSSOP  L (1915)             60

Saint-Exupery, Antoine de  NIGHT FLIGHT  P 1932 wraps          75
                                          NY (1932)            50

Saki, (Hector H. Munro)  see H. H. Munro
                THE WESTMINSTER ALICE  L 1902
                                 pictorial cloth              200
                                          wraps               75

Salamanca, J. R.  THE LOST COUNTRY  NY 1958                   50

Salas, Floyd  TATTOO THE WICKED CROSS  NY (1967)             20

Salinger, J(erome) D(avid)  THE CATCHER IN THE RYE
                                 NY (1951)                    500
                                 L 1951                       200

Sallans, G. Herbert  LITTLE MAN  T (1942)                    50

SALMAGUNDI... see Launcelot Langstaff
```

Modern Masterpieces in English

Night-Flight

by

Antoine de Saint-Exupéry

Translated by Stuart Gilbert

Crosby Continental Editions
Paris

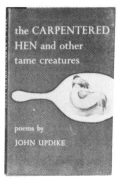

```
Salt, Sydney  THIRTY PIECES  M 1934 (500 no. cc)
              i -back panel of dw w/o reviews          75

Salter, James  THE HUNTERS  NY (1956)                 50

Saltus, Edgar Evertson  BALZAC  B 1884                50

Sanborn, Franklin Benjamin  EMANCIPATION IN THE WEST INDIES
                            Concord 1862  wraps       150
                            (2 prev broadsides)

Sanborn, Pitts  VIE DE BORDEAUX  Ph 1916 boards       40

Sanchez, Thomas  RABBIT BOSS  NY 1973                 25

Sandburg, Carl (Charles August)  IN RECKLESS ECSTASY
                            Galesburg 1904          6,000
              INCIDENTALS  Gales (1907) wraps       2,500
              CHICAGO POEMS  NY 1916 i -ads dated 3/16 150

Sanders, Ed  POEM FROM JAIL  (SF 1963) wraps          50

Sanders, Lawrence  THE ANDERSON TAPES  NY (1970)      40

Sandoz, Mari  OLD JULES  B 1935                       60

Sandoz, Paul  LEGEND  Geneva 1925 wraps               50

Sandy, Stephen  CAROMS  Groton MA 1960  wraps (70 cc) 60

Sanford, John  see Julian L. Shapiro
              THE OLD MAN'S PLACE  NY 1935  25 sgd no. cc 125
                                             unsigned   75

Sansom, Clive  THE UNFAILING SPRING  L 1943           35
```

```
Sansom, William  FIREMAN FLOWER  L 1944                           125
                 (previous collaboration)

Santayana, George  see LINES ON LEAVING...
                   SONNETS AND OTHER VERSES   C/Ch  1894
                                        60 no. 1pc          400
                                      trade  (450 cc)       100

Santee, Ross  MEN AND HORSES  NY (1926)                           150

Saroyan, Aram  POEMS  NY 1963 (with J. Caldwell and
                                      R. Kolmer)             25
              IN   Eugene, Oregon  1964                      25

Saroyan, William  THE DARING YOUNG MAN...  NY 1934               150

Sarton, May  ENCOUNTER IN APRIL  B 1937                          200

Sassoon, Siegried  see POEMS
                   Also see Saul Kain

Savage, Thomas  THE PASS  GC 1944                                 40

Savoy, Willard  ALIEN LAND  NY 1944                               50

Saxe, John Godfrey  PROGRESS: A SATIRICAL POEM  NY 1846 bds      100

Sayers, Dorothy  OP. 1  Oxford 1916 wraps (350 cc)              500
                 WHOSE BODY?  NY (1923) i -w/o "Inc."
                        after Boni & Liveright on title       1,500
                                      L (1923)                1,000

Sayles, John  PRIDE OF THE BIMBOS  B 1975                         50

Scarfe, Francis  INSCAPES  L (1940)                               40

Schaefer, Jack  SHANE  B 1949                                    250
                       L 1963                                     40

Schevill, James  TENSIONS  (Berkeley 1947)                        60

Schiff, Sydney  CONCESSIONS  L 1913                               50

Schlesinger, Arthur M., Jr.  ORESTES A. BROWNSON  B 1939          40

Schneider, Isidor  see I.S.

Schoolcraft, Henry Rowe  A VIEW OF THE LEAD MINES...
                                       NY 1819               400

Schoonover, Lawrence  THE BURNISHED BLADE  NY 1948                35

Schorer, Mark  A HOUSE TOO OLD  NY (1935)                         75

Schreiner, Olive  see Ralph Iron

Schulberg, Budd  WHAT MAKES SAMMY RUN  NY (1941)                 200

Schuyler, James (Marcus)  ALFRED AND GUINEVERE  NY 1958           50
                 SALUTE  NY (1960) folio (prints by Grace
                        Hartigan) 225 sgd no. cc   glassine dw   400

Schwartz, Delmore  IN DREAMS BEGIN RESPONSIBILITIES
                                       N (1938)              200

Schwartz, Lynne Sharon  ROUGH STRIFE  NY  1980                    20

Scott, Alexander  THE LATEST IN ELEGIES  Glasgow 1949
                                       300 no. cc            60
```

```
Scott, Duncan Campbell  THE MAGIC HOUSE+  L 1893           125

Scott, Evelyn  PRECIPITATIONS  NY 1920                     100

Scott, Michael  see TOM CRINGLE'S LOG

Scott, Paul  JOHNNIE SAHIB  L 1952                         200

Scott, Winfield Townley  ELEGY FOR ROBINSON  NY (1936)
                             (100 cc) wraps                175

Screen, Robert Martin  WE CAN'T RUN AWAY FROM HERE
                                      NY (1958)             25

Scully, James  THE MARCHES  NY 1967                         25
               (edited 2 prev books 1965/66)

Seabrook, William  see DIARY OF SECTION...

Seale, Bobby  SEIZE THE TIME  NY (1970)                     30

Searle, Ronald  CO-OPERATION IN A UNIVERSITY TOWN  L (1939)
                   Searle's first illus, bk by W. Henry Brown  100
                   FORTY DRAWINGS  Cambridge 1946           200

Seaver, Edwin  THE COMPANY  NY 1930                         40

Seeger, Alan  POEMS  NY 1916                                60
                     L 1917                                 40

Segal, Erich  THE BRAGGART SOLDIER...  NY (1963) wraps
                      (translation of play by Plautus)      30
                   ROMAN LAUGHTER  C 1968                   50

Seitz, Don C(arlin)  SURFACE JAPAN  L 1911                  60

Seizen Press  LOVE AS LOVE, DEATH AS DEATH by Laura Riding
                                      L 1928               400

Selby, Hubert  LAST EXIT TO BROOKLYN  NY (1964)             35
                                      L 1966                35

Seltzer, Charles Alden  THE COUNCIL OF THREE  NY 1900       60

Sendak, Maurice  ATOMICS FOR THE MILLIONS  NY (1947) by
                   Eidinoff & Ruchlis (1st bk illus by MS)
                   (statement on paper quality on c p
                         omitted in later printings)       250

SENSE AND SENSIBILITY  (Jane Austen)  L 1811  3 vols bds
          i  -ruled lines on half title in vol 1, 4/5"  12,000
          ii -lines 1-1/7"                               3,000

Serling, Rod  PATTERNS  NY 1957                             40

Service, Robert  SONG OF A SOURDOUGH  T 1907 "Author's
                             Edition" on title page        600

Serviss, Garrett P(utnam)  THE MOON METAL  NY 1900          75

Seton, Anya  MY THEODOSIA  B 1941                           50

Seton, Ernest Thompson  A LIST OF THE MAMMELS OF MANITOBA
                             T (1886) wraps             1,500
                          STUDIES IN THE ART OF ANATOMY OF
                                 ANIMALS  L 1896          300

Settle, MaryLee  THE LOVEEATERS  L (1954)                  200
                          NY (1954) (first not stated)    100
```

Seuss, Dr. (Theodore Geisel) AND TO THINK THAT I SAW IT
          ON MULBERRY STREET NY 1937 pictorial bds, dw
                              (1st children's book)   250

Sewell, A(nna) BLACK BEAUTY... L 1877 wraps
          i -red, green or blue pictorial cloth,
            horse's head in gilt looking right
            (see Carter's More Binding Variants
            for more detail)   1,200
                              B 1890   300

Sexton, Anne TO BEDLAM AND PART WAY BACK B 1960   100

Shaara, Michael THE BROKEN PLACE NY (1968)   60

Shaffer, Peter see Peter Anthony

Shange, Ntozake FOR COLORED GIRLS WHO HAVE CONSIDERED
            SUICIDE... (San Lorenzo 1976) wraps
          i -name spelled Ntosake; $.95 cvr price   125
                              NY (1977)   35

Shanks, Edward SONGS L 1915 wraps   100

Shannon, Dell (Barbara Elizabeth Livington) CASE PENDING
                                        NY 1960   50

Shapiro, David JANUARY NY (1965) First reg publ book   35
          (preceded by three privately pr books)

Shapiro, Harvey THE EYE Denver (1953)   35

Shapiro, Julian L. (John Sanford) THE WATER WHEEL Ithaca
                                              (1933)   350

Shapiro, Karl (Jay) POEMS BA 1935 (200 sgd no. cc)   900
                     PERSON PLACE AND THING (NY 1942)   75

Sharp, Luke (Robert Barr) FROM WHOSE BOURNE? L 1893   75

Sharp, William see Fiona MacLeod

Shattuck, Roger THE BANQUET YEARS... NY (1958)   40

Shaw, George Bernawd CASHEL BYRON'S PROFESSION (L) 1886
                          wraps (2 prev pamphlets)   500

Shaw, Irwin BURY THE DEAD NY (1936)   100

Shaw, Robert THE HIDING PLACE L (1959)   50
                              CL/NY (1959)   35

Sheckley, Robert E. UNTOUCHED BY HUMAN HANDS NY (1954)
                                            cloth   75
                                            wraps   15

Sheed, Wilfred JOSEPH NY (1958)   60

Shelley, Mary Wollstonecraft see HISTORY OF A SIX...
                    also see FRANKENSTEIN

Shepard, Odell A LONELY FLUTE B 1917 boards   50

Shepard, Sam FIVE PLAYS I (1967)   90
                         L (1969)   60

Sheppard, Elizabeth Sara see CHARLES AUCHESTER

Sheridan, Richard Brinsley see THE LOVE EPISTLES...

Sherwin, Judith Johnson URANIUM POEMS NH 1969   20

Sherwood, Robert E(mmet) THE ROAD TO ROME NY 1927   50

Shiel, M.P. PRINCE ZALESKI L 1895 (16 pg catalog at rear)   200

Shippey, Lee WHERE NOTHING EVER HAPPENS B 1935   75

Shorthouse, J. Henry JOHN INGLESANT Birmingham (Eng) 1880
                                        1 vol or 3 vols   300

Shulman, Irving THE AMBOY DUKES NY 1947   50

Shute, Nevil (Norway) MARAZAN L 1926   300

Sidney, Margaret (Harriet Mulford Stone Lothrop)
              FIVE LITTLE PEPPERS AND HOW THEY GREW
                                        B (1880)
              i -caption p.231 reads "said Polly"   350

Sigal, Clancy WEEKEND IN DINLOCK B 1960   40
                                   L 1960   35

Sigourney, Lydia Huntley see Lydia Huntley

Silkin, Jon THE PORTRAIT + Ilfracombe (1950) wraps   150
             THE PEACEABLE KINGDOM L 1954   60

Sill, Edward Rowland see POEM AND VALEDICTORY ORATION...
                      THE HERITAGE + NY 1868   125

Sillitoe, Alan WITHOUT BEER OR BREAD Dulwich Village 1957
                                               wraps   350
                SATURDAY NIGHT AND SUNDAY MORNING L 1958 100

Siluriensis, Leolinus (Arthur Machen) THE ANATOMY OF
                      TOBACCO L (1884) 2nd book   200

Silverberg, Robert REVOLT ON ALPHA C NY (1955)   60

Silverstein, Shel TAKE TEN (Tokyo) 1955   60

Simak, Clifford THE CREATOR (LA 1946) wraps   50

Simenon, Georges THE CRIME OF INSPECTOR MAIGRET NY 1932 100
                  THE DEATH OF MONSIEUR GALLET NY 1932   100

Simic, Charles WHAT THE GRASS SAYS Santa Cruz (1967)
                               wraps (1000 cc)   60

Simms, William Gilmore LYRICAL + Charlestown 1827   500

Simon, (Marvin) Neil HEIDI NY 1959 wraps (with Wm.
                                        Friedburg)   75
                  COME BLOW YOUR HORN NY 1963
                               (with Danny Simon)   60

Simon, Roger LICHTENBERG HEIR NY (1968)   25

Simpson, Helen LIGHTNING SKETCHES B 1918 wraps   50

Simpson, Louis (Aston Marantz) THE ARRIVISTES NY (1949)
                               wraps (500 cc)   200
                                        P (1950)   175

Simmons, Charles POWDERED EGGS NY 1964   25

Simmons, Herbert CORNER BOY B 1957   25

Sims, George R(obert) THE TERRIBLE DOOR L (1964)   75

Sinclair, Andrew THE BREAKING OF BUMBO NY 1959   40
                                          L 1959   35

Sinclair, Clive BIBLIOSEXUALITY L 1973   35

Sinclair, Upton SAVED BY THE ENEMY NY 1898   150

Singer, Burns (James Hyman) THE GENTLE ENGINEER Rome 1952   40

Singer, Isaac Bashevis THE FAMILY MUSKAT NY 1950
                               (1st trans in Eng)   100

Singer, I. J. THE SINNER NY 1936 (1st trans in Eng)   125

Sinjohn, John (John Galsworthy) FROM THE FOUR WINDS
                            L (1897) (500 cc)   500

SIR JOHN CHIVERTON (Wm. H. Ainsworth and John P. Aston)
                                          L 1826   250

Siringo, Charles Angelo A TEXAS COWBOY... CH 1885   7,500

Sisson, C(harles) H(ubert) AN ASIATIC ROMANCE L 1953   40

Sissman, L. E. DYING: AN INTRODUCTION B (1967)   25

Sitwell, Edith THE MOTHER + O 1915 (500 cc, 200 pulped)
                                                 wraps   500

Sitwell, Osbert TWENTIETH CENTURY HARLIQUINADE + O 1916
                    (with Edith Sitwell) (500 cc) wraps   200
              THE WINSTONBURG LINE L 1919   pic wraps   150

Sitwell, Sacheverell THE PEOPLE'S PLACE O 1918 wr (400 cc)   150

SIX TO ONE: A NANTUCKET IDYL (Edward Bellamy) NY 1878
                                          cloth   300
                                          wraps   200

SIXTY YEARS OF THE LIFE OF JEREMY LEVIS (Laughton Osborn)
                                          NY 1831   100

SKETCHES BY "BOZ" (Charles Dickens) L 1836/7 3 vols
                    (2 vols -1836, 1 vol -1837)   3,500
                    L 1837-39 20 parts wraps   10,000

SKETCHES OF HISTORY, LIFE AND MANNERS...(Anne Royall)
                                          NH 1826   400

Skinner, M.L. BLACK SWAN L 1925   60
              (previous book with D.H. Lawrence)

SLAVE (THE); OR, THE MEMOIRS OF ARCHY MOORE (Richard
                    Hildreth) B 1836 2 vols   300

Slesinger, Tess THE UNPOSSESSED NY 1934   50

Smith, A. J. M. POETRY OF ROBERT BRIDGES Montreal n-d
                            (early 1930's) wraps   1,200
                    NEWS OF THE PHOENIX + T 1943   100

Smith, Adam THE THEORY OF MORAL SENTIMENTS L 1759   1,000

Smith, Alexander POEMS L 1853 i -ads dated Nov 1852   60

Smith, Clark Ashton THE STARTREADERS + SF 1912   125

Smith, Cordwainer (Paul Linebarger) see Felix Forrest

Smith, Edward E. THE SKYLARK OF SPACE (Buffalo Book Co.
                  Prov 1946) (with Mrs. Lee Hawkins Garby)   175
                                    Hadley Co. Prov (1947)   50

Smith, F(rancis) Hopkinson OLD LINES IN NEW BLACK B 1885   60

Smith, George O. VENUS EQUILATERAL Ph 1947   60

Smith, Johnston (Stephen Crane) MAGGIE A GIRL OF THE
                                 STREETS (NY 1893) wraps   7,500

Smith, Joseph, Jr. THE BOOK OF MORMON Palmyra NY 1830   5,000

Smith, Kate Douglas (Wiggin) THE STORY OF PATSY...
                                  SF 1883 wraps   500

Smith, Lee THE LAST DAY THE DOGBUSHES BLOOMED   NY 1968   100

Smith, Lillian STRANGE FRUIT NY 1944   35
                               L 1945   25

Smith, Logan Pearsall THE YOUTH OF PARNASSUS +   L 1895
                       blue & red cloth priority unknown   125

Smith, Mark TOYLAND B (1965)   40

Smith, Martin Cruz GYPSY IN AMBER NY (1971)   35

Smith, Robert Paul SO IT DOESN'T WHISTLE NY (1941)   40

Smith, Stevie (Florence Margaret Smith) NOVEL ON YELLOW
                                 PAPER L (1936)   300
                                         NY 1937   150

Smith, J. Thorne BILTMORE OSWALD NY (1918)   50

Smith, Wilbur WHEN THE LION FEEDS   L (1964)   60

Smith, William Gardner LAST OF THE CONQUERERS NY 1948   75

Smith, William Jay POEMS Banyon Press Pawlett, Vermont
                                 1947 500 no. cc   75

Smollett, Tobias THE ADVENTURES OF RODERICK RANDOM
                            L 1748 2 vols   750

Snelling, William J. see TALES OF THE NORTHWEST...

Snider, Denton Jacques CLARENCE St. Louis 1872 wraps   125

Snodgrass, W(illiam) D(ewitt) HEART'S NEEDLE NY 1959
                                         (1500 cc)   150
                                    Hessle (Eng) 1960   100

Snow, Charles Wilbert SONGS OF THE NEUKLUK Council,
                       Alaska 1913 with Ewen MacLennan   250

Snow, C(harles) P(ercy) DEATH UNDER SAIL L (1932)   300
                                          GC (1932)   125

Snyder, Gary (Sherman) RIPRAP (Ashland MA) 1959 wraps
                                          (500 cc)   300

Solano, Solita THE UNCERTAIN FEAST NY 1924   40

Solomon, Carl MISHAPS PERHAPS (SF 1966) wraps   20

Solzhenitsyn, Alexander ONE DAY IN THE LIFE OF IVAN
                         DENISOVICH L 1963 (1st Eng trans)   75
                                     NY 1963 cloth   50
                                             wraps   10

SOMEBODY see John Neal

Sommerfield, John THEY DIE YOUNG L 1930   50

Sommer, Scott NEARING'S GRACE NY 1979   25

Sontag, Susan THE BENEFACTOR NY (1963)   35

Sorrentino, Gilbert THE DARKNESS SURROUNDS US Highlands,
                                    NC 1960 wraps   40

Soto, Gary THE ELEMENTS OF SAN JOAQUIN (Pitts 1977)
               50 sgd no. cc in unprinted dw   50

Souster, (Holmes) Raymond WHEN WE WERE YOUNG Montreal
                                     1946 wraps   500

SOUTH-WEST (THE) (Joseph Holt Ingraham) NY 1835 2 vols   400

Southern, Terry FLASH & FILIGREE (L 1958)   100
                 NY (1958) (dw price $3.50) full cloth   50

Southey, Robert POEMS... (with Robert Lovell) Bath 1795   300
                                                 B 1799   150

Southworth, Emma Dorothy RETRIBUTION... NY 1849   100

Spackman, W. M. HEYDAY NY (1953) cloth   75
                         wraps   20

Spade, Mark (Nigel Balchin) HOW TO RUN A BASSOON FACTORY
                                     L 1934   50

Spark, Muriel (Sarah) TRIBUTE TO WORDSWORTH L (1950)
                          edited with Derek Stanford   75
                       CHILD OF LIGHT Essex (1951)   150
                       THE FANFARLO + Kent 1952 wraps
                       i -wraps printed in red   100

SPECIMENS (Joaquin Miller) (Canyon City, OR 1868) wraps
                           (preface sgd C. H. Miller)   3,000

Speicher, John LOOKING FOR BABY PARADISE NY (1967)   40

Spencer, Bernard AEGEAN ISLAND + L (1946)   30

Spencer, Claire GALLOW'S ORCHARD L (1930)   35
                                   NY (1930)   30

Spencer, Elizabeth FIRE IN THE MORNING NY 1948   200

Spencer, Herbert SOCIAL STATISTICS L 1851   150

Spencer, Scott LAST NIGHT AT THE BRAIN THIEVES BALL
                                     B 1973   40

Spencer, Theodore STUDIES IN METAPHYSICAL POETRY NY 1939
                            (with Mark Van Doren)   60
                THE PARADOX IN THE CIRCLE N (1941) wr   40

Spender, Stephen (Harold)   see S.H.S.
                            TWENTY POEMS O (1930) 75 sgd cc   750
                                           60 unsgd cc   400
                            POEMS L (1933)   175
                                   NY 1934   100

Speyer, Leonora HOLY NIGHT (by Hans Travsil) NY 1919
                 (paraphrased into English by LS)
                      (500 cc) (cover by Eric Gill)   75
                 A CANOPIC JAR NY (1921)   75

Spicer, Jack CORRELATION METHODS OF COMPARING IDOLECTS...
                    (offprint of "Language" 1952) wraps
                 (with David W. Reed) (less than 100 cc)   400
                 AFTER LORCA (SF 1957) wraps (26 sgd cc)   300
                                           (474 cc)   125

Spillane, Mickey (Frank Morrison Spillane) I, THE JURY
                                            NY 1947   200

Springs, Elliott White NOCTURNE MILITAIRE NY (1927)   200

Squires, James RADCLIFFE CORNAR Ph (1940) (in printed
                                             tissue dw)   50

Stacton, David AN UNFAMILIAR COUNTRY (Swinford 1953) wr   225

Stafford, Jean BOSTON ADVENTURE B (1944)   50

Stafford, William E(dgar) DOWN IN MY HEART Elgin, Il
                                               (1947)   850
                 WEST OF YOUR CITY Los Gatos
                                   1960 cloth/bds   500
                                        wraps   300

Standish, Robert THE THREE BAMBOOS L 1942   50

Stanford, Ann IN NARROW BOUND Denver (1943) wraps   125

Stanford, Donald E. NEW ENGLAND EARTH + SF (1941) wraps   125

Stanford, Theodore Anthony DARK HARVEST Ph (1936) no dw   35

Stapledon, W(illiam) Olaf LATTER-DAY PSALMS L 1914   150

Starbuck, George BONE THOUGHTS NH 1960   25

Stark, Freya BAGHDAD SKETCHES Baghdad 1932   150

Starrett, (Charles) Vincent (Emerson) ARTHUR MACHEN
                        Ch 1918 (250 sgd no. cc)   200

Stead, Christina (Ellen) THE SALZBURG TALES L (1934)   150
                                              NY 1934   100

Steadman, Ralph STILL LIFE WITH RASPBERRY...   L 1969
                 (50 sgd no. cc with original drawings)   200

Stedman, Edmund Clarence POEMS, LYRICAL AND IDYLLIC
                                          NY 1860   100

Stefansson, Vilhjalmur MY LIFE WITH THE ESKIMO NY 1913   175
                              L 1913 (U.S. sheets)   125

Steffens, (Joseph) Lincoln THE SHAME OF THE CITIES
                                          NY 1904   150

Stegner, Page ESCAPE INTO AESTHETICS... NY 1966   25

Stegner, Wallace (Earle) REMEMBERING LAUGHTER   B 1937   125

Steig, Henry SEND ME DOWN NY 1941   35

Steig, William ABOUT PEOPLE NY (1939)   40

Stein, Gertrude THREE LIVES NY 1909   (700 cc) issued
                                           without dw   900
                  L 1915 (300 cc from Amer. sheets)   200

Steinbeck, John (Ernst) CUP OF GOLD NY McBride 1929
                  i -top edge stained   3,500
                  ii -NY Covici Friede (1936)
                     remainder sheets -maroon cl   400
                                       -blue cl   125
                                       L (1937)   1,200

Steinem, Gloria THE BEACH BOOK NY 1963   40

Steiner, F(rancis) George POEMS (Fantasy Poets #8) O 1952   100

Stephanchev, Stephen THREE PRIESTS IN APRIL BA 1956   50

Stephens, Ann Sophie HIGH LIFE IN NEW YORK (NY 1843) wr   150

Stephens, James INSURRECTIONS D 1909   75

Sterling, George THE TESTIMONY OF THE SUNS + SF 1903   100

Stern, Richard G(ustave) GOLK NY (1960)   25

Stevens, Shane GO DOWN DEAD NY 1966   25

Stevens, Wallace HARMONIUM NY 1923
                  i -checkered bds (500 cc)   1,000
                  ii -striped bds   (215 cc)   500
                  iii -blue cl (715 cc)   400

Stevenson, Adlai E. MAJOR CAMPAIGN SPEECHES... NY 1953   75

Stevenson, Robert Louis see THE PENTLAND RISING
                  AN INLAND VOYAGE L 1878   400

Stewart, Donald Ogden A PARODY OUTLINE OF HISTORY NY 1921   35

Stewart, Fred Mustard THE MEPHISTO WALTZ NY (1960)   35

Stewart, Mary MADAM, WILL YOU TALK? L 1955   60

Still, James HOUNDS ON THE MOUNTAIN NY 1937 (750 cc)   150

Stockton, Frank R(ichard) TING-A-LING NY 1870   250
                  (previous pamphlet)

Stoddard, Charles Warren POEMS SF 1867 (750 cc)   100
                  SOUTH-SEA IDYLS B 1875   75

Stoddard, Richard Henry FOOTPRINTS NY 1849 wraps   1,500

Stoker, Bram ADDRESS... DINING HALL... TRINITY COLLEGE...
                                      D 1872 wraps   500
                  THE DUTIES OF CLERKS... D 1879 wraps   400
                  UNDER THE SUNSET L 1882   200

Stone, A. R. A BOOK OF LETTERING L 1935   60

Stone, I. F. (Isador Feinstein) THE COURT DISPOSES
                                      NY (1937)   75

THREE LIVES

STORIES OF THE GOOD ANNA, MELANCTHA AND THE GENTLE LENA

BY

GERTRUDE STEIN

THE GRAFTON PRESS

NEW YORK   MCMIX

Harmonium

by Wallace Stevens

New York Alfred · A · Knopf Mcmxxiii

```
Stone, Irving  PAGEANT OF YOUTH  NY 1933                    75

Stone, Robert  A HALL OF MIRRORS  B 1967                   150
                           L (1968)                         75

Stopes, Marie C(harlotte)  THE STUDY OF PLANT LIFE FOR
                           YOUNG PEOPLE  L 1906            100

Stoppard, Tom  LORD MALQUIST AND MR. MOON  L (1966)        125
                                           NY 1968          40

Storey, David (Malcolm)  THIS SPORTING LIFE  (L 1960)      125

Storm, Hans Otto  FULL MEASURE  NY 1929                     50

Story, Joseph  THE POWER OF SOLITUDE  B (1800)             200

Stout, Rex(Tod Hunter)  HOW LIKE A GOD  NY 1929           350

Stow, Randolph  A HAUNTED LAND  L 1956                      75

Stowe, Harriet (Elizabeth) Beecher  see Harriet Beecher

Strachey, Lytton  LANDMARKS IN FRENCH LITERATURE  L (1912)
                  i -top edge stained green (prev pamphlet)  150

Strachey, Mrs. Richard  NURSERY LYRICS  L 1893            200
                        (Reissued with new title pg and
                        binding - "LADY STRACHEY")        100

Strand, Mark  SLEEPING WITH ONE EYE OPEN  Iowa City 1963
                                          (225 cc)        300

STRATFORD-BY-THE-SEA (Alice Brown)  NY 1844                 75

Straub, Peter  ISHMAEL  L(1972) wraps 100 sgd no. cc in dw  200

Strauss, David Friedrich (George Eliot)  THE LIFE OF JESUS
                        L 1846  3 vols (translated by
                                Eliot (Evans)             750

Strauss, Theodore  NIGHT AT HOGWALLOW  B 1937              35

Strawberry Hill Press  ODES (Thomas Gray)  1757           600

Street, Cecil John Charles  see John Rhode

Street, George Edmund  BRICK AND MARBLE IN THE MIDDLE AGES
                                          L 1855          400

Street, James H.  LOOK AWAY  NY 1936                       50

Street, Julian (Leonard)  MY ENEMY THE MOTOR  NY 1908      40

Streeter, Edward  DERE MABLE: Love Letters of a Rookie
                  NY (1918) pictorial bds                  25

Stribling, T(homas) S(igismund)  CRUISE OF THE DRY DOCK
                                 Ch (1917) (250 copies
                                 published per Author)     75

Strong, Jonathan  TIKE +  B 1969                           25

Strong, L.A.G.  DALLINGTON RHYMES (200 cc priv pr 1919)   300
                DUBLIN DAYS  O 1921  wraps                  75

Stroud, Robert  DISEASES OF CANARIES  Kansas City 1933
                                (Birdman of Alcatraz)     125
```

by
Frank R. Stockton.

Illustrated by
E.B. Bensell.

New York:
Hurd and Houghton,
Riverside Press Cambridge,
1870

Struther, Jan (Joyce Maxtone Graham) BETSINDA DANCES +
O/L 1931 wraps   75

Stuart, H. (Francis Stuart) WE HAVE KEPT THE FAITH D 1923   350

Stuart, Jesse (Hilton) HARVEST OF YOUTH Howe, OK (1930)   2,000
MAN WITH A BULL TONGUE PLOW
(NY 1934)   400

Sturgeon, Theodore WITHOUT SORCERY NY 1948
i -29 page brochure "It"   500
ii -80 sgd cc--red buckham, slipcase   300
iii -unsgd   125

Styron, William LIE DOWN IN DARKNESS I (1951)   150

Suckow, Ruth COUNTRY PEOPLE NY 1924 (600 cc)   100
trade   50

Sullivan, Frank THE LIFE AND TIMES OF MARTHA HEPPLETWAITE
NY 1926   50

Summers, Hollis (Spurgeon) CITY LIMIT B 1948   50

Swados, Harvey OUT WENT THE CANDLE NY 1955   50

Swallow, Alan XI POEMS Prairie Press Muscatine 1943
(300 no. cc) wraps   60

SWALLOW BARN (Joseph Pendleton Kennedy) Ph 1832 2 vols   400
(previous collaboration)

Sward, Robert ADVERTISEMENTS CH 1958 (368 cc) wraps   30

Swarthout, Glendon THEY CAME TO CORDURA NY (1958)   50

Swenson, May A CAGE OF SPINES NY 1958   35
(appeared in Poets of Today in 1954)

Swift, Graham THE SWEET SHOP OWNER L 1980   75

Swinburne, Algernon Charles THE QUEEN MOTHER AND ROSAMOND
L 1860
i -A.G. Swinburne on spine   600
ii -B.M. Pickering imprint   400
iii -J.C. Hotten title page   300

Swingler, Randall DIFFICULT MORNING L(1933)   60

Sykes, Gerald THE NICE AMERICANS NY 1951   35

Symonds, J(ohn) A(ddington) THE ESCORIAL O 1860 wraps   200

Symons, A.J.A. EMIN L 1928 300 no. cc (issued w/o dw)   100

Symons, Arthur AN INTRODUCTION TO THE STUDY OF BROWNING
L 1886 (ads dtd Jan 1887)   100
DAYS AND NIGHTS L 1889   1,000

Symons, Julian (Gustave) CONFUSIONS ABOUT X L (1939)   250

Synge, John M(illington) IN THE SHADOW OF THE GLEN
NY 1904 wraps (50 cc)   1,000
THE SHADOW OF THE GLEN...
L 1905 wraps   225

Tabb, John Banister POEMS (BA 1882)   400

```
Taggard, Genevieve  WHAT OTHERS HAVE SAID...  BE (1919)
                                             wraps          150
                    FOR EAGER LOVERS  NY 1922              100

Taine, John (Eric Temple Bell)  THE PURPLE SAPPHIRE
                                             NY (1924)      150

TALES OF THE NORTHWEST... (William J. Snelling)  B 1830    500

Talese, Gay  NEW YORK: A SERENDIPITER'S JOURNEY  NY (1961)  35

TAMERLANE By a Bostonian (Edgar Allan Poe)  B 1827 wraps  250,000
               also see Poe

TARCISSUS, THE BOY MARTYR OF ROME... (Baron Corvo
        Frederick Wm. Rolfe)  (Essex, Eng 1880) wraps     3,000

Tarkington, (Newton) Booth  THE GENTLEMAN FROM INDIANA
                                             NY 1899
                    i -p.245:12 last word "eye" and
                       p.245:16 reads "so pretty"           75

Tarn, Nathaniel  OLD SAVAGE/YOUNG CITY  L (1964)            50

Tate, Allen (John Orley)  THE GOLDEN MEAN +  (Nashville
                          1923) (with R. Wills)
                                 (200 no. cc)             3,500
                    STONEWALL JACKSON  NY 1928             400
                    MR. POPE +  NY 1928                    450

Tate, James (Vincent)  CAGES  Iowa City 1966 45 no. cc wr   250
                       THE LOST PILOT  NH 1967            100

Tauber, Peter  THE SUNSHINE SOLDIERS  NY (1971)             25

Taylor, (James) Bayard  XIMENA +  Ph 1844                  250

Taylor, Eleanor Ross  WILDERNESS OF LADIES  NY (1960)       50

Taylor, Elizabeth  AT MRS. LIPPINCOTE'S  L 1945           125
                                          NY (1946)         75

Taylor, Peter (Hillsman)  A LONG FOURTH +  NY (1948)       150
                                           L (1948)        150

Taylor, Philip Meadows  CONFESSIONS OF A THUG  L 1939 3 v  200

Taylor, Phoebe Atwood  THE CAPE COD MYSTERY  I (1931)      250

Taylor, Robert Lewis  ADRIFT IN A BONEYARD  GC 1947         60

Teasdale, Sara  SONNETS TO DUSE +  B 1907                  200

Tennant, Emma  THE TIME OF THE CRACK  L 1973               40

Tennyson, Lord Alfred  see POEMS BY TWO BROTHERS
                    TIMBUCTOO (Cambridge Pr Poem) wr      1,250
                    POEMS, CHIEFLY LYRICAL  L 1830
                    i -"19" for "91"                      1,000

Tennyson, Frederick  DAYS AND HOURS  L 1854               100

TENTH MUSE, LATELY SPRUNG UP IN AMERICA (THE)
               (Anne Bradstreet)  L 1650                 5,000

Terhune, Albert Payson  SYRIA FROM THE SADDLE  NY 1896     150

Terkel, Studs  GIANTS OF JAZZ  NY (1957)                   75
```

```
Tevis, Walter  THE HUSTLER  (NY 1959)                          75
                L (1960)                                       40

Thackeray, William Makepeace  see Theophile Wagstaff  THE
                YELLOW PLUSH CORRESPONDENCE  PH 1838        1,500

Thaxter, Celia  POEMS  NY 1872                                100

Thayer, Lee  THE MYSTERY OF THE THIRTEENTH FLOOR  NY 1919      25
                (2 juveniles preceded)

Theroux, Alexander  THREE WOGS  B 1972                         60

Theroux, Paul  WALDO  B 1967                                  150
                L 1968                                        125

Thom, Robert  VIATICUM  Columbus 1949  200 no. cc  wr          30

Thoma, Richard  GREEN CHAOS  Seine (1931) wr 100 sgd no. cc   150

Thomas, D(onald) M(ichael)  PERSONAL AND POSSESSIVE  L 1964   350
                TWO VOICES  L 1968 cloth in
                glassine dw (50 sgd no. cc)                   250
                        wraps in glassine dw                  75
                NY 1968 wr in glassine dw                     50

Thomas, Dylan (Marlais)  18 POEMS  Sunday Referee &
                Parton Bookshop  L(1934)
                i -flat spine (250 cc)                      2,000
               ii -rounded spine (1936) (250 cc)             750

Thomas, Edward  WOODLAND LIFE  L 1897                         400

Thomas, Gwyn  WHERE DID I PUT MY PITY  L 1946 stiff wr & dw    60

Thomas, Hugh  THE WORLD'S GAME  L 1957                         60

Thomas, Jerry  THE BARTENDER'S GUIDE  NY 1862                 125

Thomas, Leslie  THIS TIME NEXT WEEK  L 1964                    40

Thomas, Norman  THE CONSCIENTIOUS OBJECTOR IN AMERICA
                                        NY 1923              100

Thomas, Piri  DOWN THESE MEAN STREETS  NY 1967                35

Thomas, R. S.  THE STONES OF THE FIELD  Carmarthen 1946      300

Thomas, Robert Bailey  THE FARMER'S ALMANAC  No. 1...
                                        B (1793)             200

Thomas, Ross  THE COLD WAR SWAP  NY 1965                     200

Thomas, Will  GOD IS FOR WHITE FOLKS  NY (1947)               60

Thomason, John W.  FIX BAYONETS  NY 1926                     150

Thomes, William Henry  see THE GOLD-HUNTER'S...

Thompson, A.C. (Alice Meynell)  PRELUDES  L 1875
                i -brown endpapers                            75

Thompson, Daniel Pierce  see THE ADVENTURES OF TIMOTHY
                                        PEACOCK...
                THE LAWS OF VERMONT  Montpelier 1835         250

Thompson, Dorothy  THE DEPTHS OF PROSPERITY  NY (1925)
                                with P. Bottome               150
```

A WEEK

ON THE

CONCORD AND MERRIMACK RIVERS.

BY

HENRY D. THOREAU.

BOSTON AND CAMBRIDGE:
JAMES MUNROE AND COMPANY.
NEW YORK: GEORGE P. PUTNAM.   PHILADELPHIA : LINDSAY
AND BLACKISTON.   LONDON : JOHN CHAPMAN.
1849.

```
Thompson, Dunstan  THE SONG OF TIME  C (1941) (50 cc) wr      100

Thompson, Earl  A GARDEN OF SAND  NY (1970)                    40
                                  L 1971                       40

Thompson, Francis  POEMS  L 1893  12 sgd cc                 1,000
                   (500 cc) i -ads dated Oct                  300

Thompson, Hunter S.  HELL'S ANGELS  NY (1967)                 90

Thompson, (James) Maurice  HOOSIER MOSAICS  NY 1875           75

Thompson, James  THE CITY OF DREADFUL NIGHT +  L 1880
                                     (40 lpc)                500
                                regular edition               125

Thompson, Lawrence  THE NAVY HUNTS THE CGR  GC 1944           40

Thomson, Virgil  THE STATE OF MUSIC  NY 1939                  60

Thoreau, Henry David  A WEEK ON THE CONCORD AND MERRIMACK
                          RIVERS  B 1849 (294 cc bound)    1,250

THOUGHTS IN THE CLOISTER AND THE CROWD (Sir Arthur Helps)
                                           L 1835           150

Thurber, James  IS SEX NECESSARY?  (with E.B. White)
                                      NY 1929               350
                                      L (1930)              200
                THE OWL IN THE ATTIC  NY 1931               250
        (Also 6 musical scores between 1922 and 1924, all
                  for Ohio State Scarlet Mark Club)

Thurman, Wallace  NEGRO LIFE IN NEW YORK'S HARLEM  Little
                  Blue Book #494  Girard, KS (n-d) wraps    150
                  THE BLACKER THE BERRY  NY 1929            300

Thwaites, Anthony  THE FANTASY POETS No. 17  Eynsham 1952
                                               wraps         50

Thwaites, Reuben Gold  HISTORIC WATERWAYS... Ch 1888        100

Tietjens, Eunice  PROFILES FROM CHINA  Ch 1917             125

Timrod, Henry  POEMS  B 1860                               150

Tinker, Chauncey Brewster  DR. JOHNSON AND FANNY BURNEY...
                                            NY 1911          60

Todd, Mabel (Loomis)  FOOTPRINTS  Amherst 1883  wraps      200

Todd, Ruthven  OVER THE MOUNTAIN  L (1939)                 100

Tolkien, J(ohn) R(onald) R(euel)  A MIDDLE ENGLISH
                    VOCABULARY  O 1922 wraps
          i -ads dated October 1921 (186 orna-
                       ments in cover design               850
            ii -ads undated; "Printed in England"
             at bottom of title pg, 184 ornaments          400

Toller, Ernest  MASSES AND MEN  L 1923 (1st Eng trans)     125

Tolson, Melvin B.  RENDEZVOUS WITH AMERICA  NY 1944         60

Tolstoy, Leo  CHILDHOOD AND YOUTH  L 1862 (1st Eng trans)  500


TOM BROWN'S SCHOOL DAYS (Thomas Hughes)  C 1857
              i -"nottable" for "notable"  p.24:15         350
```

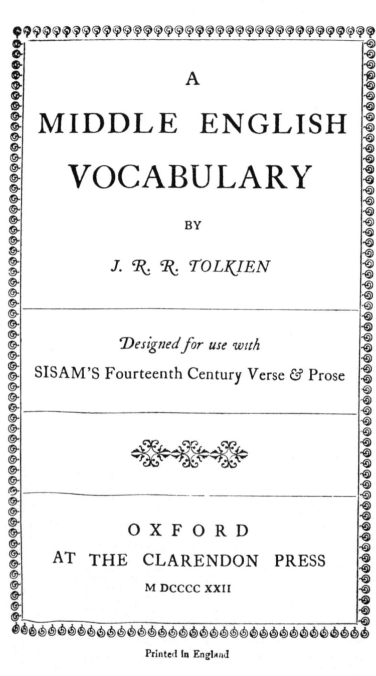

A
MIDDLE ENGLISH
VOCABULARY

BY

J. R. R. TOLKIEN

Designed for use with
SISAM'S Fourteenth Century Verse & Prose

OXFORD
AT THE CLARENDON PRESS
M DCCCC XXII

Printed in England

202

```
TOM CRINGLE'S LOG (Michael Scott)  L 1833  2 vols                    200

Tomkins, Calvin  INTERMISSION  NY 1951                               35

Tomlinson, Charles  RELATIONS AND CONTRARIES  Aldington
                                  (Eng) (1951) wraps                 75

Tomlinson, H(enry) M(ajor)  THE SEA AND THE JUNGLE
                                  L (1912) (350 cc)
                          i -10 leaves of ads at back               100
                                        NY 1913                      60

Tooker, Richard  THE DAY OF THE BROWN HORDE  Payson &
                                  Clarke  NY 1929                    75
                          Brewer & Warren  NY 1929                   50

Toole, John Kennedy  A CONFEDERACY OF DUNCES  Baton Rouge
                                  1980 (2500 cc)                    175
                          (L 1981) (1500 cc)                         75

Toomer, Jean  CANE  NY 1923                                       2,000

TOPSYS & TURVEYS (Peter Newell)  NY 1893 pictorial boards          250

Torrey, Bradford  BIRDS IN THE BUSH  B 1885                         50
```

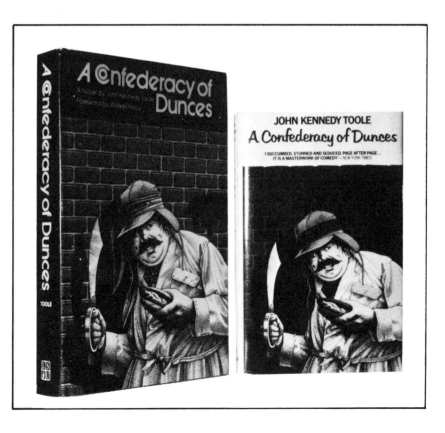

Tourgee, Albion W.   BOOK OF FORMS (Raleigh 1868) wraps   200
                     also see Henry Churton

Toynbee, Arnold J.   GREEK POLICY SINCE 1882   L 1914 wraps   100

Train, Arthur (Chesney)   McALLILSTER AND HIS DOUBLE
                                              NY 1905   50

Traven, B.   THE DEATH SHIP   L 1934 (1st Eng trans by
                                              Sutton)   450
                     NY 1934 (Eng trans by Traven, revised)   350

Traver, Robert (John Donaldson Voelker)   TROUBLE-SHOOTER
                                              NY 1943   125

Travers, P.L.   MARY POPPINS   (L 1934)   350
                               NY (1934)   250

TREATISE OF HUMAN NATURE (A) (David Hume) L 1739-40 3 vols 9,000

Tree, Iris   POEMS   Nassau 1917 wraps   75

Treece, Henry   38 POEMS   L (1940)   100

Trelawny, Edward John   see ADVENTURES OF A YOUNGER SON

Tremayne, Sydney   FOR WHOM THERE IS NO SPRING   L 1946 wr   50

Trevanian (Rodney Whitaker) THE EIGER SANCTION NY (1972)   40

Trevor, William (William Trevor Cox)   A STANDARD OF
                                  BEHAVIOR   L 1958   350
                          THE OLD BOYS   L (1964)   150

Trillin, Calvin   AN EDUCATION IN GEORGIA...   NY (1964)   35

Trilling, Diana   CLAREMONT ESSAY   NY (1964)   25

Trilling, Lionel   MATTHEW ARNOLD   NY (1939)   75

Trocchi, Alexander   see Frances Lengel

Trollope, Anthony   THE MACDERMOTS OF BALLYCLORAN   L 1847
                                              3 vols 4,000

Trotsky, Lev Davydovich   FROM THE WORKERS MOVEMENT...
                                         Geneva 1900   350

Trowbridge, John Townsend   see Paul Creyton

Trumbo, Dalton   ECLIPSE   L (1935)   1,000
                 WASHINGTON JITTERS   NY 1936 (noted in
                 blue & yellow cloth -priority unknown)   100

Tryon, Thomas   THE OTHER   NY 1971   25

Tully, Jim   EMMETT LAWLER   NY (1922)   150

Turbyfill, Mark   THE LIVING FRIEZE   Evanston (1921)
                                  350 no. cc   100
                     (also see Samuel Putnam)

Turner, Frederick Jackson   THE CHARACTER AND INFLUENCE
                            OF THE FUR TRADE...(Madison
                                     1889) wraps   500

Tutuola, Amos   THE PALM-WINE DRINKARD   L 1952   50

```
Twain, Mark (Samuel Langhorne Clemens)   THE CELEBRATED
     JUMPING FROG OF CALVERAS COUNTY   NY 1867
        i -ad before title page                          4,000
                              L 1867 wraps               1,500

TWO PHILOSOPHERS (THE)   (John Jay Chapman)   B (1892) wr   200

TWO YEARS BEFORE THE MAST   (Richard Henry Dana)   NY 1840
        i -perfect "i" first line of copyright          2,000

Tyler, Anne   IF MORNING EVER COMES   NY (1964)           400

Tyler, Parker   see Charles Ford

Tynan, Katherine (K.T. Hinkson) LOUIS DE LA VALLIERE +
                                        L 1885             90

Tynan, Kenneth   HE THAT PLAYS THE KING   L 1950           50

Ullman, James Ramsey   MAD SHELLEY   PR 1930               30

Untermeyer, Louis   FIRST LOVE   B 1911                    50

Updike, D. B. (Printer)   VEXILLA REGIS QUOTIOE   B 1893
                                        100 cc            150

Updike, John (Hoyer)   THE CARPENTERED HEN   NY (1958)    350
                       HOPING FOR A HOOPEE   L 1959
                                        (new title)        75

Upfield, Arthur W(illiam)   THE HOUSE OF CAIN   L 1928    600
                                        NY 1928           200

Upson, William Hazlett   THE PIANO MOVERS   St. Charles, IL
                                        1927               60

Upward, Allen   SONGS IN ZIKLAG   L 1888                  200

Upward, Edward   JOURNEY TO THE BORDER   Hogarth Press
                                        L 1938            150
              (prev. verse work in 1924)

Urdang, Constance   CHARADES AND CELEBRATIONS   NY 1965 wr  30

Uris, Leon   BATTLE CRY   NY (1953)                       100
                         L 1953                            50

Ustinov, Peter (Alexander)   HOUSE OF REGRETS   L (1943)   50

Vail, Amanda (Warren Miller) LOVE ME LITTLE   NY (1957)
              (2nd bk, also see Warren Miller)             25

Valin, Jonathan   THE LIME PIT   NY 1980                   35

Van, Melvin (Pebles)   THE BIG HEART   SF 1957             40

Van Der Post, Lawrence   IN A PROVINCE   L 1934   (1250 cc)  150
                                        NY (n-d)          100

Van Dine, S.S. (Willard Huntington Wright)   THE BENSON
                    MURDER CASE   NY 1926                 400
              (first under this name)

Van Doren, Carl   THE LIFE OF THOMAS LOVE PEACOCK   B 1911  150
                                        L 1911            100

Van Doren, Mark   HENRY DAVID THOREAU   B 1916            150
```

Van Dyke, Henry LADIES OF THE RACHMANINOFF EYES NY (1965)   40

Van Gulik, Robert (Hans)   DEE GOONG AN Tokyo 1949
                              (1200 sgd no. cc)   750
                    THE CHINESE MAZE MURDERS
                              The Hague 1956   400
                                      L 1957   300

Van Loon, Hendrik Willem THE FALL OF THE DUTCH REPUBLIC
                                      B 1913   100

Van Pebles, Melvin see Melvin Van

Van Vechten, Carl MUSIC AFTER THE GREAT WAR   NY 1915   75
     (previous musical score and promotional pamphlet)

Van Vogt, A. E. SLAN SC 1946   150

Vance, Jack (John Holbrook) THE DYING EARTH (1950) wraps   150

Veblen, Thorstein THE THEORY OF THE LEISURE CLASS L 1899   400
                                             NY 1899   250

Velikovsky, Immanuel WORLDS IN COLLISION NY 1950   50

Verne, Jules FIVE WEEKS IN A BALLOON   NY 1869 (1st Eng.) 200

VERSES BY TWO UNDERGRADUATES (Van Wyck Brooks and John
                  Hall Wheelock) (C 1905) wraps   500

Vestal, Stanley FANDANGO... B 1927   150

Vidal, Gore WILLIWAW NY 1946   175

Vidocq, Francois Eugene MEMOIRS OF VIDOCQ... L 1829 4 vol 600

Villa, Jose Garcia FOOTNOTE TO YOUTH NY 1933   75

Vinal, Harold WHITE APRIL NH 1922 stiff wraps   40

Visiak, E. H. BUCCANEER BALLADS L 1910 intro by John
                                             Masefield   40

Visscher, William Lightfoot BLACK MAMMY... Cheyenne 1885   250

Vliet, R. G.   EVENTS & CELEBRATIONS NY (1966)
               (3rd book - 1st reg publ)   50

Vonnegut, Kurt, Jr. PLAYER PIANO NY 1952
               i -"A" and seal on c pg   300
                                      L 1953   200

Voynich, E. L. THE GADFLY L 1897   30

W., E.B. (E.B. White) THE LADY IS COLD NY 1929
               i --Plaza Hotel statue on cover,
                         spine lettered in gold   300
               ii -city skyline on cover, spine
                         lettered in green   250

Waddell, Helen THE SPOILED BUDDHA D 1919 wr   35

Waddington, Miriam GREEN WORLD Montreal 1945
                         stiff wraps & dw   250

Wade, Henry (Henry Lancelot Aubrey-Fletcher) THE VERDICT
                         OF YOU ALL L 1926   100

206

```
Wagoner, David  DRY SUN, DRY WIND  Bloomington 1953          75

Wagstaff, Theophile (Wm. Makepeace Thackeray)  FLORE ET
            ET ZEPHR  L 1836 (wrapper folio with
                        nine unnumbered plates)         1,500

Wakefield, Dan  ISLAND IN THE CITY  B 1959                 30

Wain, John (Barrington)  MIXED FEELINGS: NINETEEN POEMS
                    U. of Reading for Subscribers,
                    1951  wraps  120 no. cc              250
                    HURRY ON DOWN  L 1953                100
                    BORN IN CAPTIVITY  NY 1954
                               (new title)               50

Wakefield, Dan  ISLAND IN THE CITY  B 1959                 40

Wakefield, H(erbert) R(ussell)  GALLIMAUFRY  L (1928)     150
                    THEY RETURN AT EVENING
                               NY 1928                   125

Wakoski, Diane  JUSTICE IS REASON ENOUGH  (BE priv pr)
                    1959 (50 mimeographed cc)          1,500
            COINS AND COFFINS  (NY 1962)  wraps          100

Waldman, Anne  ON THE WING  NY 1967  wraps 25 sgd no. cc   75
                                     475 no. cc           35
            GIANT NIGHT (NY 1968) stapled wr (100 cc)     35
                                     NY 1970              15

Waley, Arthur  see Chinese Poems

Walker, Alice  ONCE  NY (1968)                            200

Walker, Margaret (Abigail)  FOR MY PEOPLE  NY 1942        150

Wallace, (Richard Horatio) Edgar  THE MISSION THAT FAILED
                               Cape Town 1898 wraps      500

Wallace, Irving  THE FABULOUS ORIGINALS  NY 1955          50
                                          L 1956          40

Wallace, Lew(is)  THE FAIR GOD  B 1873                   100

Wallant, Edward Lewis  THE HUMAN SEASON  NY (1960)        75

Waller, Mary Ella  THE ROSE BUSH OF HILDESHEIM  B (1889)  100

Walpole, Sir Hugh Seymour  THE WOODEN HORSE  L 1909       50

Walrond, Eric  TROPIC DEATH  NY 1926                     150

Walsh, Chad  THE FACTUAL DARK  Prairie City (1949)        75

Walsh, Ernest  POEMS AND SONNETS  NY (1934)              150

Walton, Izaak  THE COMPLEAT ANGLER... L 1673           7,500
                    L/Edin./PH 1837 (2 vols)             250
                    NY 1847 ("First American Edition")   350

Walton, Todd  INSIDE MOVES  GC 1978                       25

Wambaugh, Joseph  THE NEW CENTURIONS  NY 1971             25
                                       L 1971             25

Wandrei, Donald  ECSTASY  Athol 1928                     400
```

```
Ward, Lynd   GOD'S MAN   NY (1929) 409 sgd cc boxed          400
                                   trade edition              150

Ware, Eugene Fitch   see Rhymes of Ironquill

Warhol, Andy   LOVE IS A PINK CAKE BY CORKIE & ANDY (n-pl,
                          n-d) 23 leaves in folder            250

Waring, Robert Lewis   AS WE SEE IT   Wash 1910               75

Warner, Charles Dudley   MY SUMMER IN A GARDEN   B 1871       75

Warner, Rex (Ernest)   THE KITE   Oxford 1936                 125

Warner, Sylvia Townsend   THE ESPALIER   L 1925               175

Warren, Robert Penn   JOHN BROWN   NY 1929                    750

Warren, Samuel   see PASSAGES FROM THE DIARY...

Washington, Booker T(alliaferro)   DAILY RESOLVE   L/NY 1896
                    "Booker T. Washington" on title page      400
                  BLACK BELT DIAMONDS   NY 1898               400
                  THE FUTURE OF THE OF THE AMERICAN NEGRO
                                              B 1899          250

Waterhouse, Keith   THE CAFE ROYAL... L 1955 (with
                                    Guy Deghy)                75
                  THERE IS A HAPPY LAND   L 1957              50

Waters, Frank   FEVER PITCH   NY (1930)                       400

Waters, (William Russell)   RECOLLECTIONS OF A DETECTIVE
                        POLICE OFFICER   NY 1852              300
                                         L 1856              750

Watkins, Vernon (Phillips)   BALLAD OF THE MARILWYD +
                                         L (1941)            75

Watson, Wilfred   FRIDAY'S CHILD   L (1955)                   35

Watson, William   THE PRINCE'S QUEST   L 1880                 75

Watts, Alan W.   AN OUTLINE OF ZEN BUDDHISM   L (1932) wraps  125
              BUDDHISM IN THE MODERN WORLD   L (n-d 1933)
                                         wraps              50

Watts, Sunton Theodore   THE COMING OF LOVE +   L 1898        50

Waugh, Alec   THE LOOM OF YOUTH   L 1917                      100
                          NY (1917)                          60

Waugh, Auberon   THE FOXGLOVE SAGA   L 1960                   35
                          NY 1961                            25

Waugh, Evelyn (Arthur St. John)   THE WORLD TO COME (priv.
                          printed) 1916                    7,500
                  P.R.B. AN ESSAY ON THE PRE-RAPHAELITE
                          BROTHERHOOD (priv printed)  1926  2,500
                  ROSSETTI - HIS LIFE AND WORKS   L 1928    1,000
                                         NY 1928            600
                  DECLINE AND FALL   L 1929                  600

Waugh, Frederic J.   THE CLAN OF MUNES   NY 1916              400

Weaver, John V.   IN AMERICA - POEMS   NY 1921               50

Webb, Charles   THE GRADUATE (NY 1963)                       40
```

Webb, James FIELDS OF FIRE Englewood Cliffs (1978)   35

Webb, Mary THE GOLDEN ARROW L 1916   125

Weber, Max CUBIST POEMS L 1914 cloth (100 no. cc)   250
                              blue pictorial cloth   200
                                            wraps   100

Webster, John White A DESCRIPTION OF THE ISLAND OF ST.
                              MICHAEL   B 1821   200

Weedon, Howard SHADOWS ON THE WALL Huntsville 1899   50

Weegee, (Arthur Fellig) NAKED CITY NY (1945)   125

Weidman, Jerome I CAN GET IT FOR YOU WHOLESALE NY 1937   250

Weinbaum, Stanley G(rauman) DAWN OF FLAME (Jamaica, NY
                              1936) issued w/o dw
                     i -intro by Palmer (5 cc)   1,750
                    ii -intro by Keating (250 cc)   1,000

Weiss, Ehrich see Harry Houdini

Weissmuller, Johnny SWIMMING THE AMERICAN CRAWL B 1930   125

Weissner, Carl MANIFESTO FOR THE GREY GENERATION (n-pl)
                   1966 (with D. Georgakas & Poessnecker)   35

Welch, Denton MAIDEN VOYAGE L 1943   200
                                   NY 1945   60

Welch, James RIDING THE EARTHBOY FORTY World NY/Cl
                    (1971) - reportedly not distributed   40
                              Harper NY (1976) - revised   20

Welch, Lew WOBBLY ROCK (SF) 1960 wraps (500 cc)   60

Weldon, Fay THE FAT WOMAN'S JOKE L 1967   30

Wellman, Manley Wade THE INVADING ASTEROID NY (1932) wr   100

Wells, Carolyn (Mrs. Hadwin Houghton) THE STORY OF BETTY
                                            NY 1899   125

Wells, H(erbert) G(eorge) TEXT BOOK OF BIOLOGY L (1893)
                                            2 vol   600
                              (prev. doctoral dissertation)
              SELECT CONVERSATION WITH AN UNCLE L 1895   350
                                            NY 1895   250

Wells, Winifred THE HESITANT HEART NY 1919   40

Welty, Eudora THE KEY (GC 1941) wraps   2,000
              A CURTAIN OF GREEN GC 1941   750

WERTHER'S YOUNGER BROTHER... (Michael Fraenkel) NY/P
                              (1931) stiff wraps   100

Wescott, Glenway THE BITTERNS Evanston (1920) wr (200cc)   500

West, Anthony THE VINTAGE B 1950   30

West, Mae BABE GORDON NY 1930   75

West, Morris see Julian Morris

West, Nathanael (Nathanael W. Weinstein) THE DREAM LIFE OF
                    BALSO SNELL P (1931) (500 cc) 15 cc in cl   1,750
                                      485 cc in wraps   1,000

West, Rebecca (Cicily Isabel Fairfield Andrews)
                         HENRY JAMES L 1916   60
                                      NY 1916   40
            THE RETURN OF THE SOLDIER NY 1918   60
                                       L 1918   50

Westcott, Edward Noyes   DAVID HARUM NY 1898
                    i -perfect "J" in "Julius"
                         penultimate line p.40   60

Westlake, Donald THE MERCENARIES NY (1960)   125
                                    L 1961   75

Weston, Patrick (Gerald Hamilton) DESERT DREAMERS L (1914)
                                           (250 cc)   125

Westwood, Thomas POEMS L 1840   60

Weyman, Stanley THE HOUSE OF THE WOLF L 1890   75

Whalen, Philip THREE SATIRES (Portland, OR 1951) wraps   400
            SELF-PORTRAIT FROM ANOTHER DIRECTION
                                    (SF) 1959 wraps   35

Whaler, James HALE'S POND + NY 1927   35

Wharton, Edith Newbold Jones see Edith Newbold Jones
            THE DECORATION OF HOUSES (with O. Codman)
                                      NY 1897   350
                                      L 1898   250
                THE GREATER INCLINATION NY 1899   125

Wharton, William BIRDY NY 1979   35
                         L 1979   35

Wheatley, Dennis THE FORBIDDEN TERRITORY L (1933)   75

Wheatley, Phillis POEMS ON VARIOUS SUBJECTS, RELIGIONS
                            AND MORAL L 1773   2,000
                                 Ph 1785   1,000

Wheeler, Ella (Wilcox) DROPS OF WATER NY 1872   50

Wheelock, John Hall see VERSES BY TWO UNDERGRADUATES
                THE HUMAN FANTASY B 1911   75

Wheelwright, John Brooks NORTH ATLANTIC PASSAGE (Florence,
                                      Italy 1924)   750

Whistler, James Abbott McNeill WHISTLER V. RUSKIN Chelsea
                1878   wraps   first edition - 12mo   350
                               second edition - 4to   200

White, Antonia FROST IN MAY L (1933)   200

White, E(lwyn) B(rooks) see Sterling Finney, James Thurber
                and E.B.W.

White, Edmund FORGETTING ELENA NY (1973)   40

White, Edward Lucas NARRATIVE LYRICS NY/L 1908   30

White, Grace Miller A CHILD OF THE SLUMS Ogilvie 1904 wr 200

White, Margaret Bourke   EYES ON RUSSIA   NY 1931   300

White, Patrick (Victor Martindale)   THE PLOUGHMAN +
                                      Sydney 1935   1,000
                           HAPPY VALLEY   L 1939   600
                                          NY 1940   300

White, Stewart Edward   THE BIRDS OF MACKINAC ISLAND
                                      NY 1893   wr   400
                        THE CLAIM JUMPERS   NY 1901
                            pictorial cloth   75
                        (Town & Country Lib)   wr   60

White, T(erence) H(anbury)   THE GREEN BAY TREE (C 1929)
                                          wraps   350
                           LOVED HELEN +   L (1929)   300

White, T(heodore) H.   THUNDER OUT OF CHINA   NY 1946 with
                                      Annalee Jacoby   25

White, Walter F(rancis)   THE FIRE IN THE FLINT   NY 1924   150

White, William Allen   RHYMES BY TWO FRIENDS   Fort Scott
                        (1893) (with A.B. Paine) (500 cc)   75
                        THE REAL ISSUE   Ch 1896   40

White, W(illiam) L(indsay)   WHAT PEOPLE SAID   NY 1936   35

Whitehead, E.A.   THE FOURSOME   L 1972   wraps   30

Whitehead, Henry S(t.Clair)   JUMBEE +   (SC) 1944   175

Whitlock, Brand   THE 13TH DISTRICT... I (1902)   25

Whitman, Sarah Helen (Power)   POEM   (Providence 1847) wr   50

Whitman, Walt(er)   FRANKLIN EVANS: OR, THE ENEBRIATE
                                      (NY 1842) wraps
                        i -12 1/2 cent price   5,000
                       ii -6 1/2 cent price   4,000
                        also see Leaves of Grass

Whittier, John Greenleaf   LEGENDS OF NEW ENGLAND Hartford
                                                    1831
                        i -last line, p 98 "The go" for
                                          "They go"   250

Whittemore, (Edward) Reed   HEROS AND HEROINES   NY (1946)   50

Whyte-Melville, George John   DIGBY GRAND   L 1853   2 vols   200

Wideman, John Edgar   A GLANCE AWAY   NY (1967)   75

Wiener, Norbert   CYBERNETICS...   NY (1948)   125

Wieners, John (Joseph) THE HOTEL WENTLY POEMS (SF) 1958 wr
                        i -censored   50
                       ii -unexpurgated (press listed at
                                  "1334 Franklin Street")   30

Wiesel, Elie   NIGHT   P 1958   75

Wiggin, Kate Douglas   see Kate Douglas Smith

Wilbur, Richard (Purdy)   THE BEAUTIFUL CHANGES +   NY (1947)
                                          (750 cc)   250

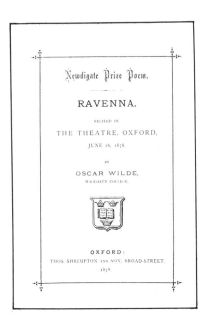

Newdigate Prize Poem,

RAVENNA.

RECITED IN

THE THEATRE, OXFORD,

JUNE 26, 1878.

BY

OSCAR WILDE,

MAGDALEN COLLEGE.

OXFORD:

THOS. SHRIMPTON AND SON, BROAD-STREET.

1878.

Battle of Angels

A Play by Tennessee Williams

With a note on the play by Margaret Webster and an account of its production in the City of Boston by the author. This publication being the first number of

Pharos

A magazine dedicated to creative writing, which is published intermittently at the pleasure of its editor from Box 215 at Murray, Utah. This is a double number.

Spring, 1945

THE TEMPERS

BY

WILLIAM CARLOS WILLIAMS

LONDON

ELKIN MATHEWS, CORK STREET

M CM XIII

```
Wilde, Oscar (Fingal O'Flahertie Wills)  RAVENNA  O 1878 wr
               i -Oxford Univ arms on title and cover      600

Wilder, Amos N(iven)  BATTLE-RETROSPECT +  NY 1923          150

Wilder, Thornton  THE CABALA  NY 1926   i -"conversation
                    for "conversion" on p.196:13,
                 "explaininn" for "explaining" p.202:12
                    (blue patterned cloth reportedly
                              scarcer than red)            250
                                       L 1926               75

Wilkinson, Sylvia  MOSS ON THE NORTH SIDE  B 1967           60

Wilkins, Mary E. (Mary E. W. Freeman)  DECORATIVE PLAQUES
               B (1883) (with George F. Barnes)            600

Will, George  THE PURSUIT OF HAPPINESS +  NY 1979           35

Williams, Alfred  SONGS IN WILTSHIRE  L 1909 (500 cc)       40

Williams, Ben Ames  ALL THE BROTHERS WERE VALIANT  NY 1919  50
                    (much more with N.C. Wyeth dw)

Williams, C. K.  A DAY FOR ANNE FRANK  Ph (1968)            40

Williams, Charles (Walter)  THE SILVER STAIR  L 1912       300

Williams, Emlyn  A MURDER HAS BEEN ARRANGED  L 1931         50

Williams, Heathcote  THE SPEAKERS  L 1964                   35

Williams, Joan  THE MORNING AND THE EVENING  NY 1961        25
                                             L 1962         25

Williams, John  THE BROKEN LANDSCAPE  Denver 1949 (500 cc)  50

Williams, John A(lfred)  THE ANGRY ONES +  NY (1960) wraps  50

Williams, Jonathan (Chamberlain)  PAINTING & GRAPHICS
                 Highlands 1950 (exhibition folder)        500
                 (previous pamphlet may exist)

Williams, Joy  STATE OF GRACE  GC 1973                      25

Williams, Oscar  THE GOLDEN DARKNESS  NH 1921 wr over bds   60

Williams, Tennessee (Thomas Lanier)  BATTLE OF ANGELS
                 Murray, Utah 1945 as Pharos Nos.
                              1 & 2   wraps                350

Williams, Thomas  CEREMONY OF LOVE  I (1955)                40

Williams, William Carlos  POEMS  (Rutherford NJ) 1909 wr
                              (100 cc)                  15,000
                         THE POEMS  L 1913                 800

Williamson, Henry  THE FLAX OF DREAMS: THE BEAUTIFUL YEARS
                              L 1921  (750 cc)             300

Williamson, Jack  THE GIRL FROM MARS  NY (1929) wraps
                              (with Dr. M. Breuer)          75
                 THE LEGION OF SPACE  Reading 1947
                              500 sgd no. cc                90
                              trade edition                 35

Willingham, Calder (Bayard)  END AS A MAN  NY (1947)
                 i -back panel of dw blank                  75
```

Willington, James (Oliver Goldsmith) MEMOIRS OF A
                              PROTESTANT L 1758   2,000

Willis, N(athaniel) P(arker) SKETCHES B 1827   100

Willis, George TANGLEWEED GC 1943   35

Wills, Garry CHESTERTON NY (1961)   50

Willson, Meredith AND THERE I STOOD WITH MY PICCOLO
                                     NY 1948   50

Wilson, Angus (Frank Johnstone) THE WRONG SET + L 1949 60

Wilson, Augusta Jane Evans see INEZ...

Wilson, Carroll Atwood VERDENT GREEN (n-pl) 1933 wraps 40

Wilson, Colin (Henry) THE OUTSIDER L 1956   75
                                     B 1956   40

Wilson, Edmund THE UNDERTAKER'S GARLAND NY 1922 (with
          J.P. Bishop) 50 cc "Bookseller Friends"
                              issued w/o dw   250
                              regular edition   350
          DISCORDANT ENCOUNTERS NY (1927)   350

Wilson, Harry Leon ZIG ZAG TALES FROM EAST TO WEST
                              NY 1894 wraps   100
                                       cloth   75

Wilson, (Thomas) Woodrow CONGRESSIONAL GOVERNMENT B 1885
                    i -publ monogram on spine   100

Windham, Donald YOU TOUCHED ME   NY (1947) wraps
                    (with Tennessee Williams)   75
                 THE HITCHHIKER (Florence 1950)
                    (250 sgd no. cc) wraps   125

Winsor, Justin A HISTORY OF THE TOWN OF DUXBURY... B 1849 150

Winsor, Kathleen (Herwig Shaw Porter) FOREVER AMBER NY 1944 60

WINTER IN THE WEST (A) By A New Yorker (Charles Fenno
                    Hoffman) NY 1835 2 vols   150

WINTER SHIP (A) (Sylvia Plath) Edinburgh 1960 wraps   1,000

Winter, William POEMS B 1855   150

Winters, Yvor DIADEMS AND FAGOTS Sante Fe (1920) (trans
                         by Winters) (50 copies)   500
               THE IMMOBILE WIND Evanston (1921) wraps 450

Wister, Owen THE LADY OF THE LAKE (C) 1881 (chorus book) 200
             THE NEW SWISS FAMILY ROBINSON (C 1882)   250

Witwer, Harry Charles FROM BASEBALL TO BOCHES B (1918) 40

Wodehouse, P(elham) G(renville) THE POTHUNTERS L 1902 1,750

Woiwode, Larry WHAT I'M GOING TO DO... NY (1969)   40
                                         L 1970   40

Wolfe, Bernard REALLY THE BLUES NY (1946) with Milton
                                     Mezzrow   75
              LIMBO   NY (1952)   75

214

Wolfe, Humbert   THE COUNT OF SALDEYNE   L 1915   50

Wolfe, Thomas (Clayton)   THE CRISIS IN INDUSTRY
                         Chapel Hill 1919   6,000
                   LOOK HOMEWARD, ANGEL NY 1929
                   i -dw has author's pix on back   1,500
                   ii -dw w/o pix   750
                         L 1930 (few textual changes) 650

Wolfe, Tom   THE KANDY-KOLORED... NY (1965)   60

Wolff, Geoffrey   BAD DEBTS   NY 1969   20

Wolff, Maritta M.   WHISTLE STOP   NY (1941)   40

Wolff, Tobias   IN THE GARDEN OF THE NORTH AMERICAN MARTYRS
                                            NY (1981)   40

Wolheim, Donald A(llen)   THE SECRET OF SATURN'S RINGS
                                            PH (1954)   35
                         (prev edited anthologies)

Wood, Charles Erskine Scott   IMPERIALISM VS. DEMOCRACY
                         NY 1899 (offprint from
                                "Pacific Monthly")   100
                         A MASQUE OF LOVE   CH 1904   60

```
Wood, Clement  GLAD OF EARTH  NY 1917                         40

Woodberry, George Edward  HISTORY OF WOOD-ENGRAVING
                                       NY 1883               125

Woodford, Jack  EVANGELICAL COCKROACH  NY 1929               60

Woodward, W(illiam) E.  BUNK  NY 1923                        60

Woolf, Douglas  THE HYPOCRITIC DAYS  Divers Press 1955 wr    50

Woolf, L(eonard) S.  THE VILLAGE IN THE JUNGLE  L (1913)    250

Woolf, Virginia  THE VOYAGE OUT  L 1915                     500
                 NY (1920) text revised by Woolf           400

Woollcott, Alexander  MRS. FISKE... NY 1915  i -author's
                      name misspelled on title pg           50

Woolrich, Cornell  COVER CHARGE  NY 1926                    750

Woolsey, Gamel  MIDDLE EARTH  NY 1932                       100

Wordsworth, William  AN EVENING WALK  L 1793             5,000

Wouk, Herman  THE MAN IN THE TRENCH COAT  NY (1941) wraps   750
             AURORA DAWN  NY 1947                           100
                          L 1947                             75

Wright, Austin Tappan  ISLANDIA  NY (1942) with
                       INTRODUCTION TO ISLANDIA  2 vols     300

Wright, Charles (Stevenson)  THE MESSENGER  NY (1963)        40

Wright, Frank Lloyd  THE JAPANESE PRINT  CH 1912            600

Wright, Harold Bell  THAT PRINTER OF UDELL'S  CH 1903        40

Wright, James (Arlington)  THE GREEN WALL  NH 1957          250

Wright, Judith  THE MOVING IMAGE  Melbourne (1946)         100

Wright, Richard (Nathaniel)  UNCLE TOM'S CHILDREN  NY 1938  600

Wright, Richard B.  THE WEEKEND MAN  NY (1970)              30

Wright, S(ydney) Fowler  THE AMPHIBIANS  L (1925)          100

Wright, Willard Huntington  SONGS OF YOUTH  NY 1913         60
                            also see S.S. Van Dine

Wurlitzer, Rudolph  NOG  NY (1968)                          35
                    THE OCTOPUS  L 1969 (new title)         30

Wylie, Elinor (Hoyt)  see INCIDENTAL NUMBERS
                      NETS TO CATCH THE WIND  NY 1921
                      i -unwatermarked paper               300

Wylie, Philip (Gordon)  HEAVY LADEN  NY 1928               150

Wyndham, John (John Beynon Harris)  see John Beynon
             THE DAY OF THE TRIFFIDS  NY 1951 (1st novel)   150
                   L (1951) (contains textual revisions)   200

Yates, Edmund Hodgson  MY HAUNTS AND THEIR FREQUENTERS
                                       L 1854  wraps       125

Yates, Elizabeth  QUEST IN THE NORTH-LAND  NY 1940          35
```

THE
BACHELORS' CLUB

BY

I. ZANGWILL

JOINT-AUTHOR OF 'THE PREMIER AND THE
PAINTER,' ETC.

WITH ILLUSTRATIONS BY GEORGE HUTCHINSON

' *A slavery beyond enduring,*
But that 'tis of their own procuring.
As spiders never seek the fly,
But leave him of himself t' apply ;
So men are by themselves employed,
To quit the freedom they enjoyed,
And run their necks into a noose,
They d break 'em after to break loose.'

HUDIBRAS.

' *A man may have a quarrel to marry when he will.'*

BACON'S ESSAYS.

London

HENRY & CO.

6 BOUVERIE STREET

1891

```
Yates, Richard   REVOLUTIONARY ROAD   B (1961)                    60
                                     (L 1962)                    50

Yeats, Jack B(utler)   JAMES FLAUNTY   L (1901)   wraps         200

Yeats, W(illiam) B(utler)   MOSADA   D 1886 (100 cc)        35,000
                            THE WANDERING OF OISIN +
                                     L 1889 (500 cc)          1,000

Yerby, Frank (Garvin)   THE FOXES OF HARROW   NY 1946           60

Yglesias, Jose   A WAKE IN YOUR CITY   NY (1963)                30
                 (previous translations)

Yorke, Henry Vincent   see Henry Green

Young, Al   DANCING   NY (1969)   wraps  50 sgd no. cc         150
                                         regular edition        30

Young, Marguerite   PRISMATIC GROUND   NY 1937                  50

Young, Stark   THE BLIND MAN AT THE WINDOW +   NY 1906         100

Yount, John   WOLF AT THE DOOR   NY 1967                        40

Yurick, Sol   THE WARRIORS   NY(1965)                           40

Zagat, Arthur Lee   SEVEN OUT OF TIME   Reading 1949            25

Zangwill, I.   THE BACHELOR'S CLUB   L 1891                    150

Zeitlin, Jake   FOR WHISPERS AND CHANTS   SF 1927   (500 cc)   200

Zugsmith, Leane   ALL VICTORIES ARE ALIKE   NY 1929           100

Zindel, Paul   THE PIGMAN   NY (1968)                          35

Zukofsky, Louis   see Anton Reiser
                 LE STYLE APOLLINAIRE   P 1934 wraps         4,000
                 FIRST HALF OR 'A'--9   NY 1940
                         (55 mimeographed sgd cc)            1,500
```

Abbreviations

Cities of Publication

B	—Boston, Mass.
BA	—Baltimore, Md.
BE	—Berkeley, Calif.
BL	—Bloomington, Ind.
C	—Cambridge, Mass.
CH	—Chicago, Ill.
CI	—Cincinnati, Ohio
CO	—Columbus, Ohio
D	—Dublin
DV	—Denver, Colo.
GC	—Garden City, NY
I	—Indianapolis, Ind.
L	—London, England
LA	—Los Angeles, Calif.
M	—Majorca, Spain
MIL	—Milwaukee, Wis.
N	—Norfolk, Conn.
NH	—New Haven, Conn.
NY	—New York, NY
O	—Oxford, England
P	—Paris, France
Ph	—Philadelphia, Pa.
PR	—Princeton, NJ
SC	—Sauk City, Wisc.
SP	—Springfield, Ill.
St. P.	—St. Paul, Minn.
W	—Washington, D.C.

Bindings are Cloth Unless Otherwise Noted

bds	—boards
cl	—cloth
stwr	—stiff paperwraps
hb	—hardback (cloth)
mag	—magazine
ph	—pamphlet
pic	—pictorial
wr	—flexible paperwraps as in a current paperback book

Other Abbreviations

app	—appeared or appearance
b	—bottom
c	—copyright page
cc	—copies
des	—destroyed
dw	—dustwrapper
ed	—edition or edited
ep	—endpapers or flyleaf
fwd	—forward, introduction, preface
fn	—fine book under author's own name
i,ii,iii	—indicates first, second, third issue "points"
l	—line number (on page)
ll	—lettering
lpc	—large paper copies
n-d	—no date on title page and not known
n-pl	—no city of publication on title page and not known
p	—page number
pc	—previous collaboration
pre	—preceded
pp	—pages
Reg	—first regularly published book
sgd	—signed by author
sp	—spine of book
supp	—supplement
t	—top
teg	—top edges of pages are gilt
tr	—translated by the author
v	—volumes
w	—written in collaboration with (others)
w/o	—without
( )	—indicates that information contained therein is not on the title page of the book. Also used when showing the number of copies the first book was limited to or other miscellaneous information
+	—used at the end of a title to indicate that the complete title includes the words "And Other Stories (Poems/Essays)"
?	—a question in my mind of whether the information given is correct
. . .	—at the end of title indicates that the title has been abbreviated

Appendix A

First Edition Identification by Publisher

There are two methods used by most publishers to indicate first editions. In both cases, the date on the title page should match the copyright date in 99% of the cases. When a book does not have a date on the title page, one should carefully check out the particular book. It is true that many publishers do not place a date on the title page, but in my experience many of the books without a date on the title page or with a date that is later than that of the copyright date have turned out to be later printings. In cases involving books printed in the 19th century in the U.S. and many British books printed as late as the early 20th century, there may be a date on the title page, but no copyright date or information. These books are normally first editions but must be carefully researched to verify this.

The two most common are:

(A) To leave the copyright page devoid of any information except copyright information and only on subsequent printings to list the complete printing history. Publishers which follow or have followed this method include:

A.S. Barnes	Harrison Smith
Ernest Benn	Harvard University
A. & C. Boni	Henry Holt (usually)
Boni & Liveright	Alfred A. Knopf (thru 1933/4)
Brentano's (until 1928)	J.P. Lippincott
Jonathan Cape & Harrison Smith	McGraw-Hill (to 1956)
Caxton Printers	William Morrow (to 1973, series of
Covici Friede	numbers thereafter)
Coward-McCann	Oxford University
Creative Age	Pantheon (to 1964, stated thereafter)
John Day (since 1930's)	G.P. Putnam
Devin-Adair	Reynal & Hitchcock (thru 1948/50)
Dial Press	Simon & Schuster (thru 1950's)
Dodd Mead	Alan Swallow
Four Seas	Vanguard
Harcourt Brace (thru 1930)	

(B) To state the printing beginning with the first printing. Publishers which follow or have followed this method include:

Atheneum	Jonathan Cape
Bodley Head	John Day (through 1930's)
Brentano's (1928-33)	Delacorte Press

Duell, Sloan (used "1") Hodder & Stoughton
Eyre & Spottiswoode Alfred A. Knopf (since 1956)
Faber & Faber Macmillan
Farrar Straus Cudahy Methuen & Co.
Farrar Straus Giroux New American Library
Funk & Wagnalls (used "1") New English Library
Gambit Random House (also see below)
Bernard Geis Simon & Schuster (since 1950's)
Hamish Hamilton T. Fisher Unwin
Hart-Davis, MacGibbon Viking Press ("First publ by . . . in 19--"
William Heinemann or "Publ by . . . in 19--")

There are also those publishers that used both methods at various times. These publishers normally indicate later printings:

Harry Abrams Hill & Wang
Arbor House Holt, Rinehart & Winston
Beacon Press Michael Joseph
George Braziller McDowell Obolensky
Capra Press Noonday Press
Chatto & Windus Harrison Smith & Robert Haas
Crime Club (British) Lyle Stuart
Thomas Y. Crowell Swallow Press
E.P. Dutton St. Martin's Press
Grove Press

In addition, the following publishers used various other methods:

APPLETON-CENTURY: Used numerical identification (1), (2), etc., at the foot of the last page of the book.

ARKHAM HOUSE: Usually stated on last page of book.

BOBBS-MERRILL: At one time put a bow and arrow on bottom of copyright page but not consistently; also used the words "First Edition," but again, not consistently until the last few decades.

HARCOURT BRACE (& WORLD): Since 1930 "first edition" is stated on copyright page and no information is furnished on later printings; prior to 1930 did not state and normally did not put a date on title page.

HOUGHTON MIFFLIN: Always placed the year of publication on the title page of first printings and dropped the date on later printings.

LITTLE BROWN: No sure way of identifying prior to 1940's.

NEW DIRECTIONS: No sure way of identifying; occasionally they have stated on copyright page. Consult the author bibliography.

SCRIBNER: Since 1930 have placed an "A" on copyright page and either furnished no information on later printings or changed to "B," "C," etc. More recently they have a series of letters and numbers on copyright page and the first can be identified by an "A" as the first letter in the series.

The publishers that cause the greatest problems are those that identify the first printing, but then do not indicate any printing information on the subsequent printings; thus the later printings by these publishers are exactly like the first printings by the publishers in (A) above. These include:

Doubleday (in all forms including Crime Club): "First Edition" stated.

George H. Doran: GHD logo on copyright page

Farrar & Rinehart: FR logo on copyright page

Farrar & Straus: FS on copyright page

Farrar, Straus, Young: FSY on copyright page

Harcourt Brace (after 1930)

Harpers (in all forms): "First Printing" stated after 1922

Houghton Mifflin: date on title page (removed on later printings)

Rinehart & Company: R logo on copyright page.

In recent years many publishers have begun using a series of numbers or letters to identify printings. From the information available all publisers (except two) using this method start with "1" or "A", so that a first printing would state "1 2 3 4 5 6 . . ." or "A B C D E F . . . ." In addition, many of the publishers also state "First Edition" or "First Printing" on the copyright page. For the second printing, the publishers delete the words "First Edition" or "First Printing" and the initial number or letter ("1" or "A") leaving the series beginning with a "2" or "B," WHICH INDICATES SECOND PRINTING. I have noted on a few titles that the publishers deleted the number or letter in the series but forgot to take off the "First Edition" statement, so that occasionally you will find books stating "First Edition" and the series "3 4 5 6 . . .".

The two exceptions are Random House, which states "First Printing" "2,3,4 . . .", and Harcourt Brace which states "First Edition" "B C D . . .". These publishers delete the wording on the second printings (if they remember); although recently, to add further confusion, I have noted that Harcourt has started including an "A" on their books.

Unfortunately, even the most consistent publishers sometimes deviate from these guidelines. Doubleday did not state "First Edition" on John Barth's *Giles Goat Boy* and that first is identified by the code H18 on the last page. Random House did not state "First Printing" on Faulkner's *Knight's Gambit* and merely left the copyright page blank except for the copyright information. Atheneum, which normally states "First Edition," did not include this statement on Edward Albee's *Tiny Alice*. There are other such exceptions, but as a general rule the publishers are consistent with own policies.

Appendix B

Glossary

The following is a partial list of terms used in book collecting. The most complete list is contained in John Carter's *ABC FOR BOOK COLLECTORS* (see Selected Bibliography).

A.B.A.	Antiquarian Booksellers' Association (English) also the American Booksellers' Association, primarily publishers and sellers of new books
A.B.A.A.	Antiquarian Booksellers' Association of America
A.B.P.C.	American Book Prices Current (see Price Guides)
Advance Copy	A copy for booksellers and reviewers, either bound in paperwraps or a copy of the trade edition with a review slip laid-in
A.L.S.	Autographed Letter Signed—all in the author's hand
A.M.S.	Autographed Manuscript Signed—all in the author's hand
Antiquarian Books	A loose term implying collectable books versus used books. Refers to old, rare and out-of-print, which covers the waterfront
As issued	Used to emphasize original condition or to highlight something a little unusual such as recent books without dustwrappers
Association Copy	A book that belonged to the author, or that the author gave to another person with whom he was associated. The book contains some tangible identifying evidence (such as inscriptions, signatures, bookplates, letters or photographs laid-in or tipped-in)
As usual	A favorite term to describe defects which probably occur only on copies of the book the particular dealer handles, such as "lacks end-papers, as usual," or "lacks title page, as usual"
Backstrip	The spine of the book
B.A.L.	*Bibliography of American Literature* (see Bibliographies)
Bastard Title	See Front Matter and Half-Title
Biblio	From the Greek signifying or pertaining to books
Biblioclast	A destroyer of books
Bibliomaniac	Many Bookdealers and certain collectors
Bibliophile	A lover of books
Bibliophobe	A fear of books (sometimes extended to hate)
Bibliopole	The people behind the booths at the book fairs

Blind Stamped	Impressions in the bindings of books which are not colored, as in the Book-of-the-Month blind stamp on the back cover
Binding	The cover of the book
Boards	The front and back covers of the book are the boards. This term is also used to describe books that have the boards covered in paper rather than cloth or leather
Book Sizes	The following are approximate sizes in height, in inches Double Elephant folio—50 Atlas folio—25 Elephant folio—23 F—folio—15 Q—Quarto, 4to—12 O—Octavo, 8vo—9¾ D—Duodecimo, 12mo—7¾ S—Sixteenmo, 16mo—6¾ T—Twentyfourmo, 24mo—5¾ Thirtytwomo, 32mo—5 Fortyeightmo, 48mo—4 Sixtyfourmo, 64mo—3
Breaker	Either a person who breaks up books to sell the plates individually or the book itself when the covers are so bad that it either has to be rebound or broken up
Broadside	A single sheet printed on one side only
Blurb	A comment from a review (often by another author praising the particular book, printed on the dustwrapper or covers of a proof copy
Buckram	A coarse linen binding cloth
C.W.O.	Check or cash with order
Cancel	A cancel is literally any printed matter change to any part of a book, but most commonly it refers to one or more pages which are substituted for existing pages in a book that has already been bound. In other words, an error is found, a new corrected page is printed (cancel, or cancel leaf) and the original page is cut out of the book leaving a stub upon which the cancel page is glued.
Chipped	Usually used to describe the fact that small pieces on the edge of the paper dustwrapper have been torn off (chipped away)
Cloth	Refers to the binding of the book, when the boards are covered in cloth
Collate	At one time it really meant to compare one copy of a book with another to see if it was the same. Even without another copy one can determine if the book is complete by knowing how books are made. In modern times many bibliographies furnish enough

physical information to determine if the book is complete and the correct edition. It also simply means to check each page and plate to assure the book is complete, which is not a bad idea even on modern books

Colophon	derived from the Greek it means finishing touch. It was on the last page and provided facts about the production, author, title, date, etc. The title page has superceded the colophon, as an information source. In modern books the colophon page is used to refer to the page in limited editions which includes the type of paper, printer, number of copies and author's signature
Contemporary	Refers to bindings and hand-colored plates (generally of the period when the book was published) and author inscription (dated the year of publication, preferably near the publication date)
Covers	The binding of the book, most particularly the front and back panels of the book
Covers Bound-in	The original cloth covers, usually including the spine, are bound into the book when a new binding is made; normally they are mounted as pages at the end of the book. Also refers to the covers of the books originally issued in boards or paperwraps, but in these cases the covers are usually bound in their proper positions
Cut edges	Edges trimmed by machine, which applies to most modern books, versus leaving the page edges roughly cut (see uncut)
Deckled edge	Rough, irregular edges usually found on handmade paper, but it can be produced in machine-made paper
Dedication copy	A copy of a book with the author's presentation inscription to the person or persons to whom the book was dedicated
Dos-A-Dos	Two separate books bound so that each cover represents the cover for a different title. The Ace paperbacks for many science fiction books were issued this way, as was William Burroughs first book, *JUNKIE*, written under the pseudonym William Lee
Dummy	A mock-up of the book, used by salesmen in the late 19th and early 20th century to show prospective buyers what the book would look like. It usually had a title page and 10 or 20 pages of text and then blank pages to fill out the rest of the binding
Dustwrapper	The paper cover, either printed or pictorial, which is issued with the book. Also referred to as a dust jacket or dust cover. Abbreviated–dw
Edition	Actually an edition will stand until changed. There may be 20 printings of an edition before a change in the text is made that is significant enough to require a notation that it is a second edition. For the collector, though, the first edition is the first printing—or first impression—which means the whole number of books ordered by the publisher to be printed from the same set of type and issued at the same time

Else fine	Usually follows a long list of defects. One of our local book-scouts, Ralph Hirschtritt, usually refers to his copies as ex-mint, which is certainly descriptive
End papers	When a book is bound the binder adds a double leaf, half of which is pasted down to the inside covers leaving the other half to form the end papers or first and last leaves of the book
Ephemera	Perishable productions never meant to last. Pamphlets, broadsides, photos, advertisements, in fact almost anything not classified elsewhere
Errata	A printed page or slip of paper tipped or laid-in, which lists all the mistakes and misprints found after binding
First edition	The total number of copies produced in the first impression or printing of a book. Abbreviated–1st ed
First separate edition	First printing in book form of something previously published with other matter. Usually stories or poems which appeared in magazines, anthologies or collections of the same author's works. For first separate appearance see Offprint
First thus	Means not a first edition, but something is new. It may be revised, have a new introduction by the author or someone else, be the first publication in paperback form or first by another publisher
Fly leaf	The blank page following the end paper, but often used to describe the end paper itself
Fly title	see Half-title
Follow the Flag	A term which means that if one collects American authors precedence would be given to American editions, even if the chronological first edition was published in England. The practice today seems to be to either collect both editions of all titles or if a few titles were printed on the "wrong" side of the Atlantic, to collect the true first of that title or both editions of that title
Fore-edge painting	The front page edges of the book are bent back to expose a greater area and a water color painting is applied to this surface. After completion and the book is closed the painting cannot be seen
Foxing	Discoloration spots on the pages or page edges, usually brown or yellow resulting from chemical reaction of certain properties in the paper to the atmosphere
F.P.A.A.	First Printings of American Authors (see Bibliographies)
Frontispiece	An illustration at the front of the book normally across from the title page. Also referred to as the frontis
Front matter	The pages preceding the text of a book. The Bookmans's glossary gives the following order: bastard title or fly title frontispiece

title page
copyright page
dedication
preface or foreword
table of contents
list of illustrations
introduction
acknowledgements
half-title

Usually each of these are on a right-hand page except the frontispiece and copyright page which face the title page and are on the reverse or verso of the title page, respectively

Galley proofs　Early proof copies of a book on long strips of paper usually containing two or three pages of text per strip. Normally only a few copies are pulled in order for the author or editors(s) to make changes and catch typographical errors. They are also referred to as galleys or loose galleys. They preceed the perfect bound uncorrected proofs and advance reading copies. Recently many publishers have changed to galley proofs of the sheets made on copiers, which presents a problem to bookdealers and collectors because these sheets are so easily duplicated

Gathering　A group of leaves formed after the printed sheet has been folded to the size of the book for sewing or gluing into the binding. Also called a signature, section or quire

Gilt edges　The page edges have been trimmed smooth and gilt, or gold has been applied. The abbreviation g.e. means gilt edges; a.e.g. means all edges gilt; g.t. means gilt top; t.e.g. means top edge gilt

Glassine　A transparent paper dustwrapper which some people put a high value on, but is certainly unattractive and illfitting with age

Half cloth　Paper-covered boards with the spine bound in cloth

Half leather　The spine is bound in leather and the balance in cloth or paper. Also referred to as three-quarter leather when the corners are also bound, but the latter designation was supposed to imply that a good portion of the covers were bound in leather not just the corners. Also called half-bound, half binding

Half title　A page preceeding the text containing only the title of the book. There are usually two of these, one before the title page and one after the title page. The former was called a bastard or fly title, but in recent years booksellers don't seem to differentiate

Hinge　The junctions where the front and back covers meet the spine. John Carter differentiated the inner and outer junctions as hinges and joints, respectively. Book dealers refer to hinges as being weak or starting, which can mean anything from the paper making up the pastedown and end paper is starting to split at the hinge to the cover

	actually starting to come off. If the copy is also described as tight or still tight it could be assumed the break in the paper hasn't yet weakened the binding
Holograph	Means entirely in the handwriting of the author. Usually used for notes, marginal comments and partcularly manuscripts, as the term autograph is used for letters entirely in the author's hand (see A.L.S.)
Impression	The copies of an edition printed at one time. The first impression is the first edition in collector's parlance
Imprint	Originally it meant the person or firm responsible for the actual production of the book. More recently it is used to refer to the publisher (and place and date) as it appears at the foot of the title page, but can also be used to refer to the printer's name or the publisher's name on the spine
Incunabula	A Latin word for "things in the cradle." It is used to refer to books printed from movable type before 1501. Incunable is used as the singular, with incunables as an alternative plural
Inscribed copy	Means it has been inscribed by the author, for a particular person, and is not merely autographed by the author. It is often difficult to differentiate between inscribed copies and presentation copies and for the most part the terms seem to be used interchangeably
Integral	Refers to a leaf when it is part of a gathering or signature, versus being a cancel or tipped-in leaf
Interleaved	When blank leaves alternate with the printed leaves it is said to be interleaved
Issue	Issues and states of the first impression seem to be used interchangeably and the differences are at times confusing. An issue occurs when alterations, additions, or excisions are made after all the copies are printed and the book has been published or gone on sale. The most obvious examples would be books where a number of sets of sheets are run off but the sheets were bound at different times and in many cases by different publishers, books such as John Steinbeck's *CUP OF GOLD* and Dylan Thomas's *18 POEMS* (see entries in First Book List).
	States, on the other hand, occur when changes are made during printing or, at least, before publication or sale so that variant copies go on sale at the same time.
	So, if the publisher finds an error and inserts a cancel page before the first impression is distributed (of course some copies have gone out to reviewers) we have two states, but some people will call them issues and in the overall scheme of things this mistake will not be fatal.
Jacket	The printed or unprinted cover, usually paper, placed around the

	bound book. Sometimes called dust jacket (dj), dustwrapper (dw), dust cover or book jacket.
Jap(anese) vellum	A rather stiff paper with a very smooth glossy surface not unlike vellum. Japon is used to refer to French and British made imitations and American imitations are sometimes called Japon vellum
Joints	The exterior hinges of books, but are rarely referred to these days because if they're bad you can just say that the covers are off and you'll be close enough
Juveniles	Children's books
Juvenilia	Books written when the author was a child
Label	Printed paper, cloth or leather slips glued to the spine or front cover of a book
Laid-in	A photo, errata, autograph, letter, review slip, etc. laid-in the book, not attached to it
Laid paper	Paper which, when held up to the light, shows fine parallel lines (wire-marks) and crosslines (chain-marks), produced naturally by the wires of the mold in handmade papers. It can also be simulated by a pattern on the first roller in machine-made paper
Large paper edition	Produced using the same type as the regular edition but printed on larger paper resulting in larger margins.
Leaf	A piece of paper comprising one page on the front (recto, obverse) and another on the back (verso, reverse)
Limited edition	An edition which is limited to a stated number of copies, and is usually numbered (or lettered) and signed by the author and/or illustrator. It is not necessarily a first edition. If it is a first edition, it is normally issued in a different binding than the trade edition and in a slipcase, sometimes referred to as a box (although it really isn't)

Limited editions should be produced in a small number to be meaningful. 500 copies or less is usually more than enough for all but the most popular of authors. 100 to 200 copies is more realistic for many collected authors, as many collectors are satisfied with trade editions or simply do not have the money for the higher priced editions.

"Limited Editions" to have much meaning must have the total limitation noted in the book, otherwise, one must assume the "limitation" is very large, particularly if the publisher will not reveal the total limitation on request of a collector. There have been a number of "Limited Editions" of over 100,000 copies

Marbling	The process of decorating sheets of paper or cloth or edges of books with a variety of colors in a pattern which has the appearance of marble

Modern firsts	A category which seems to include all authors whose first editions were published in this century. The term has been used since the 1920's. At present it is not very descriptive. 20th Century First Editions is a much better term to define the stock of most "Modern" First Edition dealers
Mounted	Refers to illustrations which are pasted down or lightly attached to a leaf; or if referring to a damaged leaf it would mean laid down on or backed with paper, gauze or linen
No-date	is stated in book catalog entries if no date is present in the book. As I understand it, in English catalogs if the date is included in the book on the title page, copyright page, introduction, cover, etc. the dealer will state the date, e.g. "1960." If the date does not appear in the book but the dealer knows the date the entry will state "n-d (1960)." American catalogs will list the date "1960" only if it appears on the title page. If the date does not appear on the title page, but appears elsewhere in the book or on its cover, the American catalog entry will read "(1960)." If the date does not appear in the book at all the American dealer, if the date is known, will follow the English lead and state "n-d (1960)"
No-place	Similar treatment as in no-date. Abbreviated as n-p or n-pl
No publisher	Similar treatment as in no-date. Abbreviated as n-publ
Obverse	The front of a leaf, the right hand page of an open book. More commonly called the recto
Offprint	A separate printing of a section of a larger publication, generally of composite authorship, in periodicals or books. Offprints are made from the same typesetting and occasionally are given their own pagination. They normally have a separate paper cover and and sometimes a special title page. They are of interest because they represent the first separate appearance of the work, although they are not really a first separate edition
Offset	Normally describes the transfer of ink from a printed page or an engraving to the opposite page. Also used as an abbreviation for photo offset lithography
Out of print	Means the publisher no longer has copies that may be ordered. If the publisher plans on reprinting the book it will merely be out-of-stock
Out of series	Refers to overruns of limited editions which are normal as a hedge against defective copies and in order to have a few copies for the author and publisher's use and to send out for review. These copies are not numbered, but occasionally state "out of series." These are normally not signed by the author and even if signed are not usually as attractive to the collector as the numbered copies
Page	One side of a leaf
Pamphlet	A small separate work issued in paperwraps

Paperback	Refers primarily to the books in paperwraps published since the 1930's, although it can describe any book with a paper cover
Paper Boards	As used today means stiff cardboard covered in paper; otherwise, there should be a fuller description in the catalog
Parts	Refers to part issues or the practice of publishing novels in separate monthly installments in magazine format, particularly in the 19th century. Most avidly sought are the Dickens novels in parts with all the advertisements in the "proper" order
Pastedown	is that half of the paper that lines the inner sides of the cover
Perfect binding	as in a mass-market paperback book
Pictorial	describes a book with a picture on the cover versus a printed cover which implies lettering only
Pirated edition	is an edition published without the consent of the author or copyright owner. The ones we most often see are the Taiwan piracies
Plates	are the whole page illustrations printed separately from the text. Illustrations printed on the text pages are called "cuts"
Points	are misprints, corrections, advertisements, cloth color, etc. used to distinguish states, issues, impressions/printings or editions of one book from another. Catalogers seem to fall into various categories: those that assume the reader doesn't know anything; those that assume the reader knows everything; and those that assume the reader knows what the cataloger knew before that particular catalog was prepared (why repeat something in catalog 59 that you already covered in detail in catalog 23?)
Presentation copy	assumes the author meant to inscribe the copy for the recipient and actually gave or sent the copy to the recipient, rather than inscribe the book for someone the author didn't know at their request. Obviously a difficult call to make in many instances
Printed cover	used to describe a dustwrapper or paper cover that is only lettered (without any picture). Most commonly used currently to describe the covers of uncorrected proof copies, e.g. white printed wraps (white cover printed in black)
Printing	is an alternative word for impression
Private press	is one whose owner or operator prints what they like, rather than what a publisher pays them to print. The interest is in fine books. The print runs are small and although the books are sold to the public directly through subscription or occasionally through a publisher's organization, the motivation is more to make a fine book than to make a profit. Some examples would include the Baskerville, Daniel, Kelmscott, Ashendem, Cuala and Golden Cockeral presses
Privately printed	refers to a book that is not published for sale and thus it is distributed by other than the normal commercial channels

Proofs	precede the published book. The normal sequence would be a galley proof (described above), an uncorrected bound (in paperwraps) proof and an advance reading copy bound in paperwraps. The latter is not as common a form as the first two because publishers may not bother producing these but rather send out early copies of cloth bound trade editions for review
Provenance	is a record of the previous ownership of a particular copy of a book
Publication date	is the date the book is to be put on sale allowing time for distribution to stores and reviewers after the actual printing is complete
Rare	implies the book is extremely scarce perhaps only turning up once every 20 years or so
Re-backed	means the binding has been given a new spine or back strip
Re-cased	means the book was loose or out of its covers and it has been re-sewn or glued back in, usually with new end papers
Recto	the front of a leaf, the right hand page of an open book. Also called the obverse
Re-jointed	means the book has been repaired preserving the original covers including the spine. The repair is always either "almost imperceptible" or "skillfully accomplished"
Remainders	are books that publishers have decided not to stock any longer and the remainder of the stock is sold to a wholesaler which resells the books to new book stores to sell to the public significantly below the original price. You can find these books for $.99 to $4.98 at most new bookstores. Some very expensive first editions were on these shelves at one time. The definition has to be qualified somewhat, however, because occasionally a publisher will remainder a part of his stock, while retaining the title on his list at full retail price
Reverse	of a leaf is the back or the page on the left of an open book. More commonly called the verso
Signatures	are the letters or numerals printed in the margin of the first leaf of each gathering or section itself
Slipcase	a cardboard case usually covered in paper, cloth or leather which holds a book with only the spine exposed
State	see Issue
Stub	is a narrow strip of paper where the majority of a leaf has been cut away
Sunned	means the covers have been bleached or faded by sunlight
Thousands	a few publishers in the 19th century would add a notice on the title page stating "Eighth Thousand," for instance, to indicate a later printing, although they would not state second printing, third printing, etc. These are not first editions

Three-Decker	a book in three volumes, almost exclusively used to describe Victorian novels of the late 19th century
Tipped-in	means the plate, autograph, letter, photo, etc. is actually attached to the book
Top Edge Gilt	see Gilt Edges
Trade Edition	is the regularly published edition; the term is used to differentiate it from a limited signed edition of the same book
Uncut	means the edges have not been trimmed smooth by a machine. The edges are rough. It is not the same as unopened
Unopened	means the leaves of the book are still joined at the folds, not slit apart
Unsophisticated	pure, genuine, unrestored and if a book is so described it can mean trouble as far as condition is concerned
Variant	a book that differs in one or more features from others of the same impression, but a positive sequence has not been established. If the sequence were known it would be a particular state or issue
Vellum	is a thin sheet of specially prepared skin of calf, lamb or kid used for writing or printing on, or in binding
Verso	is the left page of an open book. The back of a leaf. Also called the reverse
Waterstained	means a discoloration and perhaps the actual shrinking of the leaves or binding
Working copy	you should receive most of the leaves
Wrappers	the printed or unprinted cover of a pamphlet or book bound in paper

Appendix C

Pseudonyms

The following represents a list of pseudonyms used by the authors listed herein. The sources include practically all the reference works listed in the Selected Bibliography, plus individual bibliographies.

The list has been arbitrarily limited to pseudonyms used by the authors when publishing books and does not include a number of pseudonyms used in magazine appearances.

The names are listed alphabetically. The names in **Bold Face** type are the real names of the authors.

A., T.B.	**Thomas Bailey Aldrich**
Abbott, Anthony	**Fulton Oursler**
Acre, Stephen	**Frank Gruber**
Adams, William Taylor	Warren T. Ashton; Oliver Optic
A.E.	**George Russell**
Ai	**Florence Ogawa**
Aldrich, Thomas Bailey	T.B.A.
Allen, Grace	Allen Weston (with **Alice Mary Norton**)
Allen, Hervey	Hardly Alum
Alger, Horatio	Arthur Lee Putnam; Julien Starr
Alum, Hardly	**Hervey Allen**
Ambler, Eric	Eliot Reed (with **Charles Rodda**)
Amis, Kingsley	Robert Markham; William Tanner
Anderson, Poul	A.A. Craig; Michael Karageorge; Winston P. Sanders
Andrezel, Pierre	**Karen Blixen**
Anstey, F.	**Thomas Anstey Guthrie**
Antoninus, Brother	**William Everson**
Anthony, Peter	**Peter** and **Anthony Shaffer**
Arno, Peter	**Curtis Arnoux Peters**
Arnow, Harriette	**Harriett Simpson**
Ashdown, Clifford	**R. Austin Freeman** and **John Jame Pitcairn**
Ashton, Warren T.	**William Taylor Adams**
Asimov, Issac	George E. Dale; Paul French
Ashe, Gordon	**John Creasey**
Aston, James	**T.H. White**
Atherton, Gertrude	Frank Lin
Aubrey-Fletcher, Henry L.	Henry Wade
Auchincloss	Andrew Lee
August, John	**Bernard De Voto**
Austin, Mary H.	Gordon Stairs
B., E.C.	**Edmund Blunden**
B., J.K.	**John Kendrick Bangs**
Bachman, Richard	**Stephen King**
Baker, Asa	**Dresser, Davis**
Bangs, John Kendrick	J.K.B.

Banks, Edward	**Ray Bradbury**
Banshuck, Grego	**Hugo Gernsback**
Baraka, Imamu Amiri	**Leroi Jones**
Barbellion, W.N.P.	**Bruce Frederick Cummings**
Barbette, Jay	Bart Spicer (with **Betty Spicer**)
Barnes, Julian	Dan Kavanagh
Barnsley, Alan	Gabriel Fiedling
Barr, Robert	Luke Short
Baxter, George Owen	**Frederick Faust**
Beaton, George	**Gerald Brenan**
Beecher, Harriet	Harriet Beecher Stowe
Bell, Acton	**Ann Bronte**
Bell, Currer	**Charlotte Bronte**
Bell, Ellis	**Emily Bronte**
Bell, Eric Temple	John Taine
Benson, A.C.	Christopher Carr
Benson, E.C.	E. Clerihew
Beynon, John	**John Wyndham P.L.B. Harris**
Bierce, Ambrose	Dod Grile; William Herman
Bigby, Cantell A.	**George W. Peck**
Blair, Eric Arthur	George Orwell
Blake, Nicholas	**C. Day Lewis**
Bleeck, Oliver	**Ross Thomas**
Blixen, Karen	Pierre Andrezel; Isak Dinesen; Osceola
Bliss, Reginald	**H.G. Wells**
Blunden, Edmund	E.C.B.
Boston, Charles	**Frank Gruber**
Boucher, Anthony	**William Anthony Parker White**
Box, Edgar	**Gore Vidal**
Boyd, Nancy	**Edna St. Vincent Millay**
Boyle, Kay	Mrs. Laurence Vail
Boz	**Charles Dickens**
Bradbury, Ray	Edward Banks; Leonard Douglas
Bramah, Ernest	**Ernest Bramah Smith**
Brand, Christianna	**Mary Christianna Lewis**
Brand, Max	**Frederick Faust**
Brenan, Gerald	George Beaton
Bronte, Ann	Acton Bell
Bronte, Charlotte	Currer Bell
Bronte, Emily	Ellis Bell
Brown, Frederic	Felix Graham
Brown, Zenith Jones	Leslie Ford; David Frome
Bruce, Leo	**Rupert Croft-Cooke**
Brunner, John	Gill Hunt
Burgess, Anthony	**John Anthony Burgess Wilson**
Burke, Leda	**David Garnett**
Burn, Tex	**Louis L'Amour**
Burroughs, William	William Lee
Burton, Miles	**Cecil John Charles Street**
Butler, Walter C.	**Frederick Faust**
Bynner, Witter	Emanuel Morgan
Cabell, James Branch	Berwell Washington
Cain, Paul	**Peter Ruric**

Dannay, Frederic	Barnaby Ross (with **Manfred Lee**)
Davidson, Lawrence H.	**D.H. Lawrence**
Daviot, Gordon	**Elizabeth Mackintosh**
De La Mare, Walter	Walter Ramal
Delillo, Don	**John Creasey**
Deanne, Norman	?
Derleth, August	Stephen Grendon; Eldon Heath
De Voto, Bernard	John August
Dickens, Charles	Boz
Dickson, Carr	**John Dickson Carr**
Dickson, Carter	**John Dickson Carr**
Dinesen, Isak	**Karen Blixen**
Dodge, Mary Abigail	Gail Hamilton
Dodgson, Charles Lutwidge	Lewis Carroll
Doneglion	**Jose Garcia Villa**
Donovan, Dick	**Joyce E.P. Muddock**
Dooley, Mr.	**Finley Peter Dunne**
Doolittle, Hilda	H.D.; John Helford
Douglas, Ellen	Josephine Haxton
Douglas, Leonard	**Ray Bradbury**
Douglas, Norman	Normyx
Downes, Quentin	**Michael Harrison**
Doyle, John	**Robert Graves**
Dresser, Davis	Asa Baker; Brett Halliday; Robert Kyle
Drinan, Adam	**Joseph MacLeod**
Dunne, Finley Peter	Mr. Dooley
Dunsany, Lord	**Edward John M. Drax Plunkett**
Durrell, Claude	Claude
Durrell, Lawrence	Charles Norden
E., A.	**George Russell**
Eddy, Mary Baker	**Mary Baker Glover**
Engelhardt, Frederick	**L. Ron Hubbard**
Epernay, Mark	**Kenneth Galbraith**
Erickson, Walter	**Howard Fast**
Esse, James	**James Stephens**
Evans, Evan	**Frederick Faust**
Everson, William	Brother Antonius
Ewing, Frederick R.	**Theodore Sturgeon**
F., Inspector	**William Russell**
F., M.T.	**Katherine Anne Porter**
Fair, A.A.	**Erle Stanley Gardner**
Fairbairn, Roger	**John Dickson Carr**
Farmer, Philip Jose	Kilgore Trout
Farrell, James T.	Jonathan Titulesco Fogarty
Fast, Howard	E.V. Cunningham; Walter Ericcson
Faust, Frederick	George Owen Baxter; Max Brand; Walter C. Butler; George Challis; Evan Evans; John Frederick; Frederick Frost; David Manning; Peter Henry Morland
Feikema, Feike	**Frederick Manfred**
Feinstein, Isidor	I.F. Stone
Ferguson, Helen	**Helen Woods**
Field, Gans T.	**Manly Wade Wellman**
Finney, Jack	**Walter B. Finney**

238

Finney, Walter B.	Jack Finney
Fips, Mohammed Ulysses Socrates	**Hugo Gernsback**
Fish, Robert L.	Robert L. Pike
Fleming, Oliver	**Philip** and **Ronald MacDonald**
Fogarty, Jonathan Titulesco	**James T. Farrell**
Ford, Ford Maddox (Legally Changed)	**Ford Madox Hueffer**; Daniel Chaucer; Fenil Haig
Ford, Leslie	**Zenith Jones Brown**
Forester, Frank	**Henry William Herbert**
Forrest, Felix C.	**Paul Linebarger**
Fraze, Robert	**John Creasey**
Frederick, John	**Frederick Faust**
Freeman, R. Austin	Clifford Ashdown (with **John Jame Pitcairn**)
French, Paul	**Issac Asimov**
Frome, David	**Zenith Jones Brown**
Frost, Frederick	**Frederick Faust**
Froy, Herald	**Keith Waterhouse**
Fuller, Henry Blake	Staton Page
Galbraith, Kenneth	Mark Epernay
Galsworthy, John	John Sinjohn
Galt, Walter	**Talbot Mundy**
Gardner, Earle Stanley	A.A. Fair; Carleton Kendrake
Garnett, David	Leda Burke
Garrett, Randall	Robert Randall
Garth, Will	**Henry Kuttner**
Gashbuck, Greno	**Hugo Gernsback**
Geisel, Theodor Seuss	Dr. Seuss
Gibson, Walter	Maxwell Grant
Gibb, Lee	**Keith Waterhouse**
Gernsback, Hugo	Grego Barshuck; Mohammed V.S. Fips; Greno Gashbuck; Gus N. Habergock
Gibson, Walter B.	Maxwell Grant
Glover, Mary Baker	Mary Baker Eddy
Goldman, William	S. Morgenstern
Goldsmith, Oliver	James Willington
Goodrich, S.G.	Peter Parley
Gorey, Edward	Ogdred Weary
Gottschalk, Laura	Laura Riding
Graham, John	**David Graham Phillips**
Graham, Felix	**Frederic Brown**
Graham, Tom	**Sinclair Lewis**
Grainger, Francis Edward	Headon Hill
Grant, Maxwell	**Walter Gibson**
Graves, Robert	John Doyle; Frank Richard
Green, Hannah	**Joanne Greenburg**
Green, Henry	**Henry Vincent Yorke**
Greenburg, Joanne	Hannah Green
Grendon, Stephen	**August Derleth**
Gribben, William L.	**Talbot Mundy**
Grieve, C.M.	Hugh MacDiarmid
Grile, Dod	**Ambrose Bierce**
Gruber, Frank	Stephen Acre; Charles K. Boston
Guthrie, Thomas Anstey	F. Anstey

H.D.	**Hilda Doolittle**
H.H.	**Helen Hunt Jackson**
Habergock, Gus M.	**Hugo Gernsback**
Haig, Fenil	**Ford Maddox Ford**
Haines, William	**William Heyen**
Hales, Edward Everett	Frederic Ingham
Hall, Adam	**Elleston Trevor**
Halliday, Brett	**Dresser, Davis**
Halliday, Michael	**John Creasey**
Hamilton, Clive	**C.S. Lewis**
Hamilton, Gail	**Mary Abigail Dodge**
Harbage, Alfred B.	Thomas Kyd
Hare, Cyril	**Alfred A.G. Clark**
Harris, John Wyndham Park Lucas Beynon	John Baynon; John Beynon
	Lucas Parker; Wyndham Parkes; John Wyndham
Harrison, Michael	Quentin Downes
Haxton, Josephine	**Ellen Douglas**
Haywarde, Richard	**Frederick S. Cozzens**
Heath, Edward	**August Derleth**
Heinlein, Robert A.	Simon York
Helforth, John	**Hilma Doolittle**
Hennisart, M.	Emma Lathen (with **M. Latis**)
Henry, Edgar	**Albion W. Tourgee**
Henry, O.	**William Sydney Porter**
Herbert, Henry William	Frank Forester
Herman, William	**Ambrose Bierce**
Heyen, William	William Haines
Heyer, Georgette	**Mrs. George R. Rougier**
Hext, Harrington	**Eden Phillpotts**
Highsmith, Patricia	Claire Morgan
Hill, Headon	**Francis Edward Grainger**
Hilton, James	Glen Trevor
Hoff, H.S.	**William Cooper**
Holmes, H.H.	**William Anthony Parker White**
Holmes, Raymond	**Raymond Souster**
Honeyman, William C.	James McGoran
Hooker, Richard	**Dr. H. Richard Hornberger**
Hopley, George	**Cornell Woolrich**
Hornberger, Dr. H. Richard	Richard Hooker
Houdini, Harry	**Ehrich Weiss**
Houghton, Claude	**Claude Houghton Oldfield**
Howard, Robert E.	Sam Walser
Hubbard, L. Ron	Frederick Engelhardt; Rene Lafayette
Hueffer, Ford Maddox	Ford Maddox Ford (Legally changed)
Hunt, Gill	**John Brunner**
Hunt, Kyle	**John Creasey**
Hunter, Evan	Hunt Collins; Ed McBain; Richard Marsten
Huntley, Lydia	**Lydia Sigourney**
Ingham, Frederic	**Edward Everett Hale**
Innes, Michael	**John Innes M. Stewart**
Inspector F.	**William Russell**
Irish, William	**Cornell Woolrich**
Irving, Washington	Geoffrey Crayon; Dietrich Knickerbocker;
	Launcelot Langstaff

Lyre, Pynchbeck	**Siegfried Sassoon**
M., S.W.	**S. Weir Mitchell**
McBain, Ed	**Evan Hunter**
Mac (or Mc/M') Diarmid, Hugh	**C.M. Grieve**
MacDonald, John R.	**Kenneth Millar**
MacDonald, Philip	Martin Porlock; Philip MacDonald
MacDonald, Ronald	Oliver Fleming (with **Philip MacDonald**)
MacDonald, Ross	**Kenneth Millar**
McGivern, William P.	Bill Peters
McGovan, James	**William C. Honeymoon**
MacLeod, Fiona	**William Sharp**
MacLeod, Joseph	Adam Drinan
McNeile, Herman C.	Sapper
Machen, Arthur	Leolinus Siluriensis
Mackintosh, Elizabeth	Josephine Tey; Gordon Daviot
Manfred, Frederick	Feike Feikema
Manning, Adelaide	Manning Cole (with **Coles**)
Manning, David	**Frederick Faust**
Manton, Peter	**John Creasey**
Mara, Bernard	**Brian Moore**
March, William	**William Edward March Campbell**
Markham, Robert	**Kingsley Amis**
Marric, J.J.	**John Creasey**
Marsten, Richard	**Evan Hunter**
Martin, Richard	**John Creasey**
Marvil, Ik	**Donald Grant Mitchell**
Mason, F. Van Wyck	Geoffrey Coffin
Matheson, Richard	Logan Swanson
Meynell, Alice	A.C. Thompson
Millar, Kenneth	John R. or Ross MacDonald
Millay, Edna St. Vincent	Nancy Boyd
Miller, Warren	Amanda Vail
Mitchell, S. Weir	S.W.M.
Montgomery, Robert Bruce	Edmund Crispin
Moorcock, Michael	**Desmond Reid**
Moore, Brian	Bernard Mara
Moore, Catherine and **Henry Kuttner**	Lewis Padgett
Moore, Edward	**Edwin Muir**
Morecamp, Arthur	**Thomas Pilgrim**
Morgan, Claire	**Patricia Highsmith**
Morgan, Emanuel	**Witter Byner**
Morgan, Jane	**James Fenimore Cooper**
Morgenstern, S.	**William Goldman**
Morland, Peter Henry	**Frederick Faust**
Morris, Julian	**Morris West**
Morton, Anthony	**John Creasey**
Muddock, Joyce E.P.	Dick Donovan
Muir, Edwin	Edward Moore
Mundy, Talbot	William L. Gribben; Walter Galt
Munroe, H.H.	Saki
Mugatroyd, Matthew	**James Athearn Jones**
Nabokoff-Sirin, V.	**Vladimir Nabokov**

Q	
Queen, Ellery	Frederic Dannay and Manfred Lee
Quentin, Patrick	Richard W. Webb, et al.
Quiller-Couch, Arthur	Q
Quinn, Simon	**Martin Cruz Smith**
R., C.G.	**Christina G. Rosetti**
Ramal, Walter	**Walter De La Mare**
Randall, Robert	**Randall Garrett** and **Robert Silverberg**
Randolph, Georgiana Ann	Craig Rice; Daphne Sanders; Michael Venning
Ranger, Ken	**John Creasey**
Reed, Eliot	**Eric Ambler** and **Charles Rodda**
Reed, Ishmael	Emmett Coleman
Reid, Desmond	Michael Moorcock; Jim Cawthorn
Reilly, William K.	**John Creasey**
Rhode, John	**Cecil John Charles Street**
Rhys, Jean	Francis Carco
Rice, Anne	Anne Rampling; A.N. Roquelaure
Rice, Craig	**Georgianna Ann Randolph**
Rich, Barbara	**Laura Riding** and **Robert Graves**
Richard, Frank	**Robert Graves** (Ghostwriter)
Riding, Laura	**Laura Gottschalk**
Riley, James Whitcomb	Benj. F. Johnson
Riley, Tex	**John Creasey**
Rhodda, Charles	Eliot Reed (with **Eric Ambler**)
Rohmer, Sax	**Arthur Henry S. Ward**
Rolfe, Frederick William	Baron Corvo
Roquelaure, A.N.	**Anne Rice**
Ross, Barnaby	**Frederic Dannay** and **Manfred Lee**
Ross, J.M. and L.H.	**T.E. Lawrence**
Rosetti, Christine G.	C.G.R.
Rougier, Mrs. George R.	Georgette Heyer
Ruric, Peter	Paul Cain
Russell, George	A.E.
Rissell, William	Inspector F.; Waters
Ryder, Jonathan	**Robert Ludlum**
S., E.W.	**E.W. Sherman**
S., S.H.	**Siegfried Sassoon**
Saki	**E.W. Sherman**
Sanders, Daphne	**H(ector) H(ugh) Munro**
Sanders, Winston P.	**Georgianna Ann Randolph**
Sanford, John	**Poul Anderson**
Sanford, John	Julian L. Shapiro
Sapper	**H.C. McNeile**
Sassoon, Siegfried	Saul Kain; Pynchbeck Lyre; S.H.S.
Schreiner, Olive	Ralph Iron
Seuss, Dr.	**Theodore Geisel**
Shaffer, Anthony	Peter Anthony
Shaffer, Peter	Peter Anthony
Shannon, Dell	**Barbara Elizabeth Linnington**
Shapiro, Julian L.	**John Sanford**
Sharp, Luke	**Robert Barr**
Sharp, William	Fiona MacLeod

245

Trevor, Glen	**James Hilton**
Trevor, William	**William Trevor Cox**
Trout, Kilgore	**Philip Jose Farmer**
Trowbridge, John T.	Paul Creyton
Twain, Mark	**Samuel Langhorne Clemens**
Vail, Amanda	**Warren Miller**
Vail, Mrs. Laurence	**Kay Boyle**
Van Dine, S.S.	**Willard Huntington Wright**
Van, Melvin	**Melvin Van Pebles**
Vedder, John R.	**Frank Gruber**
Venning, Michael	**Georgiana Ann Randolph**
Vidal, Gore	Edgar Box
Villa, Jose Garcia	Doneglion
Voelker, John Donaldson	Robert Traver
W., E.B.	**E.B. White**
Wade, Henry	**Henry Lancelot Aubrey-Fletcher**
Wagstaff, Theophile	**William Thackery**
Walser, Sam	**Robert E. Howard**
Ward, Arthur Henry S.	Sax Rohmer
Washington, Berwell	**James Branch Cabell**
Waterhouse, Keith	Herald Froy, Lee Gibb
Waters	**William Russell**
Weary, Ogdred	**Edward Gorey**
Weiss, Ehrich	Harry Houdini
Webb, Richard W.	Q. Patrick (written alone and with **Martha Kelley** and others; Patrick Quentin (written with **Hugh Wheeler**); Jonathan Stagge
Wellman, Manly Wade	Gans T. Field
Wells, Carolyn	Roland Wright
Wells, H.G.	Reginald Bliss
West, Morris	Julian Morris
Westamacott, Mary	**Agatha Christie**
Westlake, Donald	Tucker Coe; Timothy J. Culver; Richard Stark
Weston, Allen	**Alice Mary Norton** and **Grace Allen**
Wharton, Edith	Edith Newbolt Jones
Wharton, William	?
Wheeler, Hugh	Jonathan Stagge (with **Richard W. Webb**)
Whitaker, Rodney	Trevanian
White, E.B.	E.B.W.
White, T.H.	James Aston
White, William Anthony Parker	Anthony Boucher; H.H. Holmes
Wiggin, Kate Douglas	**Kate Douglas Smith**
Wilde, Oscar	Fingal O'Flahertie Wills
Willington, James	**Oliver Goldsmith**
Wills, Fingal O'Flahertie	**Oscar Wilde**
Wilson, J. Anthony Burgess	Anthony Burgess; Joseph Kell
Wilson, J. Willard Huntington	S.S. Van Dine
Woods, Helen	Helen Ferguson; Anna Kavan
Woolrich, Cornell	George Hopley; William Irish
Wright, Roland	**Carolyn Wells**
Wyndham, John	**John Wyndham P.L.B. Harris**

Yin, Leslie C.B.	Leslie Charteris
York, Jeremy	**John Creasey**
York, Simon	**Robert A. Heinlein**
Yorke, Henry Vincent	Henry Green

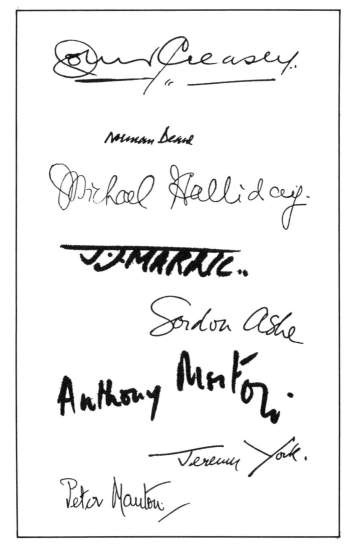

The prolific John Creasey not only used several pseudonyms but went to great lengths to make each signature as different as possible. (Reprinted from *John Creasey: Master of Mystery* published by Hodder & Stoughton.)

Appendix D

Book Dealers

The following is a list of book dealers who issue catalogs, primarily of literary (fiction, poetry, drama, science fiction, etc.) first editions. It's certainly not complete, but represents the dealers who keep our name on their mailing list.

About Books, 280 & 355 Queen Street West, Toronto, Ontario M5V 2A1, Canada

Ben Abraham Books, 97 Donnamora Crescent, Thornhill, Ontario L3T 4K6, Canada

Allen & Pat Ahearn, Quill & Brush Bookstore, Box 5365, Rockville, MD 20851

Alphabet Bookshop, 656 Spadina Avenue, Toronto, Ontario M5S 2H9, Canada

Am Here Books, 242 Ortega Ridge Road, Santa Barbara, CA 93108

The Americanist (Norman and Michal Kane), 1525 Shenkel Road, Pottstown, PA 19464

Ampersand Books (George Bixby), Box 674, Cooper Station, New York City 10276

Anacapa Books (David Wirship), 3090 Claremont Avenue, Berkeley, CA 94705

Antic Hay Rare Books (Don Stine), Box 2185, Asbury Park, NJ 07712

Argosy Book Store, 116 E. 59th Street, New York City 10022

The Associates, Box 4214, Falls Church, VA 22044

Attic Books, Second Floor, 388 Clarence St., London, Ontario N6A 3M7, Canada

Authors of the West, 191 Dogwood Drive, Dundee, OR 97115

Bert Babcock Bookseller, P.O. Box 1140, 9 East Derry Road, Derry, NH 03038

Bayside Books, Box 57, Soquel, CA 95073

Beasley Books (Beth and Paul Garon), 1533 W. Oakdale, Chicago, IL 60657

Bell, Book & Radmall, Ltd., 4 Cecil Court, London WC2 4HE England

Steven C. Bernard, 138 New Mark Esplanade, Rockville, MD 20850

Preston C. Beyer, 752A Pontiac Lane, Oronoque Village, Stratford, CT 06497

Black Sun Books (Harvey & Linda Tucker), 220 East 60th Street, New York City 10022

Peter A. Bologna Rare Books, Kilbrittain, Bandon, County Cork, Ireland

The Book Block, 8 Loughlin Avenue, Cos Cob, CT 06807

The Book Den, 15 East Anapanu Street, Santa Barbara, CA 93102

Book Dales, 46 W. 66th St., Richfield, MN 55423

The Bookpress, Box KP, Williamsburg, VA 23187

The Bookshop, 400 West Franklin Street, Chapel Hill, NC 27514

Boston Book Annex, 906 Beacon Street, Boston, MA 02215

M. Taylor Bowie, 2613 Fifth Avenue, Seattle, WA 98121

Marilyn Braiterman, 20 Whitfield Road, Baltimore, MD 21210

The Brick Row Bookshop, 278 Post Street, #303, San Francisco, CA 94108

Burkwood Books, Box 172, Urbana, IL 61801

Harold M. Burnstein & Co., 36 Riverside Drive, Waltham, MA 02154

John R. Butterworth, 742 West 11th Street, Claremont, CA 91711

Andrew Cahan Bookseller, Box 30202, Philadelphia, PA 19103

The Captain's Bookshelf (Chan and Megan Gordon), 26½ Battery Park Avenue, Asheville, NC 28801

Chaos Unlimited, Box 11002, Washington, DC 20008

Chapel Hill Rare Books, P.O. Box 456, Carrboro, NC 27510

Chloe's Books, Box 6278, Sacramento, CA 95865

Clover Hill Books, Box 6278, Charlottesville, VA 22906

The Colophon Book Shop (Robert & Christine Liska), Box E, Epping, NH 03042

Cornerstone Books, 236 Meet Street, Providence, RI 02906

Country Lane Books (Ed & Judith Myers), Box 47, Collinsville, CT 06022

Dalian Books, 81 Albion Drive, London Fields, London E8 4LT England

Joseph A. Dermont, Box 654, 13 Arthur Street, Onset, MA 02558

R & G Desmarais Books, 210 Post St., Suite 206, San Francisco, CA 94108

Detering Book Gallery, 2311 Bissonnet, Houston, TX 77005

Dinkytown Antiquarian Bookstore (Larry Dingman), 1316 SE 4th Street, Minneapolis, MN 55414

Dunn's Mysteries of Choice, Box 2544, Meriden, CT 06450

I.D. Edrich, 17 Selsdon Road, London E11 2QF England

Peter Ellis, 279 Fordhouse Lane, Stirchley Birmingham, B30 3AA England

Else Fine–Books, Box 43, Dearborn, MI 48121

Evlen Books, box 42, Centerport, NY 11721

The Fine Books Co., 781 East Snell Road, Rochester, MI 48064

R.A. Gekoski, 14 Portland Place, Leamington Spa, Warwickshire CV32 5EV England

Golden Legend, 8586 Melrose Avenue, Los Angeles, CA 90069

Grey House Books (Camille Wolff), 12A Lawrence Street, Chelsea, London SW3 England

Michael Hargraves Books, Box 291056, Los Angeles, CA 90029

Hawthorn Books, 7 College Park Drive, Westbury-on-Trym, Bristol BS10 7AN England

Heartwood Books, 9 Elliewood Avenue, Charlottesville, VA 22903

Heritage Bookshop, 8540 Melrose Avenue, Los Angeles, CA 90069

Melissa and Mark Himes, Box 309, Idyllwild, CA 92349

David J. Holmes Autographs, 230 South Broad Street, Philadelphia, PA 19102

Glenn Horowitz, 141 East 44th Street, Suite 712, New York City 10017

George Houle, 7260 Beverly Blvd., Los Angeles, CA 90036

Huntington Books (James F. O'Neil), 135 Newbury Street, Suite 3, Boston, MA 02116

In Our Time (Eugene O'Neil), Box 386, Cambridge, MA 02139

J & J House Booksellers, 632 Broadway, San Diego, CA 92101

James S. Jaffe, Box 496, Haverford, PA 19041

The Jenkins Company, Box 2085, Austin, TX 78768

David Johnson, Bookseller, 1242 Bush Street, San Francisco, CA 94109

Peter Jolliffe, 2 Acre End Street, Eynsham, Owon OX8 1PA England

Joseph the Provider, 10 West Michaeltorena, Santa Barbara, CA 93101

Priscilla Juvelis, 89 Beacon Street, Boston, MA 02108

Kenneth Karmiole Bookseller, 1225 Santa Monica Mall, Los Angeles, CA 90401

Katie Books, Box 2451, Ventura, CA 93002

Kim Kaufman Bookseller, Box 5152, FDR Station, New York City 10150

Key Books (Ray and C.L. Cooper), 2 West Montgomery Street, Baltimore, MD 21230

Leaves of Grass, 2433 Whitmore Lake Road, Ann Arbor, MI 48103

Ralph Kristiansen Bookseller, Box 524, Kenmore Station, Boston, MA 02215

Lemuria Books, 238 Highland Village, Jackson, MS 39211

Letters, 452 Queen Street West, Toronto, Ontario M5V 2A8, Canada

Ronald Levine, 15 Walter Street, Fellside, Johannesburg 2192, South Africa

Ken Lopez—Bookseller, 51 Huntington Road, Hadley, MA 01035

McClintock Books, Box 3530, Warren, OH 44485

George S. MacManus Co. (Clarence Wolff), 1317 Irving Street, Philadelphia, PA 19107

Ian McKelvie, 45 Hertford Road, London N2 9BX England

Robert A. Madle, 4406 Bestor Drive, Rockville, MD 20853

Magnum Opus (Jon Guillot), Box 1301, Charlottesville, VA 22902

David Mason, 342 Queen Street West, Toronto, Ontario M5V 2W7 Canada

William Matthews, Bookseller, 46 Gilmore Road, Fort Erie, Ontario L2S 2M1, Canada

David Mayou, 12 Oaklands Road, London W7 2DR England

Allan R. Milkerit—Books, 145 Riverway Drive, Pittsburg, CA 94565

Ming Books UK, 115 High Street, Berkhamsted, Hertfordshire HP4 2DJ England

George Robert Minkoff, RFD #3, Box 147, Great Barrington, MA 01230

Bradford Morrow Books, 33 West 9th Street, New York City 10011

Mysterious Bookshop, 129 West 56th Street, New York City 10019

Maurice F. Neville, 835 Laguna Street, Santa Barbara, CA 93101

The Old New York Book Shop, 1069 Juniper Street, NE, Atlanta, GA 30309

Nouveau Rare Books (Steve Silberman), 5005 Meadow Oaks Park Drive, Jackson, MS 39211

Oak Knoll Books, 214 Delaware Street, New Castle, DE 19720

Ohio Bookhunter (J. Stark), 564 East Townview Circle, Mansfield, OH 44907

Origin Books, 212 North Second Street, Minneapolis, MN 55409

Pan Books & Graphics, 401 Main Street, Catskill, NY 12414

Pepper & Stern Rare Books, Box 2711, Santa Barbara, CA 93120
    and Box 160, Sharon, MA 02067

R & A Petrilla Booksellers, Box 306, Roosevelt, NJ 08555

Pettler & Lieberman, 8033 Sunset Boulevard, #977, Los Angeles, CA 90046

Pharos Books, Box 17, Fair Haven Station, New Haven, CT 06513

Phoenix Bookshop (Robert Wilson), 22 Jones Street, New York City 10014

Phillip J. Pirages, 965 West 11th Street, McMinnville, OR 97128

Ralston Popular Fiction, Box 4174, Fullerton, CA 92634

Kevin T. Ransom, Bookseller, Box 176, Amherst, NY 14226

The Rare Book Room, 125 Greenwich Avenue, New York City 10014

William Reese Company, 409 Temple Street, New Haven, CT 06511

Diana J. Rendell (Autographs), 177 Collins Road, Waban, WA 02168

L & T Respess Books, Box 1284, Chapel Hill, NC 27514

Rulon-Miller, 212 North Second Street, Minneapolis, MN 55401

L.J. Sklaroff, Craiglea, The Broadway, Totland, Isle of Wight

Barry Scott, Box 207, Stonington, CT 06378

Second Life Books, Box 242, Quarry Road, Lansborough, MA 01237

Serendipity Books (Peter Howard), 1790 Shattuck Avenue, Berkeley, CA 94709

Nick Sherington—Rare Books, 11 Clifton Hill, Exeter EX1 2DJ England

Ian Sinclair, 28 Albion Drive, London E8 4ET England

Eldon P. Steeves, Box 188, Colvin Station, Syracuse, NY 13205

Christopher P. Stephens, 7 Terrace Drive, Hastings-on-Hudson, NY 10706

Eric & Joan Stevens, 74 Fortune Road, London NW6 1DS England

Sylvester & Orphanos, 2484 Cheremoya Avenue, Los Angeles, CA 90078

Taurus Books, Box 716, Northampton, MA 01061

W. Thomas Taylor Bookseller, Box 543, Austin, TX 78763

Robert Temple, 65 Mildmay Road, London N1 4PU England

Steven Temple Books, 483 Queen Street West, Toronto, Ontario M5V 2A9, Canada

Transition Books, 445 Stockton Street, San Francisco, CA 94108

H.E. Turlington Books, Box 146, Pittsboro, NC 27312

Len Unger—Rare Books, 1575 El Dorado Drive, Thousand Oaks, CA 91363

Waiting for Godot Books, 137 Magazine Street, Cambridge, MA 02139

K. Anthony Ward, Black Horse Cottage, North Lopham, Norfolk IP22 2NBE England

Watermark West, 149 North Broadway, Wichita, KS 67202

Waverly Books, 946 9th Street #E, Santa Monica, CA 90403

Jeffrey H. Weinberg—Bookseller, Box 438, Sudbury, MA 01776

E. Wharton & Co. (Sarah Baldwin), 3 Highland Terrace, Winchester, MA 01890

Wilder Books, Box 762, Elmhurst, IL 60126

J. Howard Woolmer Rare Books, Revere, PA 18953

Words Etcetera (Julian Nangle), 327 Fulham Road, London SW109 QL England

Herb Yellin, 19073 Los Alimos Street, Northridge, CA 91326

Yesteryear Book Shop, 3201 Maple Drive, N.W., Atlanta, GA 30305

Appendix E

Auction Houses

California Book Auction Galleries, Inc., 358 Golden State Ave., San Francisco, CA 94102

Christie's, 502 Park Ave., New York, NY 10022

Samuel T. Freeman and Co., 1808 Chestnut St., Philadelphia, PA 19103

Harris Auction Galleries, Inc., 875 N. Howard St., Baltimore, MD 21201

Kane Antiquarian Auctions, 1525 Shenkel Road, Pottstown, PA 19464

Richard E. Oinoner Book Auctions, Box 470, Sunderland, MA 01375

Phillips Auctioneers, 406 East 79th St., New York, NY 10021

Plandome Book Auctions, 113 Glen Head Road, Glen Head, NY 11545

Sotheby Park Bernet, Inc., 1334 York Ave., New York, NY 10021

Swann Galleries, 104 East 25th St., New York, NY 10010

Waverly Auctions, 7649 Old Georgetown Road, Bethesda, MD 20814

Samuel Yudkin & Associates, 950 Bonifant St., Silver Spring, MD 22910

Selected Bibliography

The following list represents some of the general bibliographies or price guides utilized in compiling this guide.

American Book Prices Current. Bancroft-Parkman, Inc., NY (1975-85)

Blanck, Jacob. *Bibliography of American Literature*. Yale University Press, New Haven. Seven volumes (1953-1973) (Adams through Stockton).

The Bookman's Glossary. Third Edition, Bowker, NY (1951)

Bradley, Van Allen. *Handbook of Values*, 1982-83 edition. G.P. Putnam's Sons, NY (1982)

Carter, John. *ABC for Book Collectors*, Hart-Davis, MacGibbon, London (1974)

Contemporary Dramatists, Contemporary Novelists and *Contemporary Poets*. All three edited by James Vinson and published by St. James Press, London / St. Martin's Press, NY (1973), (1976) and (1978—fourth edition), respectively.

Currey, L.W. *Science Fiction and Fantasy Authors*, G.K. Hall & Co., Boston, MA (1979).

Dunbar, Maurice. *Fundamentals of Book Collecting*, Hermes Publ. (Los Altos) 1976

First Printings of American Authors. Bruccoli, Clark, Layman and Franklin, editors. Gale Research Co., Detroit, MI (Four volumes 1977-79).

Goldstone, Adrian H. *Collection of Mystery and Detective Fiction* (Auction Catalogues). California Book Auctions Galleries, San Francisco (Dec. 9-11, 3 volumes), 1981.

Hubin, Allen J. *A Bibliography of Crime Fiction 1749-1975*, University of California, San Diego (1979).

Johnson, Merle. *American First Editions*, 4th edition revised and enlarged by Jacob Blanck. Mark Press, Waltham, MA 1969.

Kirkpatrick, D.L. (editor). *Twentieth-Century Children's Writers,* second edition, St. Martin's Press, NY (1983).

Kunitz, Stanley J. and Howard Haycraft. *Twentieth Century Authors* (1850 Biographies and Checklists) NY (1966); and *First Supplement*, NY (1967).

Lepper, Gary M. *A Bibliographical Introduction to Seventy-Five Modern American Authors*, Serendipity Books, Berkeley, CA 1976.

McBride, Bill. *A Pocket Guide to the Identification of First Editions*, McBride /Publisher, 157 Sisson Ave., Hartford, CT 06105.

McGrath, Barry. *Science Fiction and Fantasy Pseudonyms*, Misfit Press, Deerborn, MI 1976.

Minters, Arthur H. *Collecting Books for Fun and Profit*, Arco Publ., NY (1979).

Muir, P.H. *Book-Collecting as a Hobby*, Gramol Publ., London no date.

Newton, A. Edward. *This Book-Collecting Game*, Little Brown, Boston 1928.

Reilly, John M. (editor) *Twentieth-Century Crime and Mystery Writers*, second edition, St. Martin's Press, NY (1985).

Smith, Curtis C. (editor) *Twentieth Century Science Fiction Writers*, St. Martin's Press, NY (1981).

Stewart, Seumas. *Book Collecting: A Beginner's Guide*, Revised edition, Dutton, NY (1979).

Tanner, Jack. *How to Identify and Collect American First Editions.* Arco Publishing Co., NY (1976).

Wilson, Robert. *Modern Book Collecting.* Alfred A. Knopf, NY 1980.

Winterich, John T. *A Primer of Book Collecting*, Greenberg, NY (1926).

Zempel, Edward N. and Linda A. Verkler. *A First Edition?* Spoon River Press, Box 3635, Peoria, IL 61614.